Singing Masters

Singing Masters

Poets in English 1500 to the Present

Russell Fraser

Ann Arbor

THE UNIVERSITY OF MICHIGAN PRESS

To the Shades of Blackmur, Tate, and Warren

Copyright © by the University of Michigan 1999
All rights reserved
Published in the United States of America by
The University of Michigan Press
Manufactured in the United States of America
⊛ Printed on acid-free paper
2002   2001   2000   1999   4   3   2   1

A CIP catalog record for this book is available from the British Library.

Library of Congress Cataloging-in-Publication Data

Fraser, Russell A.
    Singing masters : poets in English, 1500 to the present / Russell
Fraser.
        p.   cm.
    Includes index.
    ISBN 0-472-11003-9 (cloth : alk. paper)
    1. English poetry—History and criticism.   2. English poetry—
Early modern, 1500–1700—History and criticism.   I. Title.
PR502.F73   1999
821.009—dc21   98-49294
                                                                     CIP

Preface

This account of poets in English begins four hundred years ago, but all the poets I talk about live in a perpetual present. No one more alive today than Jonson or Pope. Yeats, a modern poet, gives me my title. "Be the singing masters of my soul," he said to his instructors, suggesting for me poetry's physical side. Intellect, learning too, play into this activity, but I think of it first of all as a hymn in the throat. The phrase was R. P. Blackmur's, describing his wide-ranging course in poetics. Like Yeats, he muttered when he read, an old lion's mutter, starting out in the viscera and coming up into the larynx. He knew better than to intellectualize when he talked about the figure a poem makes. If you asked him what a poem meant, he looked down his mustache.

My first poet was already on the scene when Shakespeare arrived in London, my last, an American, overlaps the present. But I don't seek to cover the waterfront. Many of the major poets get a hearing, not all. I am not writing literary history, much less a textbook, and don't want to say more than I know. My account is personal, the distillation of a lifetime's experience of poetry. Yeats's singing masters are my masters also, and this tribute to their life and art represents the best I can do. It isn't merely impressionistic, however, but owes much to previous critics. I hope my debt to others fortifies what I have to say.

The poets I consider have in common an intense preoccupation with form. Each deserves attention for his own sake or hers, and all are representative, standing for the time that produced them. Put them together and they make a tradition. But the form they owe allegiance to may be conventional, like a sonnet by Keats, or overturn conventions, like the syllabic verse of Marianne Moore. My great tradition is elastic and has only one criterion, that the poem give pleasure, amply defined. All substantial poets do this, not least tragic poets. Like Shakespeare in *King Lear,* a tale of disasters, they discover in the worst of times "our lives' sweetness."

Readers who keep abreast of the cultural wars will be aware that the rarefied vocabulary now in vogue isn't mine. "Go in fear of abstractions" is a rubric for my book. But I am not anti-anything, only insistently pro-. Poetry means for me human activity at its highest pitch, certainly a body of knowledge but also a way of knowing things that needs defer to no other way. My ideal readers will feel as I do. In addition, they will know the poets and poems I look at, and if only sketchily, something of the historical background. This imposes obligations, but they have to be shouldered, and perhaps will seem less a burden than privilege. Though art comes first or ought to, it comes out of a context, so I try to merge background and foreground. I notice a poet's life and letters, and the critical prose, if any. But the poem is the thing, and the basic questions I explore are language centered: what kind of poetry is before us, and whether and why it works.

The obvious sequence for a book like this is temporal, beginning at the beginning of modern times, meaning in English the earlier sixteenth century, and coming down to the proximate past. But that kind of sequence argues comprehensiveness, and imposes an arbitrary order. Nothing crucial would be lost were my last poet to come first, or the book to begin *in medias res*. Poetry, unlike the physical sciences, doesn't get better and better. Important likenesses connect some poets, however, obviously Frost and Wordsworth, less obviously Herrick and Frost. Other poets differ radically, like Sidney and Yeats. Highlighting these differences and likenesses produces a taxonomic arrangement. That is the arrangement I follow, ordering poets according to kind.

My three kinds aren't judgmental nor meant as hard and fast. Partly I invoke the third for completeness' sake, needing a wild card. All the same, there is something to them. Wallace Stevens intimates what this is in his well-known anthology piece "Thirteen Ways of Looking at a Blackbird." He says he doesn't know which to prefer: "The beauty of inflections / Or the beauty of innuendoes, / The blackbird whistling / Or just after." Revising a little, I distinguish two ways poetry takes. One, the Poetry of Inflections, depends on rhetoric rather than ratiocination or the close pursuit of figures. This poetry is synthetic. The Poetry of Innuendoes is analytic. Working through figures and giving intellect priority, it features the interplay of words in their suggestive qualities. Some poetry has a foot in either camp. Like Herbert's, it celebrates or sings creation, even though its burden is misery. Not driving on a point, it gets forward only metrically, like Arnold's, or shies from an ending, like Marvell's. In this third kind, resolution is aborted and nothing precipitates out. I call it the Hymn in the Throat.

Jonson leads off among inflectional poets. Under his aegis I group a number of others who share his psychology, anyway a piece of it. Shelley and Spenser unexpectedly resemble him, each adept at a poetry of surfaces whose truth isn't educed but declared. Shakespeare is the chief exemplar of the Poetry of Innuendoes, his words reverberating in silence after the music sounds no more. That is true of Yeats and Donne, but Yeats, even more than Donne, oscillates between kinds. Prone to holding opposites in suspension, he makes you think of Marvell in some famous *Sic* and *Non* poems. Both belong with Herbert, whose devotional poetry gets nothing done. Of course, the description holds for all poetry, which makes a coherence when it succeeds, satisfying in itself and impervious to questions. But no poetry is more ambiguous or less fruitful of answers than Herbert's. He is another of my *ne-plus-ultra poets,* a reason to set him apart.

Paradigms need fleshing out, and let me illustrate mine by drawing on Shakespeare and Milton, mighty opposites for poetry in English. Milton, the prince of rhetorical poets, is necessarily superficial, not a pejorative, only descriptive. Imagery in his kind of poetry doesn't play a large role, or not an organic one. Characteristically, he uses the image as a literary figurine. His images don't point the moral, serving only to adorn the tale. Even when he ventures them, they are apt to be spare. There isn't much dilation or amplification in him (or in Jonson, Shelley, and the typical Augustan). In *Samson Agonistes,* the common rout of men perish only "as the summer fly," a typical simile; the wicked wife, whose "trains" and "gins, and toils" are noted, shears "the fatal harvest" of her husband's head, typical metaphors. Comparison with Shakespeare suggests how amplifying isn't the same as fretwork. In *Henry V,* seeing the state of man in the beehive (1.2), he finds the analogous thing absorbing in itself. But pursuing the metaphor—liking to do this—Shakespeare discovers connections. No doubt he runs on.

The heroes of these poets differ too. Milton's, lackblooded, declines "to sport with Amaryllis in the shade," Shakespeare's "to play with mammets," female breasts (*Henry IV,* pt. 1, 2.3.95). Partly, decorum dictates the difference, but the ultimate arbiter is the way an ultrafastidious artist looks at the world he lives in. Milton's eye is cursory, and his partiality is for capital-letter things. Which comes first, the dearth of interest or the partiality, is a question. It seems plausible to say that men and women in his time, throwing back to early Christian times, are out of love with our temporal place.

As a descriptive poet, Milton is refined to Shakespeare's gross. Shakespeare writes of "braying trumpets and loud churlish drums" (in *King John,* 3.1.303), Milton of "sounding alchemy" or "sonorous metal blowing martial sounds" (*Paradise Lost,* 2.517, 1.540). But truth-to-reality isn't the only truth, and Milton, like Baroque artists and Augustan poets, sponsors another. His verse suggests results rather than delineates causes. The thrilling penumbra takes priority over the palpable thing that creates it. Milton is a great composer. More than most poets, more than Pound, he is the master of verbal music. In his poetry, however, it is always "the blackbird whistling," not the pregnant silences that follow.

Earlier versions of some of my chapters have been published in the *Hudson Review, Iowa Review, Sewanee Review, South Atlantic Quarterly, Studies in English Literature, Yale Review,* and *Yeats Annual.* I thank the editors for permission to use them. I am grateful for the criticism of Lincoln Faller, Michael Schoenfeldt, Robert Weisbuch, and Mary Zwiep. Particular thanks go to the Muses, at least seven of nine, who saw to it that I had the luck to write this.

Russell Fraser
Ann Arbor and Honolulu

Contents

Part I

The Poetry of Innuendoes

Chapter 1

Shakespeare at Sonnets

I take my title from an essay of John Crowe Ransom's, collected in *The World's Body* (1938). "Shakespeare at Sonnets," Ransom decided, wasn't up to the job, "not fit for amateurs." This distinguished critic shied at "incoherence" and thought poetry should make as consistent sense as prose. Some poets, he said (in an essay on Millay, warming up for Shakespeare), adopted combinations of words that didn't quite fit into perfect meanings. That was fudging but seemed to them agreeable, the combination offering "the uncertain possibility of two meanings rather than the certainty of one." A poem was even better when you doubted what it meant "because the range of its possibilities" was wider. Civil leering, this gives the sense of Ransom's anti-Shakespeare polemic. Mild in person, he was something else in his critical prose, and didn't hold back from throwing stones at Shakespeare, aiming, he said, for the vulnerable parts.

He noticed a lot of them, for starters a confusion between non-dramatic poetry and poetry in plays. In the drama, he said, speeches and soliloquies, however poeticized, needn't work out to complete or self-determined poems. But in sonnets this requirement governs, except that Shakespeare, an imperfect logician, doesn't meet it. Not schooled in the university, he lacked Donne's or Sidney's literary training. This is where the amateur comes in. Ransom's Shakespeare is a poet in a hurry, much dash mixed with slapdash. About half his sonnets are "tolerably workmanlike" but the other half are "seriously defective." Clashing with the standard metrical organization is "some arbitrary logical organization," arbitrary because unargued. Readers who have got beyond Bardolatry will feel the justice of this, rough justice, perhaps, but full of implication. Often in the sonnets, form "makes head" against meaning or the meaning usurps on the form. This allows for different meanings, each asking primacy. Shakespeare's egalitarian art appears to demonstrate a species of Titanism, where the old unruly gods, penned under the earth, struggle to get out and the poet abets them.

The metrical pattern of the "English" sonnet (abab cdcd efef gg) is directive. Committed to three coordinate quatrains, it ends with a couplet that ties this series together. If well turned, the couplet approximates the epigram, "thus he said." Spenser in his *Amoretti,* though he uses a different rhyme scheme, gives textbook illustrations of the conventional pattern. Maybe for this reason his sonnets strike the ear, mine anyway, as humdrum. Shakespeare, blurring the pattern he inherits, frequently "elides" his quatrains, as in the Italian sonnet where the major turn occurs after line 8. Ransom, dogging his steps, detected a Shakespeare "unequal" or "insensitive" to his formal commitment. There are other ways he could have put this. But like Dr. Johnson, Shakespeare's best critic and wrong about him half the time, he raised the right questions and his hostile critique throws a light on what Shakespeare is doing.

Let us see where the light illuminates and where it may coarsen, being too clear. Shakespeare's first seventeen sonnets offer a good access point for generalizing on his practice. Intentionality links them, the summons to "breed" or have children. But the injunction laid on Shakespeare's friend, the Fair Youth, is only the *point d'appui,* and Shakespeare has other things on his mind:

> For never-resting time leads summer on
> To hideous winter and confounds him there.
>
> (V)

A little avuncular, Shakespeare prescribes for the friend: "You had a father, let your son say so" (XIII). Riveting his attention is the "coming end," however,

> stormy gusts of winter's day
> And barren rage of death's eternal cold.

In this cluster of sonnets, what is going on "inside" seems too urgent for the form, and the poems are like a reticule stuffed to bursting.

Some such description seems appropriate for later sonnets in Shakespeare's sequence. Two of them, concerned with the gift of a book (LXXVII, CXXII), go off at a tangent, devoting much energy to "razed oblivion" and "Time's thievish progress." Or is the tangential thing of these poems' essence? Intended to cheer up the friend, LV, "Not marble, nor the gilded monuments," promises him a secure abiding place in Shakespeare's powerful rhyme. But ruminations on "death and all-oblivious enmity" qualify this promise, and a sort of litotes or understatement makes it, if scrutinized, almost absurd:

> But you shall shine more bright in these contents
> Than unswept stone, besmeared with sluttish time.

Putting it mildly, this seems not much to look for.

Shakespeare at sonnets, "reverting" on himself, suggests a man at sixes and sevens. (The question is: whose eyes is he throwing dust in, his or his readers'?) Mostly the sonnets are love poems where love, a fixed star, looks on tempests and is never shaken. But fear of death or betrayal, stalking the margins, hints at some other poem, meditated but not written. In CXV, "Those lines that I before have writ do lie," paraphrase goes one way, affect another. Hyperbolic Shakespeare is saying how his love for the friend has come too short. Abruptly, though, a darker thought besets him. Creeping in between his vows, the "millioned accidents" of time "blast the sharp'st intents, / Divert strong minds . . . ," etc. Digressions like this one, or call them ebullitions, betokening the old imprisoned gods, come up often. Evidently in the sonnets, "two truths are told," remembering a line from *Macbeth*.

But Shakespeare's defective workmanship, if that is what it is, isn't involuntary, much less disabling. Assimilating discrete particulars or psychological states, his sonnets make a fruitful emulsion. Moderns (not "postmoderns") want something different, perhaps a configuration, more in keeping with their view of art. But Shakespeare doesn't concede this and his suspended thing, while it enlarges understanding, annuls declarative statement. The rubric isn't "either / or" but "and . . . and." These remarks aren't meant to describe his style, nicely reticulated as all attest, rather his psychology, "paratactic," so aloof from logical progression.

For a poet whose bias tends to qualification, the English sonnet, inflexibly progressive, is hard to cope with. Shakespeare, electing it, is working against the grain, a creative opposition. He wants a pattern to adjust or depart from, and luckily he has one. Tinkering convention, he creates the "Shakespearean" sonnet, not quite the same as the English sonnet handed up by his forebears. Received wisdom instructed him that a perfect mixture of parts into which no impurities entered formed a stable compound, proof against disordering. This oldfashioned "chemistry" (as we should call it) looked to him like moribundity, the way things fall apart. In his unlikely compound, discords, straining against each other, are "at a mortal war" (XLVI). But his internecine war, running him on difficulties, vitalizes his performance and makes it cohere.

Much admired in Shakespeare's time, sonnet II illustrates this new kind of poem. Readers copied it out in manuscript more than any other sonnet, perhaps seeing something moderns don't see. In the couplet, the point is to having offspring:

> This were to be new made when thou art old,
> And see thy blood warm when thou feel'st it cold.

Alongside the expected metrical pattern, a syntactic pattern, encountered often, conforms to the paradigm, "When. . . . Then. . . . So."

> When forty winters shall besiege thy brow
> And dig deep trenches in thy beauty's field,
> Thy youth's proud livery, so gazed on now,
> Will be a tottered weed, of small worth held:
> Then being asked where all thy beauty lies,
> Where all the treasure of thy lusty days,
> To say, within thine own deep-sunken eyes,
> Were an all-eating shame and thriftless praise.

But Shakespeare's logical series functions as a blind. Modifying the paradigm, he keeps to the letter, not the spirit, and his poem resolves to an octet and sestet. The octet is pretty bleak. In his sestet, reversing field, he means to hearten. (Or, defying logic, he means to hearten and cast down.) But his coordinates, though much attenuated, still speak to each other. Initiating the second quatrain, the "Then" clause can be heard as sardonic (among other things), Shakespeare rounding on his friend, hardly cheering him up, and the matter of time eating, conveyed in spiteful images, jostles the hopeful conclusion. This poet's last word is "cold." That doesn't say that his counsel is specious, his affection either. Only he is having it both ways.

So the end is inclusiveness and modifying the form is a means to the end. In LXIII, images, mounting up, compose a grisly picture of what time has in store for the loved one. The poet, like Marvell in his "Coy Mistress," caresses this picture lovingly, not entirely to his credit.

Against my love shall be as I am now,
With time's injurious hand crushed and o'erworn;
When hours have drained his blood and filled his brow
With lines and wrinkles; when his youthful morn
Hath traveled on to age's steepy night,
And all those beauties whereof now he's king
Are vanishing or vanished out of sight,
Stealing away the treasure of his spring.

"All those beauties," heavy with presage like Marvell's "all my lust," looks ahead to dust and ashes.

But just around the corner a palliative is waiting. The "sestet," supplying it, is ambiguous, though. Pronomial reference, not so clear as it might be, emphasizes this.

For such a time do I now fortify
Against confounding age's cruel knife,
That he shall never cut from memory
My sweet love's beauty, though my lover's life:
His beauty shall in these black lines be seen,
And they shall live, and he in them still green.

Readers alert to syntax may feel that the pledge of life after death is more efficient for the poet than the Fair Youth, also that this poet is fortifying himself. Ending the third quatrain, the concessive clause seems to read: "Age, though he cuts my lover's life from memory, has no jurisdiction over my verse." Editors, sponsoring a univocal Shakespeare, won't have that, and a footnote to my text asks the reader to supply "he takes" after "though," enforcing an antithesis between "my lover's life," forfeit to age and time, and his remembered beauty, still green. This keeps encomiastic Shakespeare at his appointed task. He is the encomiast all right, also other things, but the increment isn't generally noticed.

Editors, like tour guides but unlike poets, seek to pin things down, a habit of mind appropriate to pedagogy where the movement is to ratio (this = this). A considerable poet, Ransom spots the ambiguity in Shakespeare but temperamental bias, imperious in this clear-sighted man, insists that it isn't a virtue. His word for the Shakespearean range of possibilities is "romantic," i.e., inchoate. Shakespeare's poetry of the feelings, tainted with self-indulgence, doesn't "pursue its object with much zeal." Or is it that Shakespeare, uncommonly zealous, has more than a single object in view? You can argue that the multiplying of objects, dispersing his energies, enervates the poems, or that his poems are quickened by this accommodating instinct.

A microcosm of the sonnets, his LIX remembers a passage in the *Metamorphoses* (XV, 176ff.) where all things are flux, "changing place with that which goes before." In Shakespeare's version, the question is whether our time is better than what went before, or inferior to it, or whether flux or "revolution" is still as Ovid says it was. This sonnet, only a simulacrum of the prescribed form, is seamless except for the couplet. "Minding true things by what their mockeries be" (a phrase of Shakespeare's from *Henry V*), readers will want to pick up on that, observing how content isn't seamless but pestered. This promotes the altercation, noticed earlier, between content and form.

Shakespeare's young man, a nonpareil, suggests to the poet, his readers too, that there is something nèw beneath the sun.

> If there be nothing new, but that which is
> Hath been before, how are our brains beguiled.

Shakespeare wants us to read his "If" clause as contrary to fact. Lessoned by his Fair Youth, we are hardly "beguiled," and this present time when he flourishes is "mended" (l. 11) or improved, as against the long past.

Being mended, however, our modern time isn't radically improved, only "patched" (invoking the Clown in *Twelfth Night,* 1.5.52: "Anything that's mended is but patched"), and Shakespeare's "how" phrase, a tongue-twister, seems mimetic of beguiling. Surprisingly, that is what he denies. Even Shakespeare nods? His first line, read alone, reverses the position he appears to contend for. Syntax enjoins the reading: Now that I think about it, there is nothing new except that which is. This works out to the proposition: Everything that is is new; or (summoning Ecclesiastes and taking truce with Ovid): There is nothing new beneath the sun. This second reading doesn't cancel the first, and nothing but the whole poem precipitates out. The inclusiveness is Shakespeare's particular virtue, where virtue is power, and most of the famous poems declare it.

Antony and Cleopatra (the world well and ill lost) has a figure that clarifies what Shakespeare is up to. Saying his inclusive play, it gives the quiddity of his sonnets, at war between will and will not. The "common body," Caesar tells them,

Like to a vagabond flag upon the stream,
Goes back and forth, lackeying the varying tide,
To rot itself with motion.

The poems don't admit of resolution, however, not unless you rack them, and the back-and-forth goes on without term.

Shakespeare, every inch the modern artist, is the master of distinctions. But he is also old-fashioned in his art, non-perspectival. His sonnets are like paintings in the older time, and like much old music whose composer honors different voices, not distinguishing between background and foreground. In XV, for instance, "When I consider everything that grows." Matching or opposing his love for the friend, some occulted feeling calls it in question. I don't think we say that Shakespeare is self-indulgent, as when in certain late plays, not minding his dramatic manners, he breaks out against the new economics. E.g. in *Pericles*: "The blind mole casts / Copped hills towards Heaven to tell the earth is thronged / By man's oppression, and the poor worm doth die for't." That is digressive and readers ask where he is coming from. In his sonnets, however, the other thing that engages him speaks as loud as the "ostensible" poem. This differs from most modern art (i.e., post-Renaissance) where one point of view gets hegemony over the others.

Anguished by the "conceit" or thought of the Fair Youth's "inconstant stay," Shakespeare the loyalist engraves him anew in his verses. A familiar "topos" assures immortality through art, and for the first time in the sonnets Shakespeare takes off from this. (It speaks to his quality that in other sonnets, the consciousness is of universal wreck, everything gone, art included. "This thought is as a death," and the sonnets are helpless against it.) His enabling word as he ends, following the metaphor from husbandry with which he begins, is "engraft": as Time takes from you, "I engraft you new." But as he tells us up front, everything that grows "Holds in perfection but a little moment," and the Fair Youth's "stay," given this poem's logic, is necessarily "inconstant."

Not teasing, only searching, Shakespeare's scrutiny discloses other possibilities. "Stay" is also "support," in this context a weak reed, and "inconstant" is not merely "fleeting" but "fickle." A judgmental word, it reproves Shakespeare's friend. The conclusion he arrives at, though unexpected is seen to be just. That is, it surprises you but not like sleight-of-hand, and you find it rationalizable when you go back to the beginning. It isn't ironic either, only catholic or total, the poet taking all things in account.

"Rationalizable" is important, and nobody wants to be tricked. Shakespeare the rhetorician, practiced in declaiming, turns protest aside in an anthology piece like XVIII:

> Shall I compare thee to a summer's day?
> Thou art more lovely and more temperate.
> Rough winds do shake the darling buds of May,
> And summer's lease hath all too short a date.
> Sometime too hot the eye of heaven shines,
> And often is his gold complexion dimmed.
> And every fair from fair sometime declines,
> By chance or nature's changing course untrimmed.
> But thy eternal summer shall not fade,
> Nor lose possession of that fair thou owest,
> Nor shall Death brag thou wander'st in his shade
> When in eternal lines to time thou grow'st.
>> So long as men can breathe, or eyes can see,
>> So long lives this, and this gives life to thee.

Readers who look to their defenses will wonder how his young man can enjoy "eternal summer" when "every fair from fair sometime declines." Shakespeare has an answer, asking us to suppose that poetry preserves the friend's essence. "In eternal lines" is the way he puts it, perhaps begging the question. For poetry, even his, is subject to mortality, like the buds of May and all things beneath the sun.

> So long as men can breathe, or eyes can see,
> So long lives this, and this gives life to thee.

Perhaps Shakespeare's couplet is pious asseverating, rhetoric standing in for thought.

"So long" means forever, and most readers take heart at this. But in linguistic propriety Shakespeare's meditated words—heavy as stones—mean also "Just so long." Provisionality bears a part in his promise of immortal life, and his powerful affirmative carries its own negating. Disputed in the beginning, his comparison that verges on rodomontade is vindicated and amplified on a retrospective view. Negative and positive being immiscibles, readers with an eye for tidiness want to separate them out. In Shakespeare's sonnets, however, "there's place and means" for both. The quotation comes from *All's Well That Ends Well,* and the sonnets in this particular anticipate the plays.

Putting a question to begin his poem, Shakespeare devises an answer. The question—but it needn't be interrogative, only a taking-off point—is his given or "topos." This technical word, a good peg to hang the sonnets on, commits poets to an enterprise both exacting and essentially formal. In the nature of the enterprise, disposing counts more than inventing. Any given will do and what matters is how they assess it. We call Shakespeare sincere when his assessment checks out.

His summer's day comparison, ventured first in XVIII, diverts him again in XXXIII:

> Full many a glorious morning have I seen
> Flatter the mountain tops with sovereign eye,
> Kissing with golden face the meadows green,
> Gilding pale streams with heavenly alchemy;
> Anon permit the basest clouds to ride
> With ugly rack on his celestial face
> And from the forlorn world his visage hide,
> Stealing unseen to west with this disgrace.
> Even so my sun one early morn did shine
> With all-triumphant splendor on my brow.
> But out, alack! he was but one hour mine,
> The region cloud hath masked him from me now.
>> Yet him for this my love no whit disdaineth.
>> Suns of the world may stain when heaven's sun staineth.

This second time round, reperusal of the data dictates a change of mind or heart. The beautiful boy, assimilated to the sun, is put down remorselessly: a flatterer, "coiner" or counterfeiter, an alchemist pretending to transmute base metals, patient of himself, a culprit on the way to Tyburn, "stealing unseen to west" with his disgrace. No matter, says the last line, "Suns of the world may stain when heaven's sun staineth." We end with a democracy of insufficiency, though.

XVIII and XXXIII, complementary and opposed, salute each other from a distance. But a linear pattern overlays Shakespeare's sequence, and many of his sonnets arrange themselves in pairs, often in triads. (Some examples of the former are nos. XXVII–XXVIII, XLVI–XLVII, LVII–LVIII, LXXI–LXXII, LXXIII–LXXIV. Poems that exhibit the triad pattern include nos. XXXIII–XXXIV–XXXV, LXXVIII–LXXIX–LXXX, LXXXVIII–LXXXIX–XC, CIX–CX–CXI.) A convenient phrase for this is thesis-antithesis-synthesis, except that the synthesis is only linguistic. Shakespeare's "essays" at truth, some enormously persuasive, are "topoi," precisely, begetting different answers to a question posed.

Two well-known sonnets, XXIX and XXX, show him bending to the work. Misery is his burden in the first of these poems, "When in disgrace with fortune and men's eyes." At the end he gets rid of it, buoyed by the remembrance of his friend's "sweet love." This ending is happy. Canvassing the same materials, the next poem in his series, "When to the sessions of sweet silent thought," recites a litany of old woes or grievances. In this second poem also, thoughts of the "dear friend" make losses good. But Shakespeare, looking in the mirror, doesn't like what he sees. Down in the dumps, he is enjoying himself, watering his "chamber round / With eye-offending brine" (like his sentimental heroine in *Twelfth Night*). His woes are "sweet," called up to be exploited, a deplorable activity, at the same time refreshing. (Really that is what he tells us but readers won't trust their ears.) The couplet, a touch perfunctory, breaks off his relishing of sorrows. Another happy ending, this one is felt as too bad.

We who listen to the poet as he speaks on both sides of the question are auditors of a dramatic performance. He, if faithful to it, has to get his voices down pat. But Shakespeare, though expert in mimicry, isn't simply a mimic, and the cold-blooded artificer is also the beleaguered man, caught in a kind of hell, intolerably complete vision. More sympathetic than most or listening harder, he contains in himself all possible points of view. His special knack or unhappiness is to honor them all.

But he isn't "importunate" enough, Ransom thinks, never proposing to lose himself in the object. That isn't a saving reluctance. His considering eye is a roving eye and the willingness to hold off—Hamletesque, it might be—looks like irresolution, almost a moral failure. Why couldn't he make up his mind?

In Nashville in the Sixties, I spent an evening with "Mr. Ransom." That was how I addressed him and how he still seems to me, not a personage who asked homage but a courtly old gentleman you were glad to defer to. A bad time, the Sixties, when many of my acquaintance knew what they knew, announcing it on placards. Some in our company, raising the big questions, weren't behindhand in offering answers. Mr. Ransom, a good listener, wasn't among them.

I wanted to quiz him about his poetry, especially "The Equilibrists," his tale of two lovers who don't make it together. Fixed like painful stars, they spin in their different orbits, burning to come near. Honor beats them

back, though, and these two live out their lives in a "torture of equilib-
rium." This scenario is like Andrew Marvell's in his "Definition of Love,"
where another poet wants another mistress but Fate drives iron wedges
between them. Their love, linked in spirit, never in body, shows as the
mind's conjunction and "opposition" of the stars, separated by 180 degrees.
Perhaps "The Equilibrists" found a starting point in this seventeenth-cen-
tury poem?

But a striking young woman at the dinner table—I remember the
"honey-colored ramparts at her ear"—had questions of her own to put.
The masses of blond hair belied what she was, which only goes to show.
Issuing from a brain stocked with German philosophy, especially "the
famous philosopher Hegel," her questions bristled with capital letters.
Much about Truth and Beauty, Beauty and Truth. Smoothing out his nap-
kin, our guest attended thoughtfully, now and then murmuring answers.
They weren't really answers but her questions, politely rephrased. Where
was the sharpshooter who drew a bead on Shakespeare and unlucky Edna
Millay? One way or another, we survived the evening, but I never got to
ask about Marvell.

This was no great loss. Marvell's poem, if it gives Ransom the germ of
his idea, goes off in another direction. The older poet is anti-consummation
and his "Definition of Love" is when the lovers don't embrace. Ransom's
poem is a house divided, one reason it stands. Taking leave of logic, it goes
in two directions at once.

No lovers more passionate than the Equilibrists, her white flesh tinder
to his lecheries, her body a field of lilies beseeching him to take. But if he
plucks the lilies, he bruises or breaks them, and honor instructs him not to
do this. A gray word and officious, its counsels are ill sped. But dispute them
and you end up in Hell. Point counterpoint, and that is where great lovers
lie. But when they kiss they rend each other, a never-ending torment.

> Would you ascend to Heaven and bodiless dwell?
> Or take your bodies honorless to Hell?

This is a quandary, "Predicament indeed," except that most, strait-laced or
libertine, resolve it without ado. It wouldn't have stumped Mr. Ransom's
interlocutor. For him, the predicament is the poem, though, and you need
the whole poem to measure its sharpness. A rueful epitaph, giving and tak-
ing, remembers his lovers. "Perilous and beautiful," he calls them.

This scholar-critic, trained first in the modern sciences, came late to an interest in poetry. Vain about his early training, a whetstone for the mind, he displays it in his critical prose. There, discriminations are notably acute. Poems and plays were immiscible, like oil and water, and in the essay on the sonnets he drew a line between them. Shakespeare is the despair of tax-onomers, however. The same facts are controlling for his comedies and tragedies but not the point of vantage from which he inspects them. In *Romeo and Juliet* he makes a noble threnody, celebrating romantic love. This becomes a theme for laughter in his next play, *A Midsummer Night's Dream*. But his dream play isn't unalloyed laughter. So far, the playwright is like Shakespeare at sonnets, and readers will think of other examples.

His plays, unlike the sonnets, offer him surrogates, "circus animals," a later poet called them. Versions of himself, sometimes polar opposites, they confer greater freedom on Shakespeare the playwright. In the sonnet, a solo performance, he has to speak in propria persona. The requirement is oner-ous but he takes it on, my guess is that he courts it, liking to be in straits. The narrower compass certifies his agility, also putting the stamp of truth on what he has to say. (His saying is more credible because forced from him under pressure.) Moving up and down the gamut from comfort to despair, he plays many parts in his first-person pronoun. But where the plays need five acts to accommodate all he is, Shakespeare at sonnets does his back-and-forth in fourteen lines.

This stunning performance makes life hard on readers who prefer the certainty of one meaning to the possibility of two. Inconsistency holds no ter-rors for him, "two-headed Janus" (the god he swears by in *The Merchant of Venice*). He isn't inconsistent, though, only "circumambient." His poems are all of a piece but not coherent like prose, or they appeal to a larger coherence. (The narrow compass belies this, another instance where form and content have their useful contention.) Paraphrase, always inadequate for poetry, falsifies this poet absolutely, and if you are going to close with him you must honor his words, just the ones he uses. Involving himself with the latencies of words, he composes differences or allows them houseroom in the interest of his comprehensive truth. It isn't simply that he is better than Mr. Ransom's eruditi, Sidney and Donne, rather that he ploughs a wider furrow.

But I want to look at some poems where the larger truth absorbs him. This needs close reading, and many, satisfied with Shakespeare-in-outline, will call it perverse or myopic. Close reading has its comic side ("peeping and botanizing") but readers of the sonnets ought to be myopic, eyes right down on the page. Words being Shakespeare's medium, that is where you find him.

A good poem to begin with is LXXVI, docketed by scholars as one of Shakespeare's "Rival Poet" poems. This one introduces a dessicated Shakespeare, dried up in his invention and always harping on the one string. As his poem progresses, though, he sees how to excuse himself. Things could hardly be otherwise, since the Fair Youth is his inevitable subject. His sonnet, an integer, makes a graceful tribute to this friend.

> Why is my verse so barren of new pride,
> So far from variation or quick change?
> Why with the time do I not glance aside
> To new-found methods and to compounds strange?
> Why write I still all one, ever the same,
> And keep invention in a noted weed,
> That every word doth almost tell my name,
> Showing their birth and where they did proceed?
> Oh, know, sweet love, I always write of you,
> And you and love are still my argument;
> So all my best is dressing old words new,
> Spending again what is already spent:
>   For as the sun is daily new and old,
>   So is my love still telling what is told.

In fact, the poet's excuse, a valid one, is there from the beginning, and what he lacks and his rival has is what he is better off for not having. The "pride" he doesn't have denotes extravagant clothing, also sexual heat. This attribute, appropriate to bad actors like his Dark Lady, seducing purity with her "foul pride" (CXLIV), is morally evil. The "quick" change not open to him equates to shifty behavior, and anyway who wants to get in step "with the time," cultivating up-to-the-minute expedients and eccentric "compounds." Worse for being that, the compounds are adulterated.

But Shakespeare's integer, inspected, shows fissures, or it encloses another poem within itself. "Barren" is childless, a deprived condition, and "quick," an approbative word, tells of life. The (medicinal) compounds Shakespeare isn't learned in might help to heal him, if they weren't outside his ken. You recognize this poor poet by his ever-the-same garment, "noted" or stigmatized, also residually like a worthless plant. All his "best is dress," mere show without substance. (That is what the ear says, but intellectualizing readers rarely consult it.) He resembles an old clothes' man or "botcher," refurbishing wornout words. A fiscal image presents him, "spent" like a bankrupt; also, as the lexical range gets its due, sexually flaccid. The mutable sun to which he compares himself is, if renewing, cozening too. But the comparison includes both poet and Fair Youth, "my love" working two ways, a vice or hallmark of Shakespeare's. Each is "still" (three times repeated) telling over a tedious tale. How boring! "Why is my verse so barren of new pride?" Because, "sweet love, I always write of you."

A word about pronouns: in Shakespeare, they tend to "squint." This sows confusion, and no doubt he is doing what his critic says he shouldn't, exploiting the uncertain possibility of two meanings rather than the certainty of one. I must distinguish, however, between post-modern theory's infinite range of meanings and the ambiguity that doesn't blur but widens our horizon. Shakespeare at sonnets complicates his poems, amplifying their meaning. The primary reading is obvious, at once true and intended, the complicating or even contradicting is residually true, and the poet, a regisseur, controls both.

He gives the critics fits in his notorious sonnet XCIV, "They that have power to hurt and will do none." These icy characters, niggards of themselves and profoundly unattractive, "rightly do inherit heaven's graces." That is Shakespeare's proposal, hard to swallow. This poem's argument runs counter to that of the "procreation" sonnets with which Shakespeare's sequence begins. (Ransom, tapping his ferrule, observes this.) Vindicating the friend, a version of Narcissus or the austere Angelo of *Measure for Measure,* Shakespeare bids him hug himself to himself, keeping clear of erotic attachments. That way, he builds his credit. This counsel is disinterested but desperately partial, and the poet, with due deliberateness, is locating himself on the horns. Not confused but mimetic of confusion, the poem enacts his bifold condition.

Confusion gets its quietus in LXXXVII, "Farewell! thou art too dear for my possessing." Or is confusion aggravated to the end that Shakespeare's readers see more than before? An exercise in self-deprecating, his sonnet tells the same story over and over. Good-bye to the friend, only a "leasehold" love, not "fee simple." Ransom remarks the charm of the feminine endings but oddly doesn't "hear" what this dying fall does to the poem.

> Farewell! thou art too dear for my possessing,
> And like enough thou know'st thy estimate:
> The charter of thy worth gives thee releasing;
> My bonds in thee are all determinate.
> For how do I hold thee but by thy granting?
> And for that riches where is my deserving?
> The cause of this fair gift in me is wanting,
> And so my patent back again is swerving.
> Thyself thou gavest, thy own worth then not knowing,

Or me, to whom thou gavest it, else mistaking;
So thy great gift, upon misprision growing,
Comes home again, on better judgment making.
    Thus have I had thee, as a dream doth flatter,
    In sleep a king, but waking no such matter.

This sonnet says how meter and diction make argument, confounding the sense or enforcing a second sense. Diction means rhetorical questions (but they don't beget the expected answers), a heaping up of gerunds, gravid monosyllables in Shakespeare's last line. Also it means metaphor, legal and fiscal, a series of terms that puts a bargain before us, not a world-without-end bargain, however. Meter is that lugubrious extra syllable in all but two of Shakespeare's lines. Silences play into this, a strong hiatus after "waking" as the poem gathers itself to conclude. The gerunds accumulating, each line augurs this conclusion, and the emotional thrust, bitterly reprehending, tilts at the paraphrasable content. "Thus have I had thee": a glozing or fictive love. Damning and acquitting in the same breath, Shakespeare makes a strange panegyrist.

"Fulsome panegyric," partly strategic, dowers the young man. "Be thou the tenth Muse," Shakespeare urges him (XXXVIII), a richer source of inspiration than the other nine in aggregate. This friend gets all the praise for whatever is "worthy perusal" in the poet. The poem, concluding, says so:

If my slight Muse do please these curious days,
The pain be mine, but thine shall be the praise.

"Pains" is what we expect, as in "painstaking," but "pain" is what he gets. That is partly as his "slight Muse" points to the poet, also to his equivocal friend.

The Fair Youth is Shakespeare's alter ego, however, "two distincts, division none" (recalling his sonnet-like "Phoenix and Turtle"). In CXVI, a much-loved sonnet, handed round for a long time between boys and girls, he salutes this perfect union:

Let me not to the marriage of true minds
Admit impediments.

He is saying with the expected gravity: May I never do this. But syntax, scansion too, heard as "impedimented," allow of a subtext. I think the poem demands it. The speaker, a doubtful lover amply schooled by his friend, is saying also: Don't let me do this. We who look and listen, standing in the wings, are asked to hold him back, restraining an impulse to admit what he denies. "Love is not love," this exasperated poet thinks. (Lines in poetry, enjambed or otherwise, need their autonomy.) Truth will out, and unless we stop him he will speak as "liberal" as the north wind. That is how his Emilia speaks in *Othello*. As the play makes clear, she hasn't any recourse, and neither has Shakespeare's poet.

But poets say what they mean or ought to? That is certainly true. What they mean depends on diction and syntax, however, and it seems fair to hold the poet to this. For the criticism of poetry, words and how they go together are the only Ariadne's thread. So Shakespeare's readers have a choice, not easily evaded. (Unlike his performance in poetry, this choice comes down to either/or.) They can fault the performance, detecting in his sonnets an incoherent Shakespeare, or agree to call him "myriad-minded." Mostly, this well-worn phrase is a cliché of criticism, not really looked into, and single-minded readers will jib at what it discloses. Poems that grapple with big subjects, Shakespeare's poems, need complicatedness, however. A true marriage of minds that persist in their allegiance is hard to pull off, life instructing us endlessly how the course of true love never did run smooth. Poems that ask to be taken seriously will want to reflect this.

One of these poems is CXLVI, "Poor soul, the center of my sinful earth." Alone among the 154 sonnets that make up Shakespeare's sequence, this one, rejecting our quotidian world, appeals to the World over Yonder. Editors often compare it to Donne's Holy Sonnet, "Death, be not proud." But Shakespeare sees a logical fallacy in through-and-through conversion pieces, as when Mad Jack turns into the Dean of St. Paul's. "Anything that's mended is but patched. Virtue that transgresses is but patched with sin, and sin that amends is but patched with virtue." Or Shakespeare's ear tells him that the Platonic strain needs amplification, some judicious impurity. Truth being at issue, a monophonic composition won't do for him, and his poem, faintly dissonant, makes room for different voices.

A *De contemptu mundi* poem, CXLVI ratifies the soul's wisdom in preferring "terms divine" to "hours of dross." At the end, bizarrely feeding on death and invigorated by this, it quits the fortified place where rebel powers besiege it. Why spend such large cost on a "fading mansion"? "Is this thy body's end?" Poor body!

Shakespeare's questions have answers but readers who take thought won't speak them too quickly. The soul, not plagued by questions, thinks that life hereafter is a better bet than life in the meantime, contingent on the body's loss. Along the way to Heaven, though, it makes certain fiscal arrangements, and buying and selling portray a calculating soul. The bottom line, salvation, gets our approval. This is the meaning most pick from Shakespeare's lines but it isn't plenary, and Shakespeare sees to it that approval is tempered. Listening to him, not between the lines but consulting the lines, we are made to feel uneasy at the shopkeeper-mix of calculation and virtue.

Ransom gives high marks to Shakespeare's "Platonic" poem, "a noble revulsion" and the most "spiritual" of the sonnets. "Spiritual" is good, like "Platonic," and the body and its claims get downgraded. Shakespeare would have been better served had he employed this poem "to conclude the unhappy history, leaving quite off the eight miscellaneous and indeterminate ones that follow." But "indeterminate" is what we want, never more so than here.

Shakespeare's sonnet, singular in its concern with last things, is true to the rest of them in the way its subject is invested. He doesn't believe in the kernel of truth and doesn't strip away the husk but adds layer on layer. His multilayered performances don't preclude meaning, though, and the sonnets, however much trouble they give, aren't conundrums. But Shakespeare's meaning is comprehensive like the life his poems describe. Putting it that way seems to intimate some didactic purpose in this writer, whereas he wanted to "please many and please long." Johnson, implicative as often, used these words in his preface to Shakespeare's plays. Both the plays and sonnets depend for their special pleasure on the circus master's impulse to get everything under one tent.

Chapter 2

Sex and Science in Donne

Here is the voice of Donne, never heard before in English:

> Away thou fondling motley humorist,
> Leave me, and in this standing wooden chest,
> Consorted with these few books, let me lie
> In prison, and here be coffined, when I die;
> Here are God's conduits, grave divines; and here
> Nature's secretary, the philosopher;
> And jolly statesmen, which teach how to tie
> The sinews of a city's mystic body;
> Here gathering chroniclers, and by them stand
> Giddy fantastic poets of each land.
> Shall I leave all this constant company,
> And follow headlong, wild uncertain thee?

Primarily a speaking voice but peculiar to him, Donne's, leading off his Satires, is anti-poetic. Like Robert Frost, he dragged the intonations of colloquial speech across his pre-established accent and measure, "as waves first comb and then break stumbling on the shingle." From this contention of spontaneous and formal comes his distinctive manner, fleering, cerebral, cankered, dropping to occasional, tender, mounting to impassioned. His language, rammed with life, gives his meters something to do.

Nothing says that poets have to be better than anyone else, only on their official side, and he illustrates both propositions. He begins the mandarin tradition in poetry, wanting no such readers as he could teach. Shakespeare pleased many, he pleased a few, stooping to publish only three or four poems in a lifetime. Technique, upfront in the poems, fascinated this highbrow, but his letters are full of the man. More of them survive than from any other author of the time except Bacon. Donne's unofficial side gets free rein in the letters, bringing him down to our level. He couldn't help posturing, and waiting at death's door had himself sketched in his shroud.

In his "little world made cunningly," attention focused on the microcosm, that is, himself. Like Sir Thomas Browne, he treated the macrocosm as an artificial globe, turning it round for recreation. But though lesser than Shakespeare because felt as more personal, he gives us some things Shakespeare doesn't. His gifts and impairments swap back and forth, and how the egocentricity modifies the poems needs a case-by-case analysis. Sometimes, equating the world and the self, he makes you accept the connection.

Supplicating the great, he sought "a hole for so poor a worm as I" to creep in at, but the place he wanted escaped him, and the letters go on about it. One he addressed from "my hospital" at Mitcham, the cottage near London where he "purged and vexed" his body. He had hard words for the body, "bedded and bathed in all his ordures." Neuritis tormented him, melancholia too, and meditating suicide, he wrote a tract defending it. Other crosses he had to bear included his children, "mast" or acorns, food for swine. Hope of gain and "a rotten state," not England's, his own, sent him abroad on military service, but he came back empty-handed except for a clutch of poems.

Few of the poems owe anything to contemporary poets, and it seems he wrote in a vacuum. Or he took his cue from classical poets in the "rusty iron age." Another Persius, one reader called him, after the Roman satirist, crabbed, often elliptical, and his particular study. But he warmed to Marlowe, another pestered spirit whose damnation of Faustus spoke to him in personal ways. Some "matter in his heart" struggled up toward the light, failing to find it. This is how King Claudius diagnoses Hamlet's problem, and many see his likeness in Donne.

Early accounts of the life tell an education-of-the-hero story, first Mad Jack, "a great visitor of ladies, a great frequenter of plays, a great writer of conceited verses," then Dr. Donne, who got out of himself as he practiced salvation. The recreations of his youth were poetry, the mistress of his age divinity, according to his first biographer, Walton. But some poems postdate his ordination, only the "stamp" changing, the way "new crowned kings" altered the face, "not the money's substance" ("To Mr. Tilman"). The religious poet still has sex on the brain, and unless God enthralls him never can be free, "nor ever chaste, except you ravish me." Shockers like this famous sonnet lay "bare before us the recesses of Donne's heart," said his editor Evelyn Simpson, intending praise. Circumspection might have served him better, but he wouldn't be himself if he were tactful.

Sexual glory irradiates the love poems, "things / Extreme and scatt'ring bright." He blots it, however. Tone violates "The Funeral," its magnificent line, "that subtle wreath of hair which crowns my arm," undercut by a trivial ending. "A Valediction: of Weeping," moving toward a grave ending, decides for whimsy, "Air and Angels" for a putdown. "Love's Progress" ends with an enema. "The Relic" trails off in compliment, "The Expiration" in a quibble. In many of his poems, analogies exceed the thing they mean to clarify, and the life is in the subordinate clause. Shakespeare's portmanteau sonnets, not distracted but augmented, illustrate the difference.

Oxymoron, "the conceit of the contraries," is the trope he favors. Often dejecting us, he often freshens seeing, but his means to the end invite wonder. Moderns, making it new, take after him, sometimes for better— Eliot, for instance, laying out the evening like "a patient etherized upon a table." But Hart Crane is his scholar too, resembling love to "a burnt match skating in a urinal." Much "violent yoking" in Donne's similitudes, and if he can't always clarify, he can startle. E.g. sexual consummation, like the meeting of a lamb and the priest who embowels her. A clergyman friend of his makes "a blest hermaphrodite," knitting up in his person our father heaven and our mother earth. The poet Herbert's mother isn't yet like other women,

> Whose every tooth to a several place is gone,
>   To vex their souls at Resurrection.

This disclaimer can't have pleased. Many of his good things edge close to hysteria, and savaging old perceptions was how he cleared the ground for new ones.

Cynicism, the perversion of candor, denied him access to the resonant style. His "Progress of the Soul," disheartening, like Jonson's verses "On the Famous Voyage," follows the apple Eve plucked in the Garden until it becomes "the soul of a bitch, then of a she-wolf, and so of a woman." His poetry says he hated woman, "a grave, that's dust without and stink within." Loving went with this but the split is acidulated, not your common "odi et amo." His sexual bravado is the other side of his misogyny, and in "The Comparison," the poem I quote from here, both get rope enough to hang him. Older women were better than young ones, like the summer's sun, admired but he shunned their heat for shadow. This failing, he had a remedy, "applying worm-seed to the tail."

But he covers a lot of territory, and if you don't like his Rochester or

Swift, wait until he does Yeats and Browning. The text he chose for a late sermon, "In my Father's house are many mansions," makes a good epigraph for poetry where a hedonist, priest, and scientist find house room. More than forty different stanza forms set off the fifty-five poems of his *Songs and Sonnets*. He racked the songs deliberately, mistrusting smoothness or perhaps accessibility. Some of his constructions mimic hard thought, but some look involuntary, like a nervous tic. In the Donnean style, modifiers float free, the verb hangs back until the end of the line, and when two verbs are wanted, often a single verb spells both.

Poetry like his, said Dr. Johnson, was "only found to be verses by counting the syllables." But his ear is sure and he labored until he got the count right. A Castiglione-ish poet, all *sprezzatura,* he didn't want you to know that. You mustn't call him frivolous, though. One of the elegies, evidently a witty travelogue, deepens to tragedy when his mistress imagines and reproves him:

> I saw him, I,
> Assailed, fight, taken, stabbed, bleed, fall, and die.
>
> (XVI)

Registered as near frantic if you read the poem aloud, Donne's lines are regular, only the simulacrum of dissonance. Airing it out, he meant to subdue it. "Love was peace that now is rage," affronting his sense of decorum. Failing to bring peace, he left us a sword, but his failure is worth many others' successes.

In an age that valued artifice, he defers to none, surprising in a poet who says what comes to mind. Words were like charms. He repeats them in different forms, inverting the ordering a second time round, or repeats the same word, with or without words intervening:

> Good we must love, and must hate ill,
> For ill is ill, and good good still.
>
> ("Community")

In the Elegies and "La Corona" poems, opposites balance on a syntactic tickle point, composing what might be a quarrel between them:

> That was her torrid and inflaming time,
>   This is her tolerable tropic clime . . . .
> Here, where still evening is, not noon nor night,

Where no voluptuousness, yet all delight.

(Elegy IX, "The Autumnal")

This calipered style, surprising us, looks forward to the Augustans.

Willing our good or meditating our overthrow, a self-conscious artist tugs at the heart strings, sometimes throwing dust in the eyes. A lot of him is gamesmanship. His staple mode of building, the As . . . So construction, often seems the facade of consecutive thought, and the fun is in finding him out. Too proud to argue (in Elegy II, "The Anagram"), he fobs us off with a proverb:

Beauty is barren oft; best husbands say,
There is best land where there is foulest way—

or he answers his questions by fiat. Should he abjure Variety? He shouldn't, and here's why:

Rivers the clearer and more pleasing are,
Where their fair spreading streams run wide and far;
And a dead lake that no strange bark doth greet,
Corrupts itself and what doth live in it.

(Elegy XVII)

But what has the bark (the new lover) to do with the water, whether fresh or stagnant? Maybe, roiling the surface, it stirs up the mud. Poetry like this achieves its assent by a verbal coup de main, and he knows it.

His purview is just that, only partial in respect to the facts. Logic takes a beating in his satire "Of Religion," by design a rumination on contemporary business. Though the poem is more real than most, enlivened by questions and the dancing caesura, it isn't ruminative, and Donne's catechizing resolves to "the dialogue of one." "True religion" is his quarry, but where is it housed? He burkes this question, and though his "sentence," very Donnean, enjoins taking thought, the last couplet speaks for submission.

By common consent a problem solver, he doesn't always come up with the answers. Readers will want to ask whether the rhetorician, deceiving others, deceives himself, or whether the agnosticism is part of his signature. "What we love" is a problem "The Ecstasy" copes with, but listen:

We see by this it was not sex,
We see we saw not what did move.

The phrasing is simple but not exactly clear, and the emphatic pronouncing—all those words of one syllable, eight in each line—strikes an uncertain note. His poems protest too much.

As if getting his bearings, he glances three times at "this place" where he finds himself, Twickenham Garden. His subject in "The Blossom" provokes speculation, and pronouns, a surfeit of them, have to nail it down. The poem for St. Lucy's Day, piling "since" on "since," looks like a theme for reason, but his conclusion seems helpless, only a reprise of the line he begins with: "'Tis the year's midnight and it is the day's." As "The Canonization" ends and "The Legacy" begins, sentence structure impales his thought. Sound treads on sense ("therefore for"), and bald rhymes like "go / ago" press his point hard. Or the run of the line raises eyebrows. A heart or something like it is the legacy he leaves us:

> colors it, and corners had,
> It was not good, it was not bad.

You don't expect this rumpty-tumpty of "the monarch of wit," but he wants you to hear it, important for affect. His special affect mixes jocose brutality with profound unknowing. When he gets to Heaven, he hopes to see things all round, but only in Heaven does God proceed "to this patefaction, this manifestation, this revelation of Himself" and His creatures (*LXXX Sermons,* no. 23).

Despite the mandarin pose or bearing it out, his new Art of Loving is a primer for lay folk. But kinetic it isn't. You don't hear him proposing to "fashion" noble persons, and, though he liked to "exagitate"—one of his words, it means putting things in motion—he has no purpose but delighting. In keeping with his hermetic bias, this meant self-delighting. His *Devotions* (1624), the record of grave illness and a time for long thoughts, honor God the Metaphysical poet. "Full of comparisons," Donne calls Him. Some poets in his time, meliorist and benevolent or possibly harried, cast a wider net than he does. Spenser, assimilating his art to rhetoric and its threefold agenda ("prodesse et delectare et movere" = teaching and delighting and impelling to action), throws the last term in relief. This bump of intentionality is missing in the Donne most readers admire and quote from.

But he wanted to "do something," he said to his longtime correspondent Sir Henry Goodyer (Sept. 1608). The God of the Sermons is a Protestant God: "*actus purus,* all action, all doing" (*XXVI,* no. 24), and "Protestant" St. Augustine writes most of His lines. Anxious purpose bristles in the

"Anniversaries," one heuristic and doctrinal, the other prodding us on as we move up to Heaven. Modern scholarship shows the author lifting their three-part structure, meditation, eulogy, and exhortation, from reformers like Loyola, whose 1–2–3 sequence narrows to a point. "The greatest persons are but great wens and excrescences," Donne wrote to Goodyer, only "moles for ornament except they be so incorporated into the body of the world that they contribute something to the sustenation of the whole." In 1608, recovered from sickness, he made "a meditation in verse, which I call a Litany." This long didactic poem says how "our task is treble, to pray, bear, and do" (XIV). A praxis-minded poet, enlarging our sense of him, announces himself in the commitment.

He hefted every line, however, even noting elisions. Anointed themes and subjects crop up obsessively, among them sex and New Philosophy, i.e. modern science, but matter defers to manner or you could say to opportunity, not least when the matter is religious. The conscious problems that concern him are metrical, and more kin to music than the exposition of ideas. Like an old-fashioned poet's, his form holds his content hostage. For example, his contemporary George Wither: "If I please I'll end it here, / If I list I'll sing this year."

Hoping to fetter sexual pain in verse, he drew an analogy to the physical world, where "earth's inward narrow crooked lanes" purge the salt of the sea. But restraining grief in numbers freed it again, and the poet, who was two fools for loving and for saying so, became "the triple fool" of his poem. He is letting us know that the manner he was famous for gets nothing done, and perhaps in his own eyes he saw himself as a sciolist or trifler. But he wore his sciolism with a difference. Dryden complained that he perplexed "the minds of the fair sex with nice speculations of philosophy when he should engage their hearts and entertain them with the softnesses of love." The first clause, at least, is true.

Sex and science make an odd couple in the poems of *Songs and Sonnets*. Many are obligated to sources "not very much frequented by common readers." Dr. Johnson smelled a fault and Donne acknowledged a problem. He said he was "diverted by the worst voluptuousness" (to Goodyer, Sept. 1609). "Voluptuous" brings to mind the rake who wrote "The Indifferent"—he could love any, "so she be not true"—but he meant to describe his intellectual part, inflamed with a "hydroptic" desire of learning. The Elixer of Life, a goal of the older chemistry, gets him going in "Love's Alchemy," serious poetry that opens with an off-color joke. In "The Ecstasy," optics as he understood it offers him the chance for more sexual bantering, and at first (but not last) "pictures in our eyes to get" is all their propagation. Unexampled pretension, not a fault, only risky, characterizes his greatest love poems, and wit, a judicious lowering, allowed him to carry them off.

Like most older poets, he traded on the connection of death and sexual climax. No bad thing to experience the latter, but its pleasure comes and goes. Death of the body is permanent, though. This loose agglomerate, mixing different elements, isn't an integer, so falls to decay. Older medicine supplied the facts, and in "The Good-Morrow," the first poem of *Songs and Sonnets*, Donne rehearsed them.

> I wonder, by my troth, what thou and I
> Did, till we loved? Were we not weaned till then?
> But sucked on country pleasures childishly?
> Or snorted we in the Seven Sleepers' den?
> Twas so. But this, all pleasures fancies be.
> If ever any beauty I did see
> Which I desired and got, 'twas but a dream of thee.
>
> And now good morrow to our waking souls,
> Which watch not one another out of fear;
> For love, all love of other sights controls,
> And makes one little room an everywhere.
> Let sea-discoverers to new worlds have gone,
> Let maps to other, worlds on worlds have shown,
> Let us possess one world, each hath one, and is one.
>
> My face in thine eye, thine in mine appears,
> And true plain hearts do in the faces rest.
> Where can we find two better hemispheres
> Without sharp north, without declining west?
> Whatever dies was not mixed equally;
> If our two loves be one, or, thou and I
> Love so alike that none do slacken, none can die.

Surrogates for the rest of us, Donne's two lovers hope to outwit mortality as they appeal from difference to oneness. Being one, however, they lose the chance for orgasm, winning their triumph over death at some cost. Or perfection in them, another word for stasis, is like the tale of the Seven Sleepers, i.e. too good to be true. These primitive Christians, eluding persecution, snored out the centuries, and when the coast was clear, woke up unmarked by time's tooth.

The Platonic lie, cheerful like Donne's fairy tale, gets a hearing in his poem: "And true plain hearts do in the faces rest." This "And," pretending to sequence, is a good one. "No art to find the mind's construction in the face," said Shakespeare's King Duncan, who had reason to know, and as for the "better hemispheres" the poet means to summon, they aren't within the ken of sailors, astronomers either. Anaphoric and contemptuous, the run of the lines gives these wide-ranging men their quietus. Though paraphrase puts Donne's lovers in a class by themselves, the syntactic chase, *Let* . . . *Let* . . . *Let,* no getting round it, insists that lovers, sailors, and makers of sky maps are the same.

Maybe "two better hemispheres" are out there, not invaded like ours by coldness and change for the worse. He and we don't want to entertain them, however. His two lovers, armored in their integrity, are suspiciously marmoreal. They go on forever, like Keats's on the Urn. But consummation needs declining, and if "none do slacken, none can die." Shakespeare's character is our authority, saying how "to serve bravely is to come halting off" (*Henry IV,* pt. 2, 2.4.50). An ambiguous good-morrow, Donne's promotes the opposite of what it seems to, and his lovers wake to life as they discover its kinship to dying.

Other poems of his, yoking sex and science together, rejoice in this meditated confusion. "A Valediction: Forbidding Mourning" likens the lovers to a pair of compasses. The Metaphysical image par excellence, it isn't what you expect in a love poem. In Donne's, souls, not bodies, occupy the poet, and are joined, though you can't see this, "like gold to airy thinness beat." Or

> If they be two, they are two so
>   As stiff twin compasses are two,
> Thy soul, the fixed foot, makes no show
>   To move, but doth if the other do.
>
> And though it in the center sit,
>   Yet when the other far doth roam,
> It leans, and hearkens after it,
>   And grows erect as that comes home.
>
> Such wilt thou be to me, who must
>   Like the other foot, obliquely run;
> Thy firmness draws my circle just,
>   And makes me end where I begun.

Donne picked his conceit from Italian Guarini, always ingenious though not good for our health in poetry. He began the vogue of mongrel tragicomedy, and in a pair of envoi poems imagines a lover saying good-bye to his mistress. Though she fears that out of sight must mean out of mind, this lover-plus-geometrician assures her: "I am like the compass, and fix one foot in you as in my center; the other, while it suffers all the turns of Fortune, can only turn around yourself." Clever, otherwise not implicative, Guarini leaves it at that, but Donne adds an increment, special to him. Diction, enjoining it, makes a cluster of "stiff," "center," "grows erect," "firmness," and "circle." Freudians to the contrary, credentialed poets don't slip, and Donne's words incline us to think of sexual coupling. Looked at with a scrupulous eye, however, they don't fit the case, putting it mildly. "She," all firmness, grows erect? Meanwhile the other one—who else but "he"?—completes his circle. Perhaps an inattentive poet got his sexes wrong, leaving us to sort out the confusion. Or perhaps, confusing us, he wants to. In the opening lines, signaling his intention, good men, living just now, are dying, and you can't distinguish one state from the other. "Melt" in the second stanza continues this back-and-forth, while the image from metallurgy, denying a "breach," presents an "expansion." Meter demands that you honor all four syllables, giving each its due. Donne's reasons are more than merely exigent, though.

"Dull sublunary lovers' love," unlike our "refined" love, makes a sonantal lump. In the middle stanzas, readers are invited to distinguish between the two kinds. But distinctions aren't easy in the "Valediction," and you have to look hard to see what the pronouns refer to. This is decorous, however. Only when things are "interassured," flowing into things, is our best condition realized, and Donne's lovers, careless of eyes, lips, and hands, come to themselves as they shuck the "he" and "she." Scandalous counsel to the poet of "The Good-Morrow"! But that was yesterday, this is today, and if Donne contradicts himself, then he contradicts himself.

Contradictions are what you predicate of a poet who reasons from his hands to his head. Testing or "titrating," he made love poems that are full of becoming, and neither he nor we can be wholly certain what he will say next. Like Dante's master in the *Paradiso* (XXIV), he propounds a question "to argue it, not to conclude it." Interrogatory verse is the most of the poetry, but his questions don't precede the poems, they rise from them. Engaged with matter-of-fact, he belongs with his contemporaries Galileo, William Gilbert, and Kepler. A generation before Harvey, he knew how blood, flowing to the heart, "doth from one ventricle to the other go." Gilbert's treatise "On the Magnet" (1600) works into his "Anniversaries," while Kepler gives him a taking-off point for one of the "Paradoxes and Problems." In these young man's essays, he tortures the word until it

testifies against itself, and defending "Women's Inconstancy," discovers also
that "Virginity Is a Virtue." His science is like that, nice, i.e. niggling, an old
Scholastic's but without parti pris.

The type of the trimmer, a good thing for a poet, he got forward in
love poems by changing his course. Sex, one man's meat, is another's poi-
son, except that he is both men by turns. Take heed of loving him but take
heed of hating him. "Quirky amorists" in his time had no mistress but their
muse. His pays its respects to the body. It wasn't always the body beautiful,
and his contra-blazon is disgusting. He had a lot of Ezra Pound in his
makeup.

"Whining poetry" grated, tear-floods, sigh-tempests, etc., were passé,
and in an "Expostulation" he asked poets to "let misery be witty." His
romantic-minded predecessors got his bile flowing. Naturally, he had no
use for Sidney, Spenser either, and his marriage hymn, made at Lincoln's
Inn when he studied law there, parodies the "Epithalamion." Where
Shakespeare in sonnets teaches how "to make one twain," he dramatized
this old conceit in the body of a flea. Changed loves, he told them, were
only "changed sorts of meat," and having eaten, you flung away the shell.
After some centuries, this coarseness still shocks.

But like Pound sending up the Georgians, or like anti-Petrarchan Sid-
ney, he made a pact with the fathers, and demolishing "Petrarch," set him
back on his feet.

> What merchants' ships have my sighs drowned?
> Who says my tears have overflowed his ground?

This is the "ancient aspect," remembering Wallace Stevens in "Le Monocle
de Mon Oncle." A "new mind" inspects the old conventions, however, and
new and old, interpenetrating, sponsor "The Canonization." Among his
indispensable gifts to the future, it doesn't build monuments more lasting
than bronze, only "pretty rooms" in sonnets.

As Donne's poem concludes, saints who used to be lovers beg a pattern
of their loves from God, above the earth-centered cosmos. Going along
with the older astronomy paid off when his important sun, "rising" on the
world, finds its center in a bedroom. Elsewhere his scientist's eye notes how
a "sinewy thread," the cerebral cortex, ties one part to another. But his mis-
tress' hairs, growing from a better brain, do this better. No chemical retort
compares for efficiency with "love's alembic" ("The Nocturnal"), and
"love's natural lation"—the motion of planets—supersedes what goes on in

the heavens" ("The Autumnal"). Up there, angel-like spirits turn the crys-
talline spheres the planets are attached to. But "we," soulful lovers of "The
Ecstasy," stand in for these "intelligences," our bodies present the spheres,
and even angels lack the wit of Donne's mistress. Angelology instructed him
that looking into thoughts exceeded an angel's art. But God possessed that
power—evidence of His godhead, said Dr. Donne (*LXXX Sermons,* 11)—
and his profane mistress has it too. In "The Dream" he salutes her: "Thou
art so truth," a version of the Word but made flesh.

Donne is a casuist, making it ticklish to pronounce on the state of his psy-
che. Defending suicide (in *Biathanatos,* 1607–8), he deplored it in his attack
on Jesuit Catholics who died for the faith, "pseudo-martyrs" (1610).
Famously, he said how "New Philosophy calls all in doubt," but looking
again (in a prose polemic, *Ignatius His Conclave,* 1611), he said it mattered lit-
tle "whether the earth travel or stand still." Geo- or helio- were all the same
to him, but finding out which claim to honor banished tedium vitae. That
was how the poetry got written.

His best poems are exercise work, recalling in their method the
"quaestiones disputatae" of the medieval schools. In this disputatious
universe, the air reverberates with cries of *Sic* and *Non.* "Fantastically
contorted conclusions about trifles," said popular opinion, but the
method begets confidence exactly as it is contorted, and the respondent
and his opponent, cudgeling their brains, give you a reason to trust them.
Moderns, beginning with Milton, like to say that medieval debaters
chewed brambles and thistles, but let us say instead that particulars are
their fare. Skirmishing like theirs furnished Donne the sinews of his argu-
mentative style.

> First to break fast, then to dine,
> Is to conquer Bellarmine.

William Cartwright, a seventeenth-century poet, tells us this, adding: "Dis-
tinctions then are budding."

Sic and *Non* come together in Donne's poetry of prolusions, an old aca-
demic word, its Latin root meaning to play. Well-taught readers, never mind
that he didn't want them, are aware that the play is in earnest. Qualification is
of its essence, and ligatures (when he bothered with them) are words like
"however," "but," and "except." Talking to himself, a scrupulous poet is say-
ing: "Hold off while I think it through again." "If" / "Yet" / "Or" give him

a sequence, sometimes ending with "Thus," but only for the occasion. Most of his poems are occasional, answers to a question posed.

In "Self Love," his female speaker has a question: "Is there then no kind of men / Whom I may freely prove?" or approve. The possibilities, duly cited, don't look good, and the emerging answer reflects this. Down in the dust in "The Canonization," Donne changes his posture as new data come in. Negating becomes affirming or the other way round, and in some poems, e.g. "The Message," the ending resumes the beginning. But things have happened in the meantime, and the beginning isn't the same as it was. "Soul's language" defines his lovers as "The Ecstasy" begins, but a great prince lies in prison unless he fortifies or "alloys" it. This qualifying habit is the index of a civilized mind.

Licensed to travel ("but I know not whither," he said to Magdalen Herbert, July 11, 1607), he sailed toward home, discovering what that meant in the sailing. He wanted others to follow his serendipitous progress, detouring into lesser creeks and taking on fresh water at the Heliconian spring (verse letter "To Mr. S. B."). Shandean stopovers don't interest modern art, and Donne, though much praised by twentieth-century readers, looks backward. Or perhaps, parting company with the Age of Reason—it was mewing its youth when he came on the scene—he looks forward to our time, "post-modern." This isn't altogether matter for congratulation. In his poetry, egalitarian, on a less cordial view self-indulgent, center and circumference coincide.

Like Yeats he had his coterie of adoring females, chiefly the countesses of Bedford, Huntingdon, and Salisbury. Eulogized in verse letters, they aren't often before us, however. High-toned talk on the makeup of the soul or body crowds out panegyric, and the ladies have to shift for themselves. His best elegies, though highly sexed, entertain us with learned tangents he can't help but go off on. "Love's Progress" (XVIII) is a Mappa Mundi, more turning of the artificial globe in his study, and in "Going to Bed" (XIX), reflections on merit—do we earn it or does it drop in our lap?—compete with the sexual interest. Protestants and Catholics once argued the difference, a fatal chimera for him.

"Like an alchemist," he delighted in discoveries "by the way, though I attain not mine end." This comparison, ventured in the letters (e.g. to Goodyer, Aug. 19, 1614), comes up again in the poems when the yield his investigator hopes for doesn't precipitate out. But he "glorifies his pregnant pot, / If by the way to him befall / Some odoriferous thing, or medicinal" ("Love's Alchemy"). The parenthetical phrase gives Donne's method. "And thus long, Sir," he writes to an unknown correspondent, "whilst I have been talking of others, methinks I have opened a casement to gaze upon passengers" (July 17, 1613). Much depends on these passengers, intersecting his angle of vision. For instance, in the "Anniversaries": were there giants before the Flood and did their food taste better than ours? (Maybe it did, and all that sea water, receding, left salt in the earth.) Which came first, the morning or the evening, and how could there be days before the fourth day, when the sun and stars were created? At death, do we go to Heaven, or does Heaven come to us?

Two answers are potential and he gives both a hearing, returning to this question in sermons. Defeated temporarily, he throws up his hands: whether the soul must pass locally through the firmament or find new light in the same room, "I know not, I dispute not, I inquire not" (*LXXX*, 22). But he is the type of the inquiring man, endlessly preoccupied with "a hundred controversies of an ant." He wants to know how the stone gets in the bladder without breaking the skin, why grass is green or blood is red. Matter-of-fact enfilades his love poems, strengthening and skewing them, and in the Elegies and Satires, every rift is loaded with topical allusion. Aiming high had no meaning for him, said Allen Tate, unless he "sighted from a point below." He aimed at Paradise and hoped to be rooted there, like a lily "growing out of red earth." The adverbial phrase (from *LXXX Sermons*, 27) says where he lives, though, and "exagitating" particulars is his customary road to the truth.

Many make it a general truth—"O how feeble is man's power," etc.—but he isn't much for extrapolating, only, given his piety, fruitful of it. Piety means an ear for innuendoes, or scrutinizing details until they breed. Details, some other poet's grace note, are the warp and woof for him, "your materials, not your ornament" (verse letter to the Lady Carey and Mrs. Essex Riche). Lowering his eyes, he looks twice in "The Ecstasy" at his "single violet." This second look is lucky for meaning.

But the meaning is provincial, and his "labored particularities" forfeit the chance for conceptual truth. The Ultima Thule of the abstracting temper, it beckoned in the early centuries—"Neoplatonic"—coming round again in his lifetime. "Say not then, 'I am such and such'" (Porphyry's counsel). "If you leave out 'such and such,' you become all." The prospect of a total becoming or divining isn't visibly there to Donne.

"Direct treatment of the 'thing'" (Pound's desideratum, 1912) distinguishes his poetry, but its indigenous nature defeats annotation.

Every thy hair for love to work upon
Is much too much, some fitter must be sought.

                                              ("Air and Angels")

He isn't a *universalia ante rem* kind of poet, not Fulke Greville in his time or
Pope a century later, and doesn't employ general principles to docket his
particulars. His sometimes Augustan rhetoric, stiffening like whalebone,
does duty for the principles that ought to inform it but don't. Universals
with him are strictly *post rem* or no part of his equipment, and though
sequential clauses follow his discoveries, they hold only for the matter in
hand. "The best state of man's body is but a neutrality," he said (in *Fifty Ser-
mons,* 20), and this describes the state of his mind.

The mind is that of a hole-in-corner empiric's, one type of the scien-
tist, not the most honored one. Coleridge called him a poor metaphysician:
"that is, he never closely questioned himself as to the absolute meaning of
his words. What did he mean by the 'soul'? What by the 'body'?" He meant
different things, and with each new exercise was always at a beginning. His
imprimatur is on the centrifugal style, among his great triumphs. But it runs
him on difficulties, like Milton's demons who find no end "in wandering
mazes lost." Some poets, taking truce with finicking cerebration, find a way
to complete their "partial mind," and for an instant Yeats in "Under Ben
Bulben" stands at ease. This equanimity isn't Donne's.

He thought best things were inviolate—"simply perfectest," he called
them in "Negative Love"—and could "by no way be expressed / But neg-
atives." This is hard on relations, and Donne's effects are often more than
their causes. No poet better at the word game but it had limits. Reaching
them, he lapsed in unknowing or wrote the poetry of faith, less occupied
with problem solving than "my muse's white sincerity" ("La Corona," I).
The poet we know best reads, as we ought to read him, with eyes close to
the page, but Tate's humble particularizer is only half the story. An imper-
ial poet complements the humble one, and wants his study's fruit to be wor-
thy the sight of angels, "though blind in how they see" ("Litany," VI). "The
day of the Lord is darkness," he told himself, "not light" (Amos, v. 18).

He took this text for his first sermon at Court (*LXXX,* 14) on return-
ing from Germany in 1619, and it stands as a headnote for gnomic poems
like the "Hymn to Christ":

Churches are best for prayer that have least light;
To see God only, I go out of sight:

> And to scape stormy days I choose
> An everlasting night.

This "darkling I listen" psychology disallows what he called "De Modo" inquisitions (*Essays in Divinity,* about 1614, Simpson ed., 88). When his questions find no answers, he takes "the old broad way" ("Litany," IX), pronouncing. Divines were for hearts ("A Funeral Elegy"). That is, the job of the clergy, as Donne presents it, isn't to intellectualize but to emote. Paradoxically, "the intelligence that moves" is devotion ("Good Friday Riding Westward"). Donne's "First Anniversary" prefers praying to dissecting. If questions arise, the answers are already written. This leaves a vacuum, filled by rhetorical schemes, anaphora, for example: "Think . . . Think . . . Think" (in the "Second Anniversary"), but he wants to acquit us of thinking. "Arguing is heretic's game," dealt with by throttling ("The Progress of the Soul," XII). Ipse dixits convey his truth, matter is exhausted in conventional topoi, and holding his reader, he does this by main force.

In "A Hymn to God the Father" he plays on his own name ("When Thou hast done, Thou hast not done") and invoking science, puts it to merely lexical uses. The brain, venting by sutures through its bony walls, looks less like itself than an image of the Cross. Only an image, it might "withdraw," ceding priority to the physical world, but

> It shalt not, for it cannot; for, the loss
> Of this Cross, were to me another cross;
> Better were worse, for, no affliction,
> No cross is so extreme as to have none.

Repetition plus paradox plus punning add up to Donne's *Sic.* Stepping down the stanza in "A Hymn to Christ," he wins you musically, that is, by diminishing the line:

> Though Thou with clouds of anger do disguise
> Thy face, yet through that mask I know those eyes
>   Which, though they turn away sometimes,
>   They never will despise.

Rhythm is mesmeric, like that of old fourteeners or the Protestant Hymnal, and the Good Friday poem fortifies it with the anapestic ta-ta-tum:

> But that Christ on this Cross did rise and fall,
> Sin had eternally benighted all.

In passages like these, of great power emotionally, what you get is what you hear, not much left over.

Distinguishing two Donnes, Walton imagines one "for youth, strength, mirth, and wit," the other singing nothing but the praise of his Creator. This dichotomy has its corner of truth but the opposition is less moral/immoral than analytical/fervid. In Donne's capacious personality, emotion meets the felt presence of mind. He looks in two directions, one eye peeled for minutiae, the other synoptic. The synoptic eye takes the long view or looks inward. There, the unblinkered soul, grasping universal truth, is no longer in debt to "fantasy," the part of the mind that synthesizes sensory impressions. Yoked to the body, this inferior part peeps through lattices of eyes, hears through labyrinths of ears. But if it wants to "see all things despoiled of fallacies," Donne can tell it how to do this: "up into the watchtower get" ("Second Anniversary").

The view from the top is apt to be cursory. But cleared by "Grace and Law," Donne, an Antinomian for convenience' sake, doesn't need to check out particulars ("Litany," VII). The seeker after Truth on its steep hill breaks off his search, dignified by "imputed" merit (*Elegy* XIX), more efficient than the merit "imparted" by works. Divinest whimsy saves or damns him, and he lays everything to God:

> Impute me righteous, thus purged of evil,
> For thus I leave the world, the flesh, and devil.
>
> (Holy Sonnets VI)

Readers won't want to miss the jaunty double rhyme. It sticks the heart of Donne's particularity, telling of a poet who means what he says and mocks it.

Antinomianism holds that grace alone insures our salvation, so absolves us from niceties of conduct. Enfeebled by sin, we aren't much anyway and can't raise our stature one cubit. This beguiling doctrine—it got a lot of credit in the beginnings of the modern age—cashes for Donne in a pair of Holy Sonnets, simultaneously sacred and comic. Though angels blow their trumpets "at the round earth's imagined corners," he wants the Last Day postponed until his Creator instructs him in repentance,

> for that's as good
> As if Thou hadst sealed my pardon with Thy blood.
>
> (VII)

This impudent poet is willing to forgive the sacrifice on the Cross. Don't bother, etc. But without intercession he is certainly damned. Sex itches at him, and endowed with reason he is held to account for this, different from "lecherous goats" (IX). God, having made him, bears the blame and has the remedy, though, and if He wants to, can wash away sins in Lethe's river of forgetfulness.

> That Thou remember them, some claim as debt,
> I think it mercy if Thou wilt forget.
>
> (IX)

But Donne's joking is serious too.

On his way to Heaven in the "Second Anniversary," he takes little notice of the stars in their courses. Venus, the "multinominous star," both Hesperus and Vesper, caught his eye in his "Paradoxes and Problems." But they were for youth, and the salvationist, wiser and sadder, keeps going. "Undistinguished" speed loses something, however, and aware of that, he reins himself in. A simile, uncanny in its alertness to new science and its sense of things, tells us that his passion for matter of fact never left him. Shooting the soul from the body, death ties earth to Heaven,

> As doth the pith which, lest our bodies slack,
> Strings fast the little bones of neck and back.

Donne, even Dr. Donne, looking toward Heaven, has his eye on those vertebrae.

A year before taking orders, he said in a verse letter to the Countess of Salisbury how he still adored "the same things now which I adored before." Sex hadn't let go of him, even when age snowed white hairs on his head. Scientism still teases thought in "Good Friday Riding Westward," and pleasure, presumably the body's, marches with it. In Donne's scheme of things, souls are spheres, and a universe of them moves annually across the heavens from west to east, impelled by their "natural form." But a "first mover," the Primum Mobile, conventionally a type of God, hurries these turning spheres every day in a contrary direction. Pushed and pulled, they

Scarce in a year their natural form obey:
Pleasure or business, so our souls admit
For their first mover, and are whirled by it.

Not for the first time, syntax makes trouble, and distractions or call them evils appear to define our nature.

Sorting things out, we see that "pleasure or business" must follow the verb "admit," but inevitably they look backwards, hitching on to "natural form" and suggesting that we live in the body. A strong sense of bullying persists in the universe according to Donne, and God or His surrogate, while severe on the body, force us to live in it from birth. Heaven isn't in prospect unless He wings our hearts, and if we sin, inborn nature acquits us. This is fantastic but Donne's order-in-disorder leaves the possibility open.

Chapter 3

Herrick among the Goths

Herrick was fifty-seven before *Hesperides* (1648), his one volume of poetry, appeared. Just at this time the Quakers came on the scene, overflowing with spontaneous emotion. Their new psychology wasn't his. A year before, Puritans ejected him from his vicarage in Devon, a year later, King Charles, ruler of "this great realm of poetry" (Herrick's phrase), lost his head. In a time of the breaking of nations, the poems themselves rhymed "bowers" with "flowers." Herrick, like a contemporary of Edmund Blunden's who survived both World Wars and never read Pound and Eliot, looks to the past.

Born in 1591 just around the corner from "golden Cheapside," London's street of the goldsmiths, he shared his birthplace with Milton, younger by seventeen years. Milton's is the new voice among seventeen-century poets but Herrick doesn't hear it. The goldsmith's trade, elegant as to products but messy and dangerous, attracted his father, also a paternal uncle. At sixteen he signed articles of indenture with this uncle William, breaking off his apprenticeship after six years to read law at Cambridge, later divinity. The career he didn't follow stamps his poetry, and many poems remember the wares he polished in youth. But he is more than a clever miniaturist, executing thumbnail painting on ivory.

The "Argument" to *Hesperides* (coming first, so numbered H-1) functions as a versified topical index:

> I sing of brooks, of blossoms, birds, and bowers,
> Of April, May, of June, and July-flowers.
> I sing of May-poles, hock-carts, wassails, wakes,
> Of bridegrooms, brides, and of their bridal-cakes.
> I write of youth, of love, and have access
> By these to sing of cleanly wantoness.
> I sing of dews, of rains, and piece by piece
> Of balm, of oil, of spice, and ambergris.

> I sing of times trans-shifting; and I write
> How roses first came red, and lilies white.
> I write of groves, of twilights, and I sing
> The Court of Mab, and of the Fairy King.
> I write of Hell; I sing (and ever shall)
> Of Heaven, and hope to have it after all.

Herrick's sonnet in couplets does little with the form, resolving itself to colored beads on a string. Running substantives in series—not modified, so not differentiated—it predicts the open-ended nature of his book. But his poems are intentional, though rarely pointed or exclusive, and he wants to traverse the whole spectrum. The last poem in his collection, echoing Revelation: "I am Alpha and Omega," supplies a text for the poetry too.

An adverbial poet, he writes "how" roses came red, etc., sorting through his materials "piece by piece." Close scrutiny, the patient kind that spots resemblances missed by a synoptic eye, insures that the different pieces make a coherence. "Hock-carts," carrying home the last load of harvest, tell of fruitfulness, so complement "May-poles." But "wakes" in the same line, meaning boisterous festivals, activates another sense, and these two-in-one vehicles hearse the dead season, "borne on the bier with white and bristly beard." The coincidence of opposites, cayenne pepper on the tongue in late Metaphysicals like Cowley and Cleveland, isn't meant to titillate but pays laconic tribute to Nature's undemarcated round. *Glide* is one of Herrick's verbs and chiaroscuro his medium, proper to groves and twilights. His mood (grammatically speaking) is only declarative when he wants you to hear it as jarring. Characteristically, he favors the optative voice.

The hock-cart gives him his centerpiece in the poem of that name, familiar from anthologies. Marxists, out to demolish another "country-house" poet, think it grist for their mill, and New Historicists see it as participating in an "ideological project." According to them, Herrick is a pawn, serving the landed class. In fields around the house—property of his friend, the Earl of Westmorland—laborers work the land, insuring by their labor that "we are the lords of wine and oil." Living off this "surplus value," an ungrateful poet bites the hand that feeds him, and scorning the peasants, toadies to his patron. But Herrick's mind had little truck with ideas. Paying allegiance to beauty, he doesn't know how time's foot can fail to trample it. Politics, at its super-hopeful best and worst, means to transcend time, but can't do anything about this.

Though not rectifying life, Herrick renders it faithfully. But he isn't Breughel, and his peasants aren't naturalistic. "Sons of Summer," he calls them, no surnames or Christian names, only part of a surround that includes the poet and manor lord. He is our patron at the top of the hierarchy, but not its end-all and be-all. Like the fat beef, our feast's foundation with "upper stories" of mutton, veal, and pork, this structure has its gradations. One supports another, analogizing (says R. B. Rollin) a "mutual dependency of master and servants." All don't earn their bread in the sweat of their brow, but all are yoked together in a commonwealth more ancient than England's. Feeding and growing fat, all owe a last debt to the rough sickle and scythe.

Maybe or maybe not, Herrick tugged his forelock to Westmorland. Either way, a gap opens between his politics and his reading of physical process. Not harking back to a better social order, golden age, or earthly paradise, he looks impassively at the natural cycle, en route, says a perceptive critic, Mary Thomas Crane, to developing "an analytical gaze." Disinterested, I think we call him, like all poets of size. But I don't want to offer more praise than he can bear, and morbidity qualifies the disinterestedness and the analytical posture. He isn't Shakespeare. All the same, he has an unwinking eye, and what it sees on every hand is putrefaction, "the end / Of all that Nature doth intend" (H-432). Festivals like "The Hock-Cart's" obscure it but their pleasure is like rain, and not drowning our cares, except as "stout beer" does, makes them spring again. The poem's last lines strike the ear as cautionary, exuberant too. Death has its way but the seasons recur, and in our ending is our beginning.

Temperamentally averse to politics, unlike Dryden whom he overlaps, and not stretching the intellect like Donne and Herbert, Herrick stands comparison with all three. He left more short poems than any other important seventeenth-century poet. It comes as a shock to discover that Donne, the age's preeminent secular poet, wrote less secular verse, and only Herbert, exclusively a devotional poet, wrote more poems of devotion. If you throw in the "pious pieces," published with *Hesperides* but segregated as *Noble Numbers,* and add the "Supplemental" poetry not collected in the 1648 edition, more than fourteen hundred poems constitute his achievement. Prodigality like his anticipates Dickinson's, she of the gladstone bag stuffed with verse. The poems aren't of a piece, however, and no poet is more "schizoid." Many are highly sexual, opting for a "cleanly wantonness," while others view the body with loathing. The world that threw

them up looms out of nightmare. Herrick, who dreamed it, said he sang of
Heaven, adding that he wrote about Hell.

Everybody knows the nice old clergyman who kept a pet pig and
taught it to drink from a tankard. But he had another side, swimming up to
the light in these couplets on one of his parishioners:

> Scobble for whoredom whips his wife and cries
> He'll slit her nose. But blubb'ring she replies,
> Good sir, make no more cuts i' th' outward skin,
> One slit's enough to let adultery in.

> (H-126)

Other poems in the same vein, a lot of them, are more circumstantial.

Critics don't often say so but hatred is of his essence, much of it
devoted to the "gubbings," or peasants, who stalled with him in "this dull
Devonshire" (H-51). He took up his Devon "cure" in the fall of 1630, the
same month Herbert became rector of Bemerton. The vicar of Dean Prior
ministered to a parish of four thousand acres on the southern slopes of Dart-
moor, after London like the other face of the moon. Granite tors break the
high moorland, empty except for cattle and sheep. Thick hedgerows or
balks of mounded earth dwarf the narrow roads, and creepers and wild-
flowers bloom in the hedgerows before the farmers sickle them down. Her-
rick's church of St. George the Martyr, built of gray country stone, has a
crenelated tower going back to the Normans, but east of the tower the
church hugs the ground and leaning gravestones come up to the walls.

Dean-bourn, "a rude river," flows through the land, its bottom rocky
like the natives, "rudest salvages" (H-86). Farmers plus tightwads, they
grudged their pastor his tithes, and he rehearsed their unlovely names—
Scobble, Mudge, Dandridge, Coone—in acidulated verses. The parish reg-
ister preserves the names. For seventeen years he lived among them, then,
expelled from his vicarage, hurried off to London, "blest place of my nativ-
ity!" A "free-born Roman" (remembering exultant Cicero's "Civis
Romanus sum"), he said he would rather die than return to "the dull
confines of the drooping West" (H-713). After thirteen years' absence,
return he did, however, with the new king in 1660. He had fourteen years
more of his clerical life before the end came at age eighty-three.

Another Ovid among the Goths, he lamented the "hard fate" that dic-
tated his "long and irksome banishment," but invented his most "ennobled
numbers" in the country (H-51). Exile turned him queer, though, and

buried in his church or churchyard, he didn't stay under. Tradition, laying an ear to the pulse of his strangeness, says he haunted about the parish, the furies that possessed him still unappeased in death. Tormenting him, they put his art in motion. All poets are hobbled by defects of temper, costive Jonson, hermetic Donne, Herbert, whose smarting eyes hint at sexual "displacement." But sometimes the thing that cripples them gives their genius its bent. This is Herrick's case.

The genius comes and goes and his repertory, like Dickinson's, could do with judicious pruning. His homiletic voice is never muted for long. One of his dreary apothegm-poems directly precedes "Corinna's Going a-Maying." Moderns think such incongruities deliberate, but perhaps like Shakespeare, juxtaposing without irony the banal and profound, he allowed integrity to both. Finicking beyond the general run, he blotted every line, and manuscript copies show him hard at work in his workshop. Not getting a tough-minded critic's approval, sixty-seven lines drop from the marriage hymn for Sir Clipsby Crewe, already a great poem but he craved perfection. Luckier than some, he gets his due in all the anthologies. But his poetry, offering few handholds, hasn't much appealed to close readers, Cleanth Brooks excepted. Donne, who needs explicating, serves the teaching trade better. (Students think they have the poem if they know what it "means," and look up to the teacher who tells them.)

Some of the poems are semi-anonymous, like Jonson's echo song from *Cynthia's Revels,* and in some the masculine wit is like Donne's. For example, "Kisses Loathsome":

> I abhor the slimy kiss,
> Which to me most loathsome is.
> Those lips please me which are placed
> Close, but not too strictly laced.
> Yielding I would have them, yet
> Not a wimbling tongue admit.
> What should poking-sticks make there,
> When the ruff is set elsewhere?

"Wimbling" is when you bore a hole, a "ruff" is a gathered neckpiece, and "poking-sticks" of wood or bone, penetrating its flutings, forced them open. This version of "Love's Progress" doesn't lapse in tact, unlike Donne's, and has the virtue of being much shorter.

Outproducing his contemporaries Carew, Suckling, and Lovelace put together, Herrick worked in a greater variety of kinds. He wrote songs, the best in English, odes worthy of the Greek and Latin masters he went to school to, epitaphs, alehouse catches, scurrile epigrams, charms, pastorals, tales of fairy land, panegyrics to friends. Both grave and sexy, manly and tender, his redeem this marmoreal verse form, bringing his statues to life. Much on the point are the second wedding song and the Horatian tributes to his old schoolfellow John Wicks. Horace's "*labuntur anni*" poem (*Carmina,* II, xiv) isn't better than the one beginning

> Ah Posthumus! Our years hence fly
> And leave no sound; nor piety,
>   Or prayers, or vow
> Can keep the wrinkle from the brow.
>   But we must on
> As Fate does lead or draw us.

Partly an omnium gatherum, *Hesperides* is more than the sum of its parts, and aesthetic considerations modify its naively linear pattern. Thirty-six pages in the 1648 edition separate two paired drinking poems, "His Farewell to Sack" and "The Welcome to Sack," suggesting a real-life poet's time on the wagon. But their complementarity argues the controlling presence of a regisseur, not autobiographical, only artistic. You often hear Horace in him, and "*Non omnis moriar*" (I shall not wholly die) is one of his particular topics. Perhaps he means what he says, though praise of poetry as regenerating was already old hat when he set up as a poet. *Hesperides* voices the convention first in the motto from Ovid: "Our song alone escapes the greedy funeral pyre," and after that Herrick goes back to it often. Readers may feel that he protests too much, and a modern critic, Ann Baynes Coiro, calls him anxiety's poet.

How much the notorious hedonist loved wine and pretty girls is a question. His mistresses, at least seventeen of them, all curds and cream, seem too good to be true. The wine-bibbing and romancing come partly from Greek Anacreon and the Alexandrian poets whose lyrics went under his name. In the last poem of *Hesperides,* he said his Muse was jocund but his life was chaste. On the other hand, he was translating Ovid. His watchword is Horace's "*Nunc est bibendum,*" "Now is the time for drinking." But like Horace, he prefers a clear head to fuddled:

> When our drinking has no stint,
> There is no one pleasure in't.
>   (H-304)

James Russell Lowell called him "the most Catullan of poets," but frenzied self-mutilating, as in the terrifying Attis poem, is outside his ken. Amorous, possibly perverse, he isn't sex crazed, and love, scorching his finger, spares the burning of his heart (H-85).

Inviting you to read him autobiographically, he refers to himself by name more than any other major poet in English. Fifty titles in *Hesperides* begin with the personal possessive, *his,* and many are called "On Himself." But intimacy is always at a remove. The elegy "to the reverend shade" of his father, though chronicling this parent's suicide, muffles it beneath a cloak of latinity. Urgent poetry, Herrick's demands a hearing, at the same time stops our ears. Robert or Robin (the poet's nickname) was fourteen months old when his father Nicholas threw himself from the attic window of his London house. For thirty-five years—"seven lusters" is Herrick's phrase—his death festered in memory until the son, confronting it, heaped the grave with "smallage" (celery or parsley), nightshade, cypress, and yew. Making satisfaction for his own "debt of birth," he offers "justments" to the dead, shorn hair, a libation of tears. Imperatives and the asseverating tone ask forgiveness, but its occasion remains mysterious. Up to now, Herrick says, "I did not know / Whether thy bones had here their rest, or no," a trivial-seeming disclaimer.

A large number of poems deal with a specific mistress, and biographers identify flesh-and-blood ladies. How they relate to the poet is worth noting. Wives and daughters of family or friends make the list, plus cousins and parishioners, all safely out of bounds. Blushing prettily, they smell good, and Herrick handles and smells them (H-375). Julia, his favorite, recalls his mother Julian, also called Juliana. Another mistress, "his dear Valentine" (H-789), is still in her nonage. The man who liked little girls thought latent better than fledged, the way violets, spring's "virgins," are better than roses (H-205).

A bachelor, Herrick needed taking care of, and his widowed sister-in-law Elizabeth kept house for him in Devon until her death in 1643. Though he never touched her carnally, he doesn't decline but adjusts the idea, vowing to keep her person embraced and kissed, "but yet be chaste." His poem is entitled "No Spouse but a Sister." Later, Prudence Baldwin, an old maid, took her place. Not tempting him herself, she kept him from temptation, staying on when the "summer-birds" had flown (H-387). An old lean wife, materializing in one poem but appropriated from Ovid, kisses away his tears, while his son, supplied by Virgil, sings for them both (H-336). Elsewhere, a careful parent meditates "My Daughter's Dowry" (S-3). Imagining a wife, he supposed her harried by lustful suitors. Fly them or lose your liberty, he said, in language highly charged with images of rape, and might have been admonishing himself (H-465).

In 1640, briefly up in London, he caught the eye of an official snooper whose job was checking up on the clergy. This functionary linked him with Thomasin Parsons, lately "brought to bed" of an illegitimate child. She was daughter of a friend, organist at the Abbey, and for a time they lived under one roof. Some think Herrick fathered her bastard. But the ladies he made up to were like "yond moon,"

> Which shining in her perfect noon,
> In all that great and glorious light,
> Continues cold, as is the night.
>
> (H-136)

The coldness had its virtue, and allaying passion, preserved it, like life under glass. In one of the great poems, "Lily in a Crystal," virgins draw transparent linen over a "smiling" rose, fairer and happier, being entombed. Unmixed with color, cream is merely "naked," a pejorative for Herrick, but drop in a strawberry and it wantons with the sight. This activity is only teasing, though. Interpenetrating is out, as when Donne transplants his single violet.

Fruit in its see-through container, a "clean and subtle skin," has more beauty to commend it than when displaying "tinctures natural." Preference goes to the "broken beam," art gladdens more than nature (H-560), and life, especially female life, shows to most advantage when gilded. While the men of reform were stripping England's great churches down to naked stone, Herrick, unwilling like King Lear to reason the need, cultivated his artificial garden. There in green meadows spring embroidered the margins, and no night ever rusted day's enamel (H-575). Like those tinctures that "paint the hemisphere" (H-767), making picture-postcard sunsets, this enamel deceives us. But you had to have it; otherwise, you looked into the void.

The world, an "isle of dreams," sponsors bad ones, and "tears and terrors" beset us as we sit at water's edge (N-128). Herrick's poetry composes this chaos. The best of it lifts the heart, so cunningly does he simulate emotion, poignant, exhilarated, and comic:

> Some few sands spent, we hence must go,
> Both to be blended in the urn,
> From whence there's never a return.
>
> (H-670)

Wild I am now with heat;
    O Bacchus, cool thy rays!
Or frantic, I shall eat
    Thy thyrse, and bite the bays.

(H-201)

    We have hurled
(As with a tempest) nature through the world,
And in a whirlwind twirled her home, aghast
At that which in her ecstasy had past.

(S-4)

Saying over past times, real or imagined, a wild wicked old man flutters and crows, rearing his limbs above his chair "in a fit / Of fresh concupiscence" (H-336). Brio is Herrick's particular distinction, and whether writing youth's passion or going down with old age, he keeps our colors flying.

But though his most famous poem, "Corinna's Going a-Maying," speaks for fruition, the conventional "carpe diem" piece recoils on itself. What we seize runs through our fingers, "all love, all liking, all delight," and "decaying" and "Maying" make a rhyme. Whitethorn, the emblem of joy and pain, decks our portals, Apollo, "the god unshorn," is shorn of both hair and young manhood. Even as they greet the sun, flowers are seen as weeping. They know how vapor or a drop of rain, like the days of our life, can't be found again once you lose it. Dwelling on this rather than the cheerful sequitur sets Herrick apart from his fellow Cavaliers and Epicureans. "Song" and "shade" merge for him, and the same covering, a grave cloth, serves bed and bride (H-336, 515). "Only a little more," not wine, women, and song, is the heart of the poetry, work of a poet fascinated by the multitude who lie in vaults beneath the earth, rotting "piecemeal" (H-211). His brio is complicated.

In a trusting-to-good-verses poem (H-201), things that warm the cockles occupy him for almost ten stanzas, then, seeing a "text," he breaks off. It isn't "*Exegi monumentum,*" all that, but the death's head. Like a profane St. Jerome, he kept it before him. No flower dearer than the tulip, having "so short a stay" (H-216). He tilts at the grand Virgilian style, and "I sing," his opening gambit, indicates what he would have made of *Paradise Lost.* A minimalist who studied in Jonson's school, he exploits a narrow compass, only a pair of stanzas in "To Daffodils," short like the life they describe. Thought in this compacted poem doesn't tax us more than the mottoes on sundials, but pulling hard at its metrical tether, convinces. Dispensing with or tinkering the thus-we-see conclusion, he arrives at his point by adjusting his stanza—expanding and contracting it in "Gather Ye Rose-buds." Coming after tetrameters, his three-foot line, both diminished and augmented (feminine), makes a grave antiphon:

> And this same flower that smiles today,
>   Tomorrow will be dying.

Rhyme, often oxymoronic, stands in for comment: "flying" and "dying"/ "getting" and "setting"/ "marry" and "tarry," meaning "languish." We end as often with an imperative: "Then be not coy," worth heeding but not the heart of the poem.

Constriction tested his powers, a salutary exercise. As frugal poets can tell you, a well-wrought urn does better than half-acre tombs. Often his pentameter lines resolve to couplets, not yet closed but getting there, says Moorman, an early and able critic. In "The Christian Militant," he mediates between Chaucer's "riding rhymes" and the heroic couplet of the Augustans:

> A man prepared against all ills to come,
> That dares to dead the fire of martyrdom,
> That sleeps at home, and sailing there at ease,
> Fears not the fierce sedition of the seas.

The couplets go on like this, balanced, cinched, and chastened. For Herrick as for the Augustans, being prepared exacts a full look at the worst. Plagued by demons, he sees the need of coercing them, and this is why his style is fined down.

"Life Is the Body's Light" (H-576), a title that gives the gist of his philosophy. But rigor makes the light, not setting the house on fire. Tightly ordered structures, circumscribing his range, dictate his meaning. All poetic forms have their decorum—tetrameter for comedy or formal panegyric, blank verse for discursive thought—and Herrick, understanding this, chooses the centripetal kinds. That way, he stays close to his center of gravity.

In his most ambitious poem, among the greatest in a century where contenders are many, the center widens, also growing denser, and a limited poet discovers more than he knew before or knows elsewhere. The poem is his "Nuptial Song or Epithalamion" (H-283), celebrating the marriage of Sir Clipsby Crewe and his lady. Bride and groom "bill too long" in Herrick's earlier marriage hymn (H-149A), perhaps avoiding or postponing the moment of truth, not these two. His eyes, like a madman's, "roll about" in his head, and hers, though veiled, look "bright" with expectation. An actor in the ceremony, Herrick is his own auditor, and helping to orchestrate a theatrical performance, puts questions but addressed to himself. "Lying alone" as consummation approaches, he hears the clock toll the hours, striking "ten, eleven, twelve, one." Only once in his poetry is he man enough, as we used to say, to realize an achievement of such magnitude as this, mock-epic, homely, comic, and sober.

Sixteen turbulent stanzas urge the claim of the body, blooming and blown, treading (i.e. pacing, also copulating like a lovebird), smelling, pounded, perspiring, frying, burning to cinders with sexual heat. But though Eros gets first place, meter and a crafty rhyme scheme conspire to curb him. Matter is hectic, the manner hectic-seeming yet exerting control. Ardent Nature "melts" but does this "in numbers." "Love the confusion," says "Empedoclean" Herrick. His chaos imitates life, at the same time confers it and is the condition of form.

Menace colors the poem, as it must every true celebration, Spenser's in his marriage hymn, Shakespeare's at the end of *A Midsummer Night's Dream.* "Some gin" or snare is laid for the bride's feet, and love or luck, "spells / And magics" are needed to "shield" her. Young men and women strive to win her garters, and a playful poet bids them not to "fall / Foul" in their pastimes. For an instant, though, the admonition stands alone: "O do not fall." As the poem and its arousals subside, "two nations," twins in the womb, "may blaze the virtue of their sires." But Herrick's reminiscent phrasing summons tricky Jacob and his brother Esau, who lost his birthright for a mess of pottage. A different preview of the future, it isn't cheerful, and "bestroking" or propitiating Fate, like the anxious bridegroom, never comes amiss. Perhaps if we do that, the planets will look down benignly.

Like many "mea culpa" poets—Sidney is one—the priest appeals from our vexed condition in certain "pious pieces." Only a fifth of his total output, they have the look of an afterthought, some reprobate's retraction. But his title, *Noble Numbers,* implies a qualitative distinction, the real thing against its counterfeit, and a separate title page, dated 1647, suggests that Herrick meant to give them pride of place. Many are didactic, like Herbert's *Outlandish Proverbs,* or headed like his with frosty-sounding titles, "Wages," "Temptation," "Labor," "Prayer." Unlike Herbert's, they don't often pay more than they promise. Half are cast in couplets, others in quatrains, and some are rhymed versions of a prose commentary on Scripture. A contemporary scholar, M. K. Starkman, walks us through Herrick's metrical prayer book: "creeds and graces, confessions and thanksgivings, litanies and dirges, nativity and circumcision songs, anthems and carols, plus a large body of near-catechetical wisdom." Twentieth-century readers haven't gone back to it often.

But poems like "A Christmas Carol" keep unembarrassed company with Herbert:

> We see Him come and know Him ours,
> Who, with His sunshine and His showers,
> Turns all the patient ground to flowers.

In a "Litany to the Holy Spirit," Herrick redefines congruity, less tidy than it used to be:

> When the artless doctor sees
> No one hope, but of his fees,
> And his skill runs on the lees,
>   Sweet Spirit comfort me!

Simple enough, the religious poems mustn't be called naive, and some I know have this grace before meals by heart:

> Here a little child I stand,
> Heaving up my either hand;
> Cold as paddocks [toads] though they be,
> Here I lift them up to Thee,
> For a benison to fall
> On our meat and on us all. Amen.

> (N-95)

Praise ought to include what the poems don't do, however. They don't swoon like Crashaw's, or brim with passion like many of Donne's and a few of Jonson's. All decline to negotiate our dark night of the soul. Commentators on Herrick lay their even tenor to his uncomplicated faith. I think the circumspection tells of a pestered spirit who reined himself in as he could.

Doing that wasn't easy or always successful. Earlier editors cleaned up the poetry, Grosart (1876) culling "Selections" for the women of his family, Pollard (1891) relegating the epigrams to an appendix, Rhys (1908) omitting offensive lines, replaced with dots in the Everyman edition. But to get his quiddity you have to take the worse with the better. The sophisticated maker, delighted with perfumes and gossamer visions, is also the monstrous man-child who daubed the body with excrement, urine, and phlegm. Even in *Noble Numbers* where you expect a whitened sensibility, he can't help but soil himself and his clothing. No purifying "this my Augean stable" (N-73, 49).

Devoted to antiquity, he isn't an antiquarian but goes to the past for a literary frame, efficient in blocking off the turbid stuff his cards dealt him. His Roman censor's mask answers the need, and wearing it let him keep life at a distance. Celebrating life, this hedonist feared it. But he doesn't succeed in spite of himself, and his strength as a poet is part and parcel of his sickness. Epigrams pleased him best, among poetic forms the one he most often went back to. At least 150 of them, scattered through *Hesperides,* reveal "a coarse-minded and beastly writer whose dunghill," said Robert Southey, reviewing the 1823 edition, "ought never to have been disturbed." Moderns, smiling or bristling at this, might better consult their unexpurgated Herrick:

> Craw cracks in syrup, and does stinking say,
> Who can hold that, my friends, that will away?
>
> (H-428)

If you plunge a finger into sugar syrup, then into cold water, the hardened sugar on the finger breaks off with a crackling sound. But the "syrup" meant here is liquid feces. Herrick's biographers blame his beastliness on Saint Ben or Martial, models for satire. Natural, they say, for "the naughty mischievous" youth to fancy the epigram, a foil to the delicate beauty of his muse. The plumminess aside, this doesn't differ much from modern rationalizings of Southey's "filth and ordure."

Criticism in our time assimilates Herrick to My Lord's chaplain, buttering up his masters while reviling the hoi polloi, or thinks he meant to poke fun at his own lyrics, exploding their images of beauty, innocence, and wealth. Under the "veneer" and "artifice" of his elegant (fictitious) world lay what some call the real thing, and depicting it, he forced us to face up to the truth. Generally, words like "grim" or "brutal" describe it. But Herrick is less critiquing than savaging his subjects, and his pathological disgust or fascination with disgusting things denies the chance for any point, ameliorative or scabrous. Only on a sentimental view is the grimness he mucks about in more real than the loveliness. Turning from loveliness to "batten on this moor," he isn't aiming at truth but self-laceration. Among major poets, none backed away with more revulsion from the face he met in the mirror.

Sexual disorder seems key to his work, both begetting and disabling. Scatological Herrick is also a voyeur, inclined to masturbative fantasies, infantile, and narcissistic. Like E. M. Forster, he petered out in silence, and only a single poem marks his last twenty-six years. Drowning in delights, he couldn't "die" (H-175), i.e. experience sexual climax, but then he didn't want to. A poem called "The Frozen Heart" gives his likeness, all snow and ice. Though he thought about melting, only love could "supple" him, and rather than "be thawed or heated so," he stayed lost forever, coupling with eternal cold (H-113).

Tantalizing us is what the poems do and he calls to mind Tantalus, the fruit over his head always receding. Or he resembles the gods who don't sit down to table "yet love the smell of meat" (H-736). Dreams were his specialty, congenial though "empty," and the women he desired were like Ixion's cloud (H-105), nothing there. Fictive Electra climbing into his bed, he kisses her, panting, but calls night to witness, "that was all" (H-56). Though a warrior-mistress (virginal but masculine) gives him a good look at "the happy dawning of her thigh," he can't kiss that tempting nakedness. Waving a wand like a rap across the knuckles, his "sprightly Spartaness" forbids him, saying, "Hence, remove, / Herrick, thou art too coarse to love" (H-142). Love itself was the culprit, however, all that sweaty jigging and poking.

Erotic energy, quickening his poems, gives the body a wide berth and is dispersed among things. Clothes make the man or woman, substituting for them. If he really does "delight in disorder," he restricts it to a petticoat or shoelace. An odd kind of metonymy reduces his women to disjecta membra (Julia's leg). Much to-do about foreplay, nongenital pleasure, oral and tactile, sometimes olfactory. Like Ovid called Naso, Herrick has a nose, and it snuffs up fishy smells. Though no poet's eye sees more acutely, his doesn't act on what it sees. Frustrating the reader, this suits the voyeur.

Gliding, spectral but innocuous, he watches from the grave while his "lovely mistresses" bring him liquid refreshment (H-634). When the coast is clear, he licks up this poured-out sacrifice, no scenario wilder. The ladies turning pale, an avuncular poet says he won't hurt them; however, we don't have to be told. Perhaps they envisaged sexual coupling, but the chance for that is lost and likely never existed.

Convention, prescribing for the natural world, says that trees are male, while the plants that encircle them are female. His poem on the vine (H-41) reverses this relation or has it both ways, and "she" is also "he," a young

man but "ravished." "Soft nervelets," crawling and enthralling, "surprise /
Her body, buttocks, and her waist," and writhing, brush her forehead, their
"rich clusters hid among / The leaves." This female prisoner can't help her-
self (otherwise it's no go), but violation isn't in the cards, and the creeping /
creepy leaves conceal without invading "those parts which maids keep un-
espied." Awaking from sleep, the poet, a witty punster, finds his flesh "more
like a stock than like a vine." But this erection does him no good. The
snakelike thing goes through all the motions, and the real thing, though
tumescent, is dead.

Weird and often edged with pathos, much of Herrick is fun, however,
like this couplet "Upon Julia's Breasts":

> Between whose glories, there my lips I'll lay,
> Ravished in that fair Via Lactea.

You could call this puerile, but readers with an ear will want to listen to the
rhyme, self-conscious, absurd, and attractive. The Herrick we remember
gratefully is too big for a clinical casebook. It took clarity on his part, says
Gordon Braden, "to make his favorite poet-figure into an impotent, drunk
old man."

In poems like the "Farewell" and "Welcome" to sack, some unnamed
"thing" is his subject, only wine, but he keeps mum on its nature. Power-
ful similitudes conceal it, leading us on ("the warm soft side / Of the resign-
ing, yet resisting bride") or putting us off (hairy comets that foretell "the
coming of some dire events"). Efficient against his enemy, torpor, the
prodigious thing rouses the frost-bound blood, but its "witching beauties"
strike fear in a shrinking bachelor. Others desire their lips and "hers"
espoused, but he swears for the future to "smell of the lamp, not thee." His
abdication is mean, and "whimpering" a protest, the banished creature
smiles knowingly. Maybe, in his "raked-up ash-heap," no fire remains.
Wine might get him going, making him "active to do," like that deep-
drinking Hercules who "kept heat for fifty maids" a night. Is Herrick
pulling our leg?

Not always the wished-for thing, consummation has its scary side, and
a comical off-rhyme suggests it. Sea-scourged Ulysses, nearing home, is
before us, soon to greet his Penelope "after long divorcement." Off to land-
ward, "fires betray / The smoky chimneys of his Ithaca," ambiguous solace.
Possibly this hero ought to keep going, or like "prophetic Daphne" pursued

by Apollo, would do better changing into a tree. Readers who think so aren't finding Herrick out but collaborating with him, and his best poetry sponsors a rival creation. Resembling baroque churches in the century he lived in—"about the roof a siren in a sphere," one of Bernini's—it reorders the real world, lighting up vivid but surprising interiors. Nothing in nature is like them, except his comic-sinister heart.

Chapter 4

Wordsworth Pro and Con

Wordsworth had a lot of faults, and only a great poet could survive them. His art that looks inside is a lesser kind of art, subjective, "Romantic." He is its chief exponent among poets in English, so wears his major status with a difference. He wants us to live on the flying trapeze, but the epiphanic thing isn't nourishing for art, and poets who live by it die by it too. "Entire & intense selfishness" marked his character, said Southey. Wanting all the kudos, he scissored out "Christabel," his best friend's latest effort, from the second edition of *Lyrical Ballads*. But his devotion to his work is total, like Joyce's. "Verse was what he had been wedded to," he wrote of himself. It drove him along like a tempest, and on this side he is one of our heroes. To get his special quality needs a composite portrait, sorry and heroic sides together.

"A traveler I am," he said in *The Prelude* (bk. 3), but all his tale was of himself. Plumbing his own depths nonstop, sooner or later he scrapes bottom. "Three years she grew in sun and shower," then dying, left the memory "to me." "There was a Boy" who died in childhood, hard on Romantics. The poet, "looking at the grave" he lies in, grieves for himself, though. Even in "Ruth," where his hero runs to the bad, he is the hero. While yet a child, moon, sun, and streams "Had been his dearest joy." Engorging his characters, not the same as dwelling in them, he diminishes their interest, so many versions of Wordsworth.

The inside-outside dichotomy, familiar to readers of nineteenth-century fiction, gets a strong push from him. There's a heart of gold in his savage Boeotians. Older poets, scrutinizing behavior, sought "to catch the manners living as they rise," but in his asocial poetry, manners are an affectation. Artlessness is a sign of grace. Typical heroines are like his Lucy Gray, "The sweetest thing that ever grew / Beside a human door!" Coleridge, settling scores with an old colleague in the *Biographia Literaria,* saw him sinking from sublimity to bathos (1817, chap. 22). He does that often, for example in "Resolution and Independence": "My old remembrances went from me wholly; / And all the ways of men, so vain and melancholy." A Max Beerbohm-ish Wordsworth, fussy, not discriminating, handles nature with sugar tongs. Laying a glowworm on a leaf, he bears it with him through the night, "in my left hand."

Despite his humanitarian ardors, he doesn't care much for people, and the causes he promoted remain on a theoretical level. His principal object, specified in the preface to *Lyrical Ballads,* was "to choose incidents and situations from common life," tracing in them "the primary laws of our nature." But his common tends to commonplace, and he mistakes agitation for insight. The city, made by man and man's greatest glory, looked like an eyesore to him. Back to civilization! is the rallying cry of all right-thinking people, not his. Nowhere does he recollect the abasing/glorifying power of sexual love. In the 1790s he crossed over to France and fathered an illegitimate child on French Annette Vallon. Less tactful than squeamish, he kept mum on this affair, and in *The Prelude* a third-person narrative, standing in for it, conceals it. He put one of Chaucer's tales into modern English but jibbed at the frankness. "For on thy bed thy wyf I saugh hym swyve" becomes in his rendering "I saw him in guilty converse with thy wife."

Emotion "of whatever kind" triggered his poetry, some thrilling, some plaintive. Or the plaintive was thrilling, like his "Solitary Reaper." Either way, you got an "overbalance of pleasure," the end of poetry and its sole restriction. Once it had a dual function—teaching and delighting is the old Horatian formula—but Wordsworth's account shortens this by half. He told how images, rising before him, inspired feelings of delight, pure or mixed "with no unpleasing sadness" (Prospectus to *The Excursion,* 1814). "Surprised by joy" in one of the sonnets, he turns to share it with his daughter Catherine, but remembers that this favorite child lies buried in the tomb. No sorrow to rival "that thought's return." Its worst pang resembles joy's "transport," however, and each, an epiphany, turns the rest of the day to prose.

All his poems had "a worthy *purpose,*" he said, and he wanted "to be considered as a teacher or as nothing." But he is in his practice among the first poets who put aesthetic considerations up front. In a revealing phrase he identified the function of genius as "widening the sphere of human sensibility." All will agree that this is a good, and the last thing we want is a narrow-minded preceptor damping down our feelings. Wordsworth skirts this danger. But enlarging our feelings, he softpedals thought, so touches fewer bases than poets before him.

Drawn from real life, his "Affliction of Margaret" features a poor widow who buttonholes passing strangers for news of her lost son. Coleridge, a connoisseur of dejection "tempered with delight," liked the scenario. He said no mother, nor any parent, himself included, could read her story "without a tear." This chimes with Wordsworth's intention. He zeroes in on the mother's interesting plight, wondering whether her son lies dead in some dungeon, the lion's den, the deep. Poignant alternatives, they constitute his poem's reason for being.

Shakespeare at Sonnets squeezes pleasure from pain, for instance in his no. 30, "When to the sessions of sweet silent thought." But his narrator, stroking a morbid sensibility, is understood to be morbid. How much Wordsworth understands, in his ballad and elsewhere, is a question. He seems unembarrassed, reporting that "Dejection taken up for pleasure's sake . . . / Did sweeten many a meditative hour" (*Prelude,* bk. 6). More voracious than Shakespeare's, his sensibility feeds where it can.

Powerful feeling is enough for him in sonnets like "London, 1802," "The World Is Too Much with Us," "Composed upon Westminster Bridge." Though the rhyme scheme says these poems are Italian (eight lines "explained" in six more), they don't pose or resolve a problem. Ecstasy is Wordsworth's passport to knowledge, affirmed by "sensations" felt in the blood and heart. Feeling them is how he lightens the burden of the mystery. Though he makes room for intellect ("thinks and feels in the spirit of human passions"), all the money is on the qualifying phrase. No intimation in him that form creates affect. The feeling "gives importance to the action and situation, and not the action and situation to the feeling."

In Wordsworth, taking him as normative for Romantic poetry, the image of the poet as maker begins to wane. Anciently, "maker" = "wright," like a boatwright or cartwright, men who make things. Abrams, in *The Mirror and the Lamp* (1953), compares Wordsworth and Dryden on figures of speech—whether they come naturally or result from self-conscious creation. Dryden argues that the poet must put on the passion he hopes to express in his figure, Wordsworth, that the poet's own affective and mental state thrust the figure upon him. Shakespeare's character says, "The truest poetry is the most feigning," but Wordsworth makes this sentiment passé. Coolness and discretion (Dryden's desiderata) drop out in his art, replaced by sincerity. Not eager to rack his brains, he doesn't think he has to.

His nose, said the painter Haydon, announced a wonder, but he didn't always look down it, and though his moral sense is overdeveloped, he didn't winnow bad from good but took pleasure in "the endless store of things." I quote him in *The Prelude* (bk. 1), the long poem he spent a life-time revising while staying true to its accommodating bias. His affiliation to thingness doesn't argue "photographic exactitude," the conventional mis-understanding, expressed by Malcolm Elwin, and sometimes his things are appareled in "celestial light." In the famous Simplon Pass episode (*Prelude,* bk. 6), for instance, his view of them is "apocalyptic," the word he uses. Having crossed the Alps, he says what he sees,

>   The immeasurable height
> Of woods decaying, never to be decayed,
> The stationary blasts of waterfalls . . .
> The torrents shooting from the clear blue sky,
> The rocks that muttered close upon our ears . . .
> The unfettered clouds and region of the heavens,
> Tumult and peace, the darkness and the light.

He stands above the "Protestant" battle, running the gamut affectively (tumult and peace, etc.), and has little to say of good and evil. Style is para-tactic, diction laconic, matter inclusive. Though he detects in nature the workings of mind, he makes this apparition physical, and black crags, appar-ently inanimate, speak "as if a voice were in them." But looking beyond nature, he never looks through it.

Coleridge, on the other hand, wanted to part the veil. Knowing what he was, he knew what Wordsworth should be, a philosopher-poet like Mil-ton. But Wordsworth is least persuasive when he sounds most like Milton, second-rate Milton filtered through eighteenth-century verse. The year of *Lyrical Ballads,* he made a start at the long poem Coleridge required. This was *The Recluse,* "or Views of Nature, Man, and Society." Framing "views" was beyond or beneath him, however, and though he pegged away loyally for almost two decades, *The Recluse* never got written. Part of it did, notably *The Prelude,* an "ante-chapel" to his Gothic cathedral. All three versions mingle much smoke with their fire. The best is the first one, when he was only a poet. Some recent critics take exception, one, W. B. Gallie, ranking *The Prelude* as the premier philosophical poem in English, but this gives Wordsworth more and less than desert. Unlike the poetry of Coleridge and the next generation of Romantics, his is provincial.

His genius, though denying him the high intellectual wire, glorifies his reading of the natural world. Coleridge, deprecating "little things," called poetry "ideal and generic" (*Biographia Literaria,* chap. 26). But describing nature he equals Wordsworth, even surpassing him in a few great poems, "Frost at Midnight" and "This Lime-Tree Bower My Prison." In "The Ancient Mariner," when the bride enters the church, his eye is on the minstrels, "nodding their heads before her." Unluckily, however, he hunted bigger game, confusing it with conceptual truth, so sniffed at Wordsworth's matter-of-factness. "A something corporeal" in the poetry, he said, "a clinging to the palpable, or often to the petty." Both the good and bad of Wordsworth are caught in this phrase.

Each of these poets comes from the same Romantic mold, predicting their long decline after the first intense glowing. The miraculous year that culminated in *Lyrical Ballads* lasted just a year, beginning July 2, 1797 and ending July 2, 1798. This sounds like Virginia Woolf saying that human character changed "on or about" December 1910, but much anecdotage, even a surfeit of it, documents their daily round. Nobody cared that much about poets before them.

Coleridge never repeated his meteoric success, and the great days were barely past when he told William Godwin that the poet in him had died. Godwin, a political scientist, was sorry to hear it. But Wordsworth, says Margoliouth, whose little book on their collaboration is as good as anyone's, "had begun to burn with a steady light which was to grow for several years in range and intensity." In the beginning, he was willing to say that nature never betrayed the heart that loved her. But deep distress, his brother's drowning, mollified his soul and toughened his thinking. No sea existed, experience taught him, "that could not cease to smile," and in a tribute to "composition"—his friend Sir George Beaumont's painting of Peele Castle trampled by storm and waves—he made disharmony part of the canvas.

He didn't live on this tickle point for long. Soon after, in "Laodamia," he was anticipating virtue's reward, postponed to the world over yonder. There, beauty was happier, streams more pellucid, and we breathed an ampler "ether" than here. Early in the new century, he wrote his best-known sonnets and lyrics, the "immortal ode," and the powerful elegy commemorating his brother John, lost at sea. *The Recluse,* work-in-progress, yielded spinoffs, *The Excursion* plus a much augmented *Prelude*. In "The Ode to Duty" (1804), however, he addressed a newfound goddess, asking leave to serve her "more strictly, if I may." "Trust thyself," the Romantic credo, used to be his, but he discovered that this trust had been given "too blindly." Worn down by "uncharted freedom" and burdened by desire, he spoke with astonishing candor:

> My hopes no more must change their name,
> I long for a repose that ever is the same.

The languor of *The Faerie Queene* breathes in his hexameter line.

He became a patriot, not the Regulus kind, a nervous old man, and in patriotic odes saluted a famous victory, Waterloo. More than a hundred sonnets traced the history of Christianity in England (but "Mutability," a permanent poem, is among them). Other sonnets sought to legitimate capital punishment. As compassion waned, the poet lost his ear. In a great passage from the *Elegiac Stanzas,* he wrote of

> the gleam,
> The light that never was, on sea or land,
> The consecration, and the Poet's dream.

This reduced (in the four-volume *Poems* of 1820) to "a gleam, / Of lustre, known to neither sea nor land, / But borrowed from the youthful Poet's dream." Worse, he lost his poet's conscience, perhaps contingent on the loss of technique. The grieving poet of *The Excursion,* Wordsworth as we like him, takes comfort from nature, "those very plumes, / Those weeds, and the high spear-grass on that wall." By and by, however, Christianity consoles him, a secondhand model, not "felt in the blood," and grief can nowhere maintain "dominion o'er the enlightened spirit / Whose meditative sympathies repose / Upon the breast of Faith."

The declining curve that describes the poetry intersects another, plotting the transformation of indigent dropout to the Sage of Rydal Mount. First a salaried official in Britain's version of the IRS, then a recipient of honorary degrees, he ended as Poet Laureate. But he had his fill of tragedy, and the more you read him and read about him, the more his plodding onwardness compels admiration, including its oldfashioned sense, wonder. So many he loved dropped off before him. The sister he loved more than almost all others lost her mind but didn't die, and every day he had to confront her. Of himself, he wrote wearily:

> Yet I, whose lids from infant slumbers
> Were earlier raised, remain.

The years weren't altogether waste. In lines worth having on the death of the Scottish poet Hogg, he saw his friends disperse "Like clouds that rake the mountain summits, / Or waves that own no curbing hand." Any reader who cares for him will rejoice in the conclusion to his sonnet sequence of 1820, *The River Duddon:*

> Still glides the Stream, and shall forever glide;
> The Form remains, the Function never dies;
> While *we,* the brave, the mighty, and the wise,
> We Men, who in our morn of youth defied
> The elements, must vanish.

In 1831, however, he said, "The Muse has forsaken me," and must have known this had happened long before.

Sharp-eyed Harriet Martineau, who got to know him near the end, watched with incredulity as he ambled through a countryside filled with drunkenness, quarreling, and sexual license. "Here is dear good old Wordsworth forever talking of rural innocence and deprecating any intercourse with towns, lest the purity of his neighbors should be corrupted." He died at twelve noon, April 13, 1850, as his cuckoo-clock was telling the hour.

By then, Coleridge had been dead sixteen years, his every mortal power "frozen at its marvelous source." Twin stars of poetry, they belong together, but their conjunction includes opposition. Though *The Prelude* has them reaching "the self-same bourne" or goal via different roads, Wordsworth sought a goal he couldn't encompass, urged on by Coleridge, who undervalued the goal he achieved. Wordsworth, thinking back to *Lyrical Ballads* (1798), saw "no discordance" in the colors of their style. Getting older, however, they looked more like themselves. In their biographies, nature imitates Romantic art, and a bitter quarrel in 1810, though patched on the surface, put the happier past beyond recall.

Mingling tragedy and farce, Coleridge appalls and astounds us. He suffered from rheumatism, the "itch," stomach and bowel ailments, neuritis. His joints and testicles swelled. Once, when out walking, he threw himself on the ground and writhed like a worm. The opium he needed "almost every night" induced sweats and fevers. Terror, mystery, and supernatural menace stalk his poems. Moaning in grief and fear, a little child has lost her way in "Dejection." A woman wailing for her demon lover haunts the chasms of "Kubla Khan." Like the sinister witch in "Christabel," this demon acts out its awful purpose on the woman. Fiends plague his Ancient Mariner, wrenched with woeful agony. "Alone, alone, all, all alone," words for the Mariner, describe the Romantic poet. "*Desunt nonnulla,*" something missing, stands at the foot of his achievement. "Kubla Khan" is subtitled "A Fragment"; "Christabel" ends without concluding, like "The Wanderings of Cain." The bark the wanderer sets sail in, headed for the "Fortunate Isles" of the Muses, is driven off by "adverse gales" and never gets there. Not getting there becomes a point of honor for Romantics, masters of the Unfinished Symphony. "A person from Porlock," breaking in on the performance, makes sure it isn't finished. Taking thought might have remedied this, but they do best when laid asleep in mind.

Coleridge wrote half a dozen great poems, an astonishing achievement, but from a great poet you expect more. "Dejection," written at thirty, is his last major effort. Failure gave him a string he could harp on, however. Nine years before he died, he looked at nature's busy world, then turned to his own:

> And I the while, the sole unbusy thing,
> Nor honey make, nor pair, nor build, nor sing.

His couplet is descriptive, not diagnostic, and doesn't say why he couldn't or wouldn't. Wordsworth's case, looking back at it, isn't that different. Coleridge stopped, he went on, but his window on the world closed quickly. The two together, in their brief youthful flowering and unproductive age, sketch a story familiar in decades to come, all that dreary business of the *poète maudit,* no second acts in American literature, etc. "What portion in the world can the artist have / Who has awakened from the common dream / But dissipation and despair?"

Cultural historians often blame the *Zeitgeist,* bearer of a new style or new emotional or intellectual content. Pater, reading Coleridge, heard the chords of its fatal languor, summoning to discontent, homesickness, and regret. But the inclination to "despondency and madness" is there already in earlier times. Melancholy, the Elizabethan Malady, tormented Hamlet, and Chaucer's characters knew "the synne of Accidie," spiritual sloth. Words like "sin" and "malady" tell of point of view, however. The damned in Dante's Fifth Circle acknowledge a moral failing, being "sullen in the sweet air that is gladdened by the sun." That is why they are damned. The sense of a moral failing is missing in Coleridge and Wordsworth.

But not their sense of themselves as beleaguered. The personal, whether vexed or ecstatic, absorbs them, and self-consciousness, the great modern happening, gets up a full head of steam. Perhaps artists who don't see themselves as the cynosure of all eyes are luckier than those who do. Art prospers most when the claims it makes don't stupefy, but the upper registers are native to Wordsworth and Coleridge. Hazlitt remembered the text Coleridge chose, preaching the Gospel from a Unitarian pulpit in Shrewsbury: "And he went up into the mountain to pray, HIMSELF ALONE." Wordsworth, at home in the "egotistical sublime," was there before him. Not a dramatic poet like Shakespeare, or Yeats when he put on the mask, he lived in the busy solitude of his own heart, writing poetry "as if there were nothing but himself and the universe."

Both scorned popular applause, craving "fit audience, though few." In practice, this meant a voice crying in the wilderness, and they stand on the outside, telling their soul's tale alone. Beware the flashing eyes and weave a circle around them. Both kicked against the pricks, out of tune with society. "The Gods approve / The depth, and not the tumult, of the soul" (Wordsworth in "Laodamia"), and the jarring note of protest tells against them. Read in the larger context of poetry in English, their Romantic truth is only partial. "Trances of thought" are the life of *The Prelude* (bk. 1). Thought depends first on feeling, Coleridge says, and adds that "all truth is a species of revelation," e.g. "Kubla Khan." Sinking into "a profound sleep, at least of the external sense," he composes his poem from unconscious memory, "if that indeed can be called composition" that has no sensation of effort. The damsel in the poem, playing an Aeolian Harp, gives his likeness. Air currents, blowing as they list, cause the strings on the sounding board to vibrate. Wordsworth doesn't lack these "Aeolian visitations" (*Prelude,* bk. 1), and though sometimes they torment him, they insure that his poetry gets written.

In verses to Shakespeare, Jonson thinks about the difficulties that go with a poet's job, and how he must sweat and "strike the second heat / Upon the muses' anvil." Beneficiaries of "random gales / That swell and flutter" on the lute (Coleridge, in "The Aeolian Harp") needn't sweat like Jonson and Shakespeare. But Romantics have their own truth, and though not all-in-all sufficient, it asks a hearing. Offensive to intellectualizing critics like Babbitt (he thought the mind was the man), this truth is extrarational. Shakespeare entertains it in *The Tempest.* He gives every truth a hearing, sticking at none, settling for none, and Romantics relate to him like the dew on the myrtle leaf to his grand sea. Unexpectedly, Caliban is the play's best poet. His visions come to him in dream, and, waking, he cries to dream again. Much value in dreaming.

The conventional wisdom doesn't think this, and the hero, a book-man, embodies the kind of knowing it sets store by. The monster is the type of the Romantic poet. Against the sons of light, he stands for darkness. Moderns, cheering him on, are certainly sentimental, but the hypertrophied intellect has been the downfall of many. There is that Casaubon, the sixteenth-century dry-as-dust and George Eliot's updated version. Wordsworth and Coleridge know all about him. Shunning false clarity, the kind that skips holes and corners, they target one source of our trouble.

In the first *Prelude,* young Wordsworth tells how the sky, sinking down into his heart, held him like a dream (bk. 2). This is unprecedented, and brooding on phenomenal fact until it bears is his chief claim to uniqueness. But he isn't a ploughman-poet, like his version of Burns. His similes and metaphors are often literary, not what you would expect of a lover of nature. The card game in *The Prelude,* moving us away from nature, is oddly like Pope's in *The Rape of the Lock,* only less rinsed of physical impurities. Parallel passages from different states of *The Prelude* show him getting free of dusty life as he can. In 1805, back in Paris, he ranges "More eagerly than I had done before, / Through the wide city." But revising obsessed him, like old Henry James gilding the New York edition of the novels, and by 1850 he is ranging "with ardor heretofore unfelt, / The spacious city" (bk. 10). In one corner of his heart, he thought poetry ought to be high-toned.

Biographers who don't like him present a naif, but he made himself learned in Euclid's "geometric truth." De Quincey, distinguishing his special quality, locates him in "this world of bodiless abstraction." His conventionalized vocabulary is full of see-through words—*calm, free, quiet, breathless,* in the "beauteous evening" sonnet. Among his masters is Cowper, the poet of "The Task." This long poem repays reading, but the lines lack impasto, and after a while your eyes glaze. In Wordsworth's case, only the first clause holds true, not the second. God doesn't specify, and he has mastered the language God uses.

The generic mode hangs on even when something "far more deeply interfused" is before him:

> the light of setting suns,
> And the round ocean and the living air,
> And the blue sky . . . .
> . . . [and] the meadows and the woods,
> And mountains; and . . . all that we behold
> From this green earth.

Like certain poems of Jonson's, these lines from "Tintern Abbey" are enor-
mously persuasive. Its particulars are few and always dissolving: orchard tufts
that lose themselves, and while you are still looking, are gone. "His finest
passages are moral, emotional, subjective; whatever visual intensity they
have comes from his response to the object, not from his close observation
of it" (Lionel Trilling on the "Intimations Ode"). He has a great phrase, cel-
ebrating beauty as "a living presence of the earth." To our surprise the pres-
ence isn't physical, though, but superior to grosser forms "composed /
From earth's materials." Elsewhere he looks askance at the analytical tem-
per. It likes to "peep and botanize," different from his.

   In an offhanded but stunning remark, he said in old age that he was often
unable to think of things outside himself as having "external existence." His
mind is its own place, "My haunt and the main region of my song." He
describes it in *The Excursion,* another fragment of the philosophic poem he
left unfinished. Contradiction is his element, and partly he couldn't finish
because of his bent for externals. In his boyish days (remembering "Tintern
Abbey"), nature needed no remoter charm supplied by thought. Character-
istically, however, something extra makes the difference, and daffodils in
thought are better than daffodils in nature. Growing first "beside the lake,
beneath the trees," his become themselves only as an "inward eye" trans-
forms them. "Investing" the material world of *The Prelude*—a pool, a bea-
con, a girl with a pitcher—he overpaints its proper color with some "auxil-
iar light" (1799, bks. 1–2). This light "bestows" the splendors most ascribe
to nature. Indebted to it, he is like his shepherd's boy in "Michael," from
whom there came

>   Feelings and emanations—things which were
>   Light to the sun and music to the wind.

Look twice and you see that this Orphic country boy is creating the world
he lives in.

   Coleridge, seeing that, picked a quarrel with Wordsworth. "Poor
wretch," he

>   filled all things with himself,
>   And made all gentle sounds tell back the tale
>   Of his own sorrow.
>
>   ("The Nightingale")

How easily he asserts the truth of things, genial nature in "Tintern Abbey,"
the six-year-old "philosopher" of the "Intimations Ode." Coleridge in

"Dejection" has both these poems in his sights. An anonymous Lady is his addressee, but Wordsworth stands behind her. "We receive but what we give," Coleridge instructs him, "And in our life alone does Nature live."

Wordsworth's psychology makes an easy target. All that pumped-up fervor (oh! oh!), testifyng how "expletives their feeble aid do join" to fill a gap in the reasoning or meter. All that facile animizing: "sportive" hedgerows that run wild, smoke making wreaths and giving notice of "vagrant dwellers" who aren't really there. In his own person, idling like the sooty film that flutters before his fire, Coleridge offers an ironic version of the unregenerate Romantic. Seeing and hearing what he wants to, he "makes a toy of thought." Nothing more real than the "secret ministry" of frost or the redbreast on the branch of "mossy apple tree," but the lovely shapes of "Frost at Midnight" and its sounds that seem "intelligible" are owing to the poet alone.

Unless in the mind of an ingenuous poet, the "celestial light" Wordsworth goes on about never existed. No wedding garment or shroud covers earth's nakedness, and the beauty we worship is "luminous mist." Not true that stars glide across the heavens or watch over the world, or that the new moon cradles the old in her lap or swims in its lake of blue. All that is only "poetry," Coleridge thinks, and he begins with "as if." Less tortuous than Wordsworth, he has a keener eye, forbidding illusion. Or is it that he sees less far into the life of things? One way or another, he acknowledges the difference between them:

> I may not hope from outward forms to win
> The passion and the life, whose fountains are within.

Six feet after five feet, the long line says "dejection."

On April 21, 1802, he read an early draft of the poem to Wordsworth and his sister Dorothy. Early in May Wordsworth responded. He wrote "The Leech-Gatherer," later called "Resolution and Independence." Mounting high in delight as his poem begins, he sinks as low in dejection, and this is how the Leech-Gatherer finds him. The old man's glass is running, but his cheerful stoicism dispels a poet's blind thoughts and sorrows. His little homily is unremarkable, though, and the poem's "resolution" dwindles almost to bathos. But the rendering of nature—sun after rain—is fine. As often in Wordsworth, we have to do with an imperfect poem, splendors and banalities together.

His valiant old man, stout of heart, not intellectual, resembles many modern heroes, Faulkner's, for instance. Comparison to a huge stone or sea-beast suggests his strengths and limitations. But Wordsworth himself is the reverse of unselfconscious. Rime royal, his chosen vehicle, is cunningly tinkered, each stanza ending with an alexandrine, mimicking certain lines of "Dejection." His feeling-better-now conclusion will strike some as heartless, but "Resolution and Independence" qualifies itself, like other poems of his. Not canceling "the fear that kills," the old man's "apt admonishment" confronts it, frustrating closure. In today, tomorrow is potential, bearing "solitude, pain of heart, distress, and poverty." Wordsworth's habit is antiphonal, and often his demonstrations seem engineered by fiat. For a skeptical poet, this is a way out of the poem.

But these two poets are more like than unlike. Coleridge is frankly solipsistic, Wordsworth hopes not to be, but both "half perceive and half create." Self-critiquing and the optative voice ("I could wish") describe the "Intimations Ode," and its last eight stanzas meet Coleridge head on. Wordsworth's poem faces up to a diminished thing: "There was a time," no more. The heartening conclusion, though of power, is wistful. *Setting* and *sober* and *mortality, fears* and *tears,* give the affect. Clouds that gather as the sun sinks take their gorgeous color not from nature but the eye.

Though the Ode, like "Tintern Abbey," looks up, this posture is only official. "If I were sullen" means that I shouldn't be, but Wordsworth's dependent clause hangs in air. Sift him and you find the poet of lonely rooms, acquainted with the weight "of all this unintelligible world." Few in English have his poignance, regretting the hour of splendor in the grass, and fewer come near the dogged sequel:

> We will grieve not, rather find
> Strength in what remains behind.

The emphatic couplets offer to console us, but the voice we hear is gnomic, not prescriptive. If the Ode ends hopefully, that isn't for intellectual reasons. But like the *The Waste Land* or Yeats's *Tower,* it plants a brave flag on the wreckage.

Artifice is the badge of the simple poet who vowed to imitate "the very language of men." Fretting the strings, he makes sad equate to happy, and his vision of life going down, like Stevens's in "Sunday Morning" and "Le Monocle de Mon Oncle," exhilarates more than dejects us. Though the best is behind, loss is mitigated, even transformed, by the music. Ending the poem's longest stanza, the compass of the notes is from two feet to six:

> Hence in a season of calm weather
> Though inland far we be,
> Our Souls have sight of that immortal sea
> Which brought us hither,
> Can in a moment travel thither,
> And see the Children sport upon the shore,
> And hear the mighty waters rolling evermore.

The last line, showing us what the hexameter can do, makes thought all but palpable, and in the line before it the gratuitous detail is worth a thousand words.

Hewing to no fixed pattern but ever shifting in rhyme and meter, the free form of the Ode is right for its home truths. Declarative and eloquent enough, it doesn't need to support them, except rhetorically. A short poem, "My Heart Leaps Up," leading into it, forecasts its burden: "The Child is father to the Man." But Wordsworth doesn't insist and his ending is both provisional and prayerful. "So be it when . . . ." If "Tintern Abbey" is felt as blemished, turning shrill toward the end, that is because the blank verse, appropriate for discursive thought, betrays the poet when thought grows incoherent.

Many critics note Wordsworth's fondness for the conditional mode, words and phrases like "perchance," "as might seem," "I trust," "I would believe." Concluding *The Prelude,* first version, he highlights the word "if." Against the current of unfailing faith asserted by a confident poet, it eddies strongly. His syntax often undercuts what he says, as if he can't or won't speak straight on. Feelings of pleasure (remembered in "Tintern Abbey") have on our lives "no slight or trivial influence," or rather "perhaps" this is so. The "not un-" construction, or variations, ranks among his favorites. Introducing *Lyrical Ballads,* he has formed "no very inaccurate estimate" of his poems, incidentally "not unimportant" in the quality of their moral relations. The poet of *The Prelude* is "Not uselessly employed," and enters the world (in the "Intimations Ode") "Not in entire forgetfulness, / And not in utter nakedness." Though Earth is his foster mother, she undertakes his education with "no unworthy aim." This going-round-the-barn kind of writing is certainly pompous. More than a vice of style, though, it tells of a humble man who can't or won't affirm. In the Peele Castle elegy Wordsworth reaches his majority, and the poem's tentative voice declares this. "Not without hope" he suffers and mourns.

Cocksureness is never his. His recognitions are dim, involved with sad perplexity, and what he hears, "soft inland murmurs," comes from a long way off. Perhaps this is why he restricts the end of poetry to pleasure. It could hardly encapsulate truth. When his point of view shifts from affirmative to yes-and-no, his blank verse line is apt to break apart. That happens in "The Ruined Cottage," again in "Tintern Abbey," where the back and forth is like dialectic. Empowered by joy, "We see into the life of things." But in metrical propriety the line still needs its conclusion, and supplying it, he veers off in a different direction: "If this / Be but a vain belief . . . ." His trick of rephrasing, almost an involuntary stammer, makes us trust him.

Cleanth Brooks thought him at his best in long narrative poems, but composition isn't among his virtues. *The Prelude* is discrete episodes, lit by "gleams like the flashing of a shield." He renders better than he applies, in the powerful ship poem, "Where Lies the Land," for instance, or the Mutability sonnet, commonplace in thought, superb in detail. Characteristically, his sonnets don't evolve much, but the eye that plays over their content is pious. This is the best of a limited poet.

Time hangs heavy on our hands, not on his, in his tales of everyday ("Ruth," "The Ruined Cottage"). He thinks intrinsic importance ennobles them, worth his telling and our hearing. Often he seems innocent of meaning, or meaning is identical with matter-of-fact: stonecrop along the window's edge, bindweed on the wall, the border tufts: "daisy, thrift, and lowly camomile." His heroine Margaret, "last human tenant of these ruined walls," sticks in memory less than the ruin. But at his best, e.g. in "Michael," he persuades us that his prosaic story, though it has no point but itself, is enough.

His faith in nature, unsupported by proof, comes down to an ipse dixit, "thus he said." Coleridge made him smart for that. But the saying is immaculate, and he knows what he knows. Believing that "somehow his existence and vocation should be justifiable" (William Heath, 1970), he carries us with him. He wrote with authority, not "upon authority," his biographer Stephen Gill's fine and apposite phrase. The authority itself comes "from least suggestions," gathered by a watchful poet who had the faculty of being wrought on (*Prelude*, bk. 14). Not angelic but "stopped upon the wing" like an angel, he listened for celestial harmony and "after it was heard no more," bore it with him.

This aftervibration beguiled busy thoughts and whiled away the time, he said, tiresome eighteenth-century talk that tells nothing of his poetry's power. Restorative like the spittle that washed the blind man's eyes, it reveals the world as it was and might be, "place where, in the end, / We find our happiness or not at all!" (*Prelude,* bk. 11). What he sees is only a piece of the whole, and he misses the grand artificial world, domain of many older poets. But no poet before him sets such an aureole on the "simple produce of the common day" (prospectus to *The Excursion*). He is a great poet, diminished by the age that produced him.

Aiming at philosophy, he failed to hit the mark but found something better, though only fitfully. In *The Recluse,* he saw man wedded to the "outward frame" of things in love, a "great consummation." From the beginning he merged himself in his surroundings, endowing both with new life. In book 1 of the first *Prelude,* he wrote of

> The single sheep, and the one blasted tree,
> And the bleak music of that old stone wall.

Fifty years later these two lines reappear in book 12. Humbler than philosophy and unadorned like revolutions, they give the essence of Wordsworth.

Chapter 5

Frost in the Waste Land

Robert Frost is America's best poet, even though the million happens to think so. He has the great poet's power to shake us, and can make the eyes smart and lift the hairs on the neck. In his threnody with a difference, "Come In," for example:

> Too dark in the woods for a bird
> By sleight of wing
> To better its perch for the night,
> Though it still could sing.

This dark that won't lighten isn't obedient to a conjuror's tricks, either a bird's or a man's. But Frost's iambs and rising anapests, testifying to darkness, speak powerfully against it. Stevens in "Sunday Morning" has this two-in-one power:

> Passions of rain, or moods in falling snow;
> Grievings in loneliness, or unsubdued
> Elations when the forest blooms . . .

and Eliot in *The Waste Land:*

> The awful daring of a moment's surrender
> Which an age of prudence can never retract.

Preciosity in Stevens wants us to notice, though, and Eliot's bent for noisome things puts us off. More completely the artist than either, Frost keeps his failures to the level of life.

A friend of his who moved his chair to a distance called him a good poet but a bad man. He had a black side, and thought you got on as much by hating as loving. "I never forget, and I never forgive a wrong," he said, pleased that this was so. Headaches and stomach aches tormented him in boyhood, also fear of the dark. Among the books he cared for was *Robinson Crusoe,* "never quite out of my mind." The solitary man, battling savages who threatened to destroy him, gives his likeness. His father, prone to drink and violence, died early, his sister in a hospital for the insane. He had two sons, his first-born dying in infancy, the second in young manhood by his own hand. With his surviving children, he lived at swords' points. Nervous breakdowns threatened one daughter; another, outliving them, died of a fever contracted in childbirth. More than once, suicide tempted their father. Needing a gyroscope, he married at twenty, but his wife Elinor, "the unspoken half" of everything he ever wrote, left him in death when he still had miles to go. Desperate, he asked his daughter Lesley for a refuge but she wouldn't take him in. He might injure her daughters, she said, the way he had ruined her mother.

Growing up dirt-poor, he never got over it. Like Blake the paranoid, he thought friends who tried to help him were only pretending. When he taught school, his students were his enemies and he caned them freely. At first, getting up to speak filled him with terror. Time passed and he wouldn't sit down. A student in the informal class he taught at Dartmouth remembered him going on for nine hours. During the War I spent an hour in his company, and the impression is still there, like a hoof-print. He was touring the country, "saying" his poems to servicemen and criticizing their poems, if asked to. Having read mine, he looked at me thoughtfully. "Did you ever try prose?" he said.

To modern Americans he is the farmer-poet, like that Cincinnatus who left the plough to serve the state. But he didn't make much of a farmer, and later, in a mock-Virgilian eclogue, let Meliboeus the potato man describe him, a poet who used the farm as his backdrop. In 1912 he sailed for England, the dare of his life. He was in on the dawn of the modernist movement and on terms with all its holy names. Soon after his arrival, he brought out his first book, *A Boy's Will,* the year Joyce published *Portrait of the Artist.* Joyce is the type of the Modernist writer but Frost, who seems an antitype, is dipped in the same chilly waters.

To estimate his new poetry, readers will want to put it against De la Mare's or Masefield's, slipping along familiar grooves. Getting out of them, he emphasized prosaic detail,

> Magnified apples . . .
> Stem end and blossom end,
> And every fleck of russet showing clear.

The quotation comes from "After Apple-Picking," Robert Penn Warren's choice for the best of him. Though recycled in dream, the world of the poem isn't idealized, and Frost isn't a Platonist, one who believes that "the woman you have is an imperfect copy of some woman in heaven or in someone else's bed" (letter of 1938 to R. P. T. Coffin). More than once he thought back to Shelley, Platonist and philanderer: in "Birches," when ice crystals leave

> Such heaps of broken glass to sweep away
> You'd think the inner dome of heaven had fallen—

again in an earlier poem, "The Trial by Existence," where the light of heaven, "whole and white," is distinguished from our earthly light, "shattered into dyes." He is remembering "Adonais":

> The One remains, the many change and pass . . .
> Life, like a dome of many-colored glass,
> Stains the white radiance of eternity.

But no poet is less Shelleyan. In "Wild Grapes" his heroine, likened to Eurydice, isn't rescued from Hell but from "the upper regions." Up there, the light is unrefracted, synonymous with false.

His poetry stumbles coming out of the gate, much of it minor Georgian. He never did get wholly free of poetic diction and poetic inversions. But already in 1913 he is the revolutionary poet Edward Thomas detected in his pioneering review. The prose is Modernist all the way, a string of aperçus with the ligatures missing. "Strongly spent is synonymous with kept," said the lavish man, often supposed a niggard. He called grievances a form of impatience, griefs a form of patience, and took satisfaction in a sadness that didn't fish for consolation. "Give us immedicable woes," he said, "woes that nothing can be done for." This puts his antiliberal bias in perspective.

A barebones account of the life doesn't promise success, other than material. Already in his early time, he wished to reach out to "the general reader who buys books in their thousands." In 1936 he got his wish when the Book-of-the-Month Club anointed *A Further Range,* his volume of that year, assuring the sale of fifty thousand copies. No wonder the intellectuals, or some of them, snickered. But he liked coming first in popularity contests, and liked his role as America's best-loved poet. Playing up to the role, he didn't show to advantage. He turned up in the Sunday papers, "still following the road less traveled by." Dressed comfortably in a baggy suit, the white-haired poet of pastoral New England has the appearance of a kindly, small-town doctor. Though his rough-hewn face and figure suggest the austerity of a Vermont landscape, warm humanity animates his keen gray eyes. But he lowered the boom on Modernist writers, unintelligible and dwelling on "the insane fringe of things." (Combining interviews in the Rocky Mountain *News* and Denver *Post,* 1931.) All his life, their brave or foolish rejecting of old guidons confronted him, a gauntlet he might have picked up but declined.

Jealous of acclaim, he grudged it for contemporaries, but his introduction to E. A. Robinson's posthumous *King Jasper* is among his best pieces of writing. Though his sociopolitical take on the world was something he should have kept under his hat, he never tired of holding it up for inspection. The country feller liked kidding around and liked rough-and-ready talk, his own, often boorish. Khrushchev, whom he met in Russia, was "no saphead." Mistaking coarseness for wit, he went on to say: "No liberal sapheads for me." Wry humor was his fatal chimera, betraying some strong poems like "An Encounter." Better than almost all of us, he was worse than many. He knew what he was, "a selfish person who had dragged people rough-shod over life," he told a young poet, "a God-damned son of a bitch, Charlie, and don't let anyone tell you different."

Notoriously, his official biographer stalked him in three volumes (1966–76). He was "Larry" Thompson, a young Princeton professor when the two of them met, and their twenty-five years' connection makes a story worthy of Henry James. Sure to cash in when the old poet died, the young biographer grew old while he waited, digesting a ton of abuse in the meantime. They went on radio together. What does it mean, "Stopping by Woods on a Snowy Evening," the talk show host asked them. "A poem about death," said Larry Thompson. "Nonsense!" said Frost, glad to cut him down. In the biography, old scores got settled.

The trouble isn't with Thompson's matter-of-fact. But the young prig and old curmudgeon couldn't have written "Stopping by Woods," or rather to write it needed some extra thing, nowhere recorded. When one of the professoriate wanted to write about him, equating the life and art, he said the poet "projected" his poem, creating an object as independent of himself as he could make it (letter to Sidney Cox, 1932). Two truths are told of Frost, and we had better hold fast to the second. The first says his poetry reflects the private life. But what he made "in pain of his life" gets beyond its provenance, achieving a near-autonomous condition. From the gospel of Modernism, this is the second truth, and he ranks among modern masters.

Starting slowly, he came on like a natural force. Toward the end it petered out and his sententiousness turned into saws and sayings. But a masterpiece, "Directive," appears in his next-to-last book, published at seventy-two. Though everyone possesses a handful of his lyrics, he learned from Shakespeare how to speak with other voices, not his. Unlike most lyric poets, he excels at dramatic poetry. The modern American poet David Mason says he speaks "to a certain largeness in us, as to a congregation." This generally implies a message.

The message isn't often cheerful, however. *A Boy's Will,* its title saluting Longfellow, sends out misleading signals, and much of the poetry breathes desolation. "The Wood-Pile" in the second volume, a great narrative-meditative poem in blank verse, locates him in the waste land, a frozen swamp far from home. He went back to this forbidding place often. Marlowe taught him how to pray, he said: "Why, this is Hell, nor am I out of it."

In his life and art he swung between opposites, as delicate as Haiku and mordant beyond his admirers' dreams. "The first American who could be honestly reckoned a master-poet by world standards," Robert Graves called him, his judgment including Whitman, whose large claims for poetry Frost validates, minus the fanfare. Not everyone thinks this. A. Alvarez saw only "country poetry, simple language and simple wisdom." New Critics like Blackmur, brought up on T. S. Eliot, a recondite poet, didn't get him at all. I don't mean to disparage Eliot: recondite isn't bad nor is Frost superficial. But his poems are like ice that rides on its own melting. You must read them word by word, though.

His best poetry invades us viscerally, a hymn in the throat or tune caught in the ear. Ideas, the kind that flicker visibly like swamp fire, are absent. In a letter to Louis Untermeyer, he said "a poem positively must not begin thought first." A subject had to be an object, and he sought to hold the object "clear outside of me with struts." He was explaining himself to an academic colleague, who, like the most of them, preferred his thinking neat. Frost's is fortified with images, his nearest way to truth.

He lacked social conscience, and Malcolm Cowley indicts him for this, a fault more civic than artistic, still and all a fault. In curious contrast is his itch for pronouncing. A preacher went with the sensuous man and was always piping up to his cost. Nixing "thought first" in the letter to Untermeyer, he submitted this old friend to a dose of his so-to-say thinking. He knew about the preacher, detecting in himself a race between the poet "and that in me that would be flirting with the entelechies." When he doesn't make it, he isn't parochial enough. He didn't teach school for nothing, traces of it sticking to him like plaster.

A fair bit of him is cluttered with "considerations," said his friendly critic Radcliffe Squires, remembering a phrase from "Birches." In "West-Running Brook" he divulges what Bergson's philosophy has taught him, and in "Two Tramps in Mud Time" is willing to specify life's object. Mostly, however, his provincialism saves him, and both these poems live primarily in their details. In a poem from his first book, "In Hardwood Groves," his eye is on the procession of seasons:

> Before the leaves can mount again
> To fill the trees with another shade,
> They must go down past things coming up.
> They must go down into the dark decayed.

Already that has the characteristic sound of Frost, brooking no argument. The comment he appends to his matter-of-fact strikes me as jaunty, though:

> However it is in some other world
> I know that this is the way in ours.

But much of his teaching is circumscribed, only what you said or he said. The moral of "In Hardwood Groves" is largely ex post facto, and though "Two Tramps in Mudtime" offers an account of life's mingled yarn, it remains on the level of description:

> The sun was warm but the wind was chill.
> You know how it is with an April day
> When the sun is out and the wind is still,
> You're one month on in the middle of May.
> But if you so much as dare to speak,
> A cloud comes over the sunlit arch,
> A wind comes off a frozen peak,
> And you're two months back in the middle of March.

Reading passages like this one, readers extrapolate, but that is their business, not his. The impulse to naked saying qualifies our assent in sonnets like "A

Soldier," where his "Thus-we-see" conclusion avows more than the facts will sustain. But even when catechizing, he says one thing in terms of another. Partly this redeems him, also restricting him to the matter at hand. He wanted to be Kennedy's confidant or a very superior Norman Vincent Peale, but couldn't transcend special cases. Laying down the law isn't part of his purview, maybe an apothegm, not a general law, and on the whole this is lucky.

Seeking to determine our place among the infinities, he trained a telescope on the heavens, like the man in "The Star-Splitter" who fails at hugger-mugger farming. But peering through it didn't sharpen his sense of how things stood "between the night tonight / And a man with a smoky lantern chimney." This man, like Diogenes, sees only as far as the lantern throws its light. "For Once, Then, Something," among the permanent poems, shows him looking down the well to the surface of the water. He sees his image in the water, framed by summer's furniture, "a wreath of fern and cloud puffs." Absolutes he doesn't see, and of truth at the bottom of the well there is nothing. Yvor Winters in a morose critique throws sticks and stones at Frost the relativist, uncharitable, at least. Failing God's grace, none of us can come at truth except in similitudes. Still, his characters don't change and seem unwilling or unable to learn. W. W. Robson in a first-rate essay urges this against him. But tragedy "is when something terrible happens and no one is to blame," one of his apothegms, offhanded like Shakespeare's.

Discursive in some longer poems, Frost in his short rhyming poems is a poet of surfaces, like Jonson. Performance was everything, "in verse as in trapeze," and comprehends diction, pitch, line length, and metrics. The music they sponsor is suaver than anyone else's among near contemporaries, Stevens only excepted in certain poems from *Harmonium*. Partly it depends on modulation, e.g. stepping down the line from five feet to two:

> I have been one no dwelling could contain
> When there was rain.

"Nothing Gold Can Stay" shows his likeness to Jonson, first the patient anaphora ("Her . . . Her / So . . . So"), giving the sense of time's slow-chapped power, then its abrupt culminating in a reversed foot:

> Nature's first green is gold,
> Her hardest hue to hold.
> Her early leaf's a flower;

But only so an hour.
Then leaf subsides to leaf.
So Eden sank to grief,
So dawn goes down to day.
Nothing gold can stay.

You look for weak endings when matter turns grave ("flower" . . .
"hour"), also when the poet wants to buffer you against excess emotion. In
"A Drumlin Woodchuck":

If I can with confidence say
That still for another day,
Or even another year,
I will be there for you, my dear,

It will be because, though small
As measured against the All,
I have been so instinctively thorough
About my crevice and burrow.

Technique begets and allows the stirring conclusion: the alliteration, almost
mnemonic, leading off the last stanza, the double rhymes and banal meter,
suggesting the whimsy that saves the poem from portentousness, the single
departure from the prosodic norm—one longer line in the midst of all those
trimeters—that says where the money is, "my dear."

A poet who strikes off resonant sayings in an age that doesn't like them
much—"non dulce, non et decor"—he had the trick of the free-standing line.

Men work together . . .

Whether they work together or apart.

We love the things we love for what they are.

The fact is the sweetest dream that labor knows.

His line is Latin in its simplicity, like proverbs and sayings on gravestones.
Catullus, among the poets important to him, has that kind of simplicity.
Living much longer, Frost grew sparer with years, pinching off buds and
getting rid of suckers. Epigrams were his old man's pleasure.

Though he had a patent out on the colloquial style, that didn't pre-
clude the elevated style when needed. Like a didactic nineteenth-century
poet, he called one of his poems, "Happiness Makes Up in Height for What
It Lacks in Length," proceeding to illustrate in short rhyming couplets. He

"verily" believed what they told him, risky, that kind of diction in the mid-twentieth century, but his is self-conscious and his poem carries it off:

> It may be altogether
> From one day's perfect weather,
> When starting clear at dawn
> The day swept clearly on
> To finish clear at eve.

Like Yeats, the modern poet he most admired but like very few others, he could wear his heart on his sleeve without making us regret the performance.

All the same, he is the reverse of the confessional poet. He never unpacked his heart like Hardy. Miserable and then some, Hardy suffered besides from an "unaccountable and almost invincible personal prejudice," Frost said, dictating his vendetta against the "President of the Immortals." ("Personal" means that the evidence supporting the prejudice is wanting.) Both are first-person poets, but Hardy's insistently personal "I" raises questions. "What is he whose grief bears such an emphasis?" that kind of question. Frost's "I" is dramatic, a peg to hang the poem on. Sailing for home after England joined the War, he might have died on the *Lusitania,* anyway have written about it. But you don't imagine him asking, like Hardy in his *Titanic* poem, "What does this vaingloriousness down here?"

Though his poems give no quarter, the manner is always reined in. "The Oven Bird," a great tightfisted sonnet in a scheme of his own devising, illuminates his sense of what is proper to poetry and poets. He liked tackling sonnets, unusually exigent in the burdens they impose, and coping with the form gave him very little room to turn round in. Making a virtue of necessity, he raised his tremendous question: "What to make of a diminished thing," but had the tact not to stay for an answer.

The Romantic poet you hear in him is the one who has come through. His struggle bred a taste for piquancy, and he likes his sweet mixed with bitter:

> Now no joy but lacks salt,
> That is not dashed with pain
> And weariness and fault;
> I crave the stain
>
> Of tears . . . .

("To Earthward")

In some poems he stands comparison with great Ralegh, the manliest poet
I know. Here is Ralegh on Time eating:

> But Time, which nature doth despise,
> And rudely gives her love the lie,
> Makes hope a fool, and sorrow wise,
> His hands doth neither wash nor dry;
> But being made of steel and rust,
> Turns snow and silk and milk to dust.

And here is Frost, the first stanza of "I Could Give All to Time":

> To Time it never seems that he is brave
> To set himself against the peaks of snow
> To lay them level with the running wave,
> Nor is he overjoyed when they lie low,
> But only grave, contemplative and grave.

He has in his person, more critically in his poet's scrip, all you could ask of
truth, vigor, and humanity, words Elinor Frost used of his poetry in 1923.
She went on to note "a clear beauty, and even glamour," surprising, that
last, but right for him who posed as disheveled.

His short-line poems, the great ones, are touched with God's finger.
Thrilling with emotion, terse about it, however, the four-foot line seems
close to his bone. In "The Need of Being Versed in Country Things," his
modesty in form matches his content; at the same time he casts a wide net.
Metonymies go with his short stanzas: a chimney for a house once full of
people, the arm of a pump for the water that gave them life, a fence post
with a strand of wire standing for and mocking its function. Sexual feeling
is part of the scene—a chimney like a pistil like a phallus—suggesting that
nature, deflected for a while, is "renewed." Birds nest in the ruin, and if you
didn't know better, you might imagine them weeping. "For them there was
really nothing sad," though. Much modern poetry, tough and jocular, ends
on that note. But Frost's anti-sentimental poem, turning from idle tears,
brings us close to real ones. See how many poets you can think of who do
both.

He wrote a lot, more than five hundred pages in the standard Holt edi-
tion, and his facility, like his master Herrick's, doesn't always boost his
credit. Much of him, especially later on, falls over into light verse. If he is
willing to speak truth, he undercuts it, or he backs away like Milton in the

end of "Lycidas," a poem I heard him say once. Some of this is modern-tough guy, some of it defensive. Humor, his standard crowd face, was "cowardice" (he told Untermeyer), any form of it showing fear and inferiority. "Irony is simply a kind of guardedness. So is a twinkle." He hid behind these barricades.

It seems he needed much chaff for his wheat. The longer blank verse poems could do with less circumference, more center. Some aren't more than finger music, limbering up for a triumph like "The Wood-Pile." His blank verse, broken and beaten on, comes close to prose. In "A Hundred Collars":

> "You say unless."
>   "Unless you wouldn't mind
> Sharing a room with someone else."
>   "Who is it?"
> "A man."
>   "So I should hope. What kind of man?"

Poetry like this, though fluent, is pedestrian, and his natural style is expensive.

But much of his blank verse goes in another direction, indicating an anxious poet out to bring disorder to heel. Like early models in English—Surrey's is one, Gascoigne's another—it features off-rhyme and medial rhyme. Words are repeated, the same ones or in different permutations. "The stream of everything that runs away" is the culprit or energizing cause. It had a real-life model on his farm in Derry, N.H. Flowing away from the sea, this West-Running Brook trusted itself to go by contraries, though,

> "The way I can with you—and you with me—
> Because we're—we're—I don't know what we are.
> What are we?"
>   "Young or new?"
>   "We must be something.
> We've said we two. Let's change that to we three."

Insulted from his youth by death's cataract "that spends to nothingness," he threw up obstacles against it, chiefly his preoccupation with poetry's conventional forms. "When in doubt there is always form to go on with," he told his Amherst students. The artist in him, like Job in his "Masque of Reason," cried out for design, not religious but secular. He

wanted to shape things. You held the wind in your mouth—it has in mind
to be free as the wind, a mistake—then, "by measure," you blew it forth
("The Aim Was Song"). This is a poetics and puts before us a conservative
poet—not the same as reactionary—who meant to guarantee the future, so
conserved the best of the past. "West-Running Brook" in its backward
motion against the stream acts out his opposition to the drift of his time.
The contrariness is hardly enervating, and great things happen when he pays
his respects to rhyme and meter. Always "going slightly taut," a phrase from
his superb late sonnet, "A Silken Tent," his poems acknowledge a regis-
seur's controlling presence. This is true even of the most colloquial, and
gives the impression that he is pointing a moral. Up on the platform, the
homiletic poet did that, a reason they liked him. But the figure the poem
makes isn't the same as its moral. For what we call content, form makes a
difference, and there was always that to go on with. The kinetic poet who
means to open our eyes is simultaneously a poet of gratuities, whose endings
look in different directions. "Mending Wall" hardly argues for breaking
down walls, even though, as he tells us, something doesn't love a wall.

On his official side, the poet-sage is like Wordsworth, very talky. When
most himself, though, Frost is dumb, like Wordsworth's Leech-Gatherer,
seen as a sea-beast sunning on a ledge. He doesn't expound the universe; it
wraps him round like a caul, the near-shocking way he puts it in his late
poem "Skeptic." Never an intellectualizer and keeping clear of school, he
keeps his eyes on the ground, measuring stone walls "perch on perch." He
tells about himself, an ideal portrait, in "A Star in a Stoneboat," his boat
being the sled-like wagon upland farmers use to clear their stony fields. This
wagon does better for him than Pegasus, the flying horse of the Muses: it
moves slowly.

   You have to if you mean to look with eyes of devotion, and that kind
of seeing, more than precise, even amorous, denotes him. Blueberries,
"ready to drum in the cavernous pail," look amazing in the rain! their "fruit
mixed with water in layers of leaves." But this poet's eye is most piercing
when it lights on beauty that doesn't stay, spring pools, for instance, soon
gone like the flowers beside them. Self-conscious animizing is the rule: an
ax like a man, "steel-blue chin drawn down / And in," or like a snake or a
penis. "See how she's cock her head!" A grindstone thinks and tastes, has
feet and legs it boasts of; a white birch wears a headdress with an ornament
against the neck. There is the famous simile in "Birches," trees that trail
their leaves on the ground

Like girls on hands and knees that throw their hair
Before them over their heads to dry in the sun.

Some invoke the pathetic fallacy against him. But the inclination to commit it, says Robert Langbaum finely, signals that the object is loved.

Frost said all his poems were love poems, but he knows how life plays out, and they are only the least bit hopeful. Others look on the bright side; he takes sides with life. Poets don't invariably. Marlowe doesn't, or Donne, Pope either. Not less cold eyed than any of them, Frost seems temperamentally bound to affirm, like Shakespeare when he says: "World, world, o world! / But that thy strange mutations make us hate thee, / Life would not yield to age." In "The Census-Taker," set in an abandoned house in a waste land, no people dwell thereabouts, or "none not in hiding" or "that dare show themselves." The poem tells of emptiness, and as it ends the census taker has nothing to do "Unless to find that there was no one there," and "declare" this to the cliffs too far away for echo. Managed by repetitions and interior rhymes: *there . . . there . . . declare,* echo is what we get, though, challenging the poem as paraphrase. It must be, not least in this godforsaken place, that I the poet or his surrogate "want life to go on living."

Some such desire enlivens the poetry, as when it seems to say that the world has intention. Leaves, personified, warm the earth like a glove, then, like proletarians according to Marx, are trod beneath the heel of flowers ("In Hardwood Groves"). This assures their coming out again. Life chases death in the image of the Wood-Pile. Evidently purposeful, it warms the swamp as best it can with the smokeless burning of decay.

But Frost isn't Browning, the same, said Hopkins, who jumped up from the table with his mouth full of food to tell us all's right with the world. Evil advanced its power over the world he lived in, was even intrinsic to it, like the wick or snuff in *Hamlet* that lives within the flame of love. His awareness, mounting to revulsion, shows in poems like "Range-Finding," "Design," "Acquainted with the Night." The first two are Italian sonnets, their form, steeped in Petrarch's sweetness, implacably opposed to their content. So we have an oxymoron, and these appalling poems live on its interest. Darkness colors the last, a sonnet in terza rima. This form also carries literary baggage, harking back in the first place to Dante. His *Commedia,* at least comprehensive, begins in Hell but moves on.

The poem moves on for Frost, or it becomes a harmony, as he confronts his "desert places" in meter and rhyme. Scary in content but highly composed, "The Most of It" asks if we keep the universe alone. A friend of the poet, wanting things otherwise, raises this question, and Thompson's biography tells all about him. "He thought he kept the universe alone" and didn't like it. Maybe a great buck, breaking in on his solitude, means to increase the population by one, like Friday breaking in on Robinson Crusoe. Barging in by one door, this rough beast, full of menace, leaves by another, though. Maybe it was born in the mind of its perceiver.

In a last public appearance two months before he died, Frost glanced ironically at the hero of the poem who wanted "someone else additional to him." But unsatisfied desire was "all he got out of his longing, you see." A dour reading, for sure, and other poems appear to support it. Perhaps "All revelation has been ours," not from Heaven but spun of ourselves. Perhaps we create what we desire, including what we call revealed truth.

> Eyes seeking the response of eyes
> Bring out the stars, bring out the flowers.
>
> ("All Revelation")

Elsewhere, however, nature, when we cry out to her, seems to answer back. The "impervious geode," like the universe—or the vulva—isn't impervious but really gets "entered," and the "thrust" of the mind sets its inner crust aglow. A great wave of emotion, this glowing warms us again in "Two Look at Two," when a man and woman come face to face with a doe and antlered buck, and the earth returns their love "in one unlooked-for favor." That doesn't happen in "The Most of It."

Lionel Trilling, honoring Frost on his eighty-fifth birthday, saw "a terrifying poet." This improves on the Grandma Moses poet but fails to say how, in Frost, dawn, "shooting far into the bosom of dim night," holds up its quarrel with darkness. The poet and his critic make a bad fit. Coming to terms tardily with a great American provincial, Trilling brought along his New York City prepossessions. What should he do but assimilate Frost to early T. S. Eliot?

Strange bedfellows! All his life in poetry, Frost hated Eliot, darling of the intellectuals. More than once, forgetting his dignity, he let the hostility show. "In forty languages," Eliot strove for distinction by parading his learning. Worse was his stagey pessimism, "forswearing a world gone bad with war." It sounded deep. "But I don't know," Frost wrote to his daughter Lesley. "Waste Lands . . . !" Great grandmother knew about them, and he doubted if war had laid waste to anything that peace hadn't wasted before.

Over the years they circled warily. Keeping a lunch date with Eliot in Boston, Frost said he had a rendezvous with death. Early in the Thirties, Eliot came over to teach at Harvard, a class of disciples he limited to twelve. Frost attended the welcoming dinner, in company with acolytes galore. Incredulous, he heard the English accent, the pontificating, saw the admirers' fawning. In Eliot's opinion, offered that night, no good poetry had ever been written in Scotland. Well, perhaps there was the one poem by Dunbar. Frost, Scots on his mother's side, came near getting up from his chair. In 1936, when he followed Eliot as Norton lecturer at Harvard, the "Pound-Eliot-Richards" gang, one of his coinages, something like an expletive, landed on him with both feet. They called *A Further Range,* published that year, "A Further Shrinking."

But these mighty opposites made it up before the end. In the 1940s, Eliot without warning called on Frost in Cambridge. "To pay my respects," he said. A decade later, at a London banquet, he raised his glass to "*the* most eminent—the most *distinguished . . .* Anglo-American poet now living." Moved almost to tears, Frost responded: "There's nobody living in either country that I'd rather hear that from." This mustn't obscure the difference between them. In Eliot's world, livid with Baudelairean disgust, weeping multitudes droop in a hundred A.B.C.'s. An old man in a decayed house waits for rain, rats scamper over broken glass in the cellar. Psychology and all-round feel are different in Frost, anthropomorphic, even teleological, big words for him, and putting man at the center. Terrible things crowd in on him, though. He gives them the room they need, but not from proclivity. If you loved the world, you had to summon it all:

> It were unworthy of the tongue
> To let the half of life alone
> And play the good without the ill.
>
>   ("The Wind and the Rain")

Like Eliot the death dealer, he had a foot in the Waste Land. But his wasn't strewn with "Rocks, moss, stonecrop, iron, merds," and he didn't fish the dull canal behind the gashouse. An early poem reports a Ghost House, however, no trace of it remaining except the cellar walls. In his second volume, only "an old cellar hole in a byroad" remembers the generations who lived there. Sprout-lands flourish where the ax once kept them in order. An abandoned dwelling, Black Cottage or Old Barn at the Bottom of the Fogs, is almost his signature image. Auden, going through his poems, tots up the number, a large one, set at night or in winter and storm. The landscape isn't by Currier and Ives. A demon lives in his woods, "all in lines . . . Too much alike to mark or name a place by," and this spooky presence laughs at their sameness. Frost said the laughter stayed with him.

New to the cognoscenti, *The Waste Land* was old to him, and the stir that met its publication in 1922 got his bile flowing. If they wanted a Waste Land, he could oblige. His version is "Directive," the great poem of his age. Like its ironic title, it doesn't concede much to others. "Directive": a terse communiqué, Frost coming down from Mt. Sinai. His Tables of the Law aren't easy to decipher, but some critic-poets, Robert Pack and Randall Jarrell, furnish hints.

The great minatory opening, "Back . . . Back," like a summons by old Haydn in on the Creation, is adverbial, admonishing too. We go back via a "disused and forgotten road," recalling the one the Ghost House sat on. This place the poet directs us to was there before the present, rumorous with discord like Eliot's "Falling towers." The road to the house, scored by lines that look manmade but fool us, remembers the Ice Age. Coming up that chilly road on our quest, we have to feel diminished. Eyes peer from Frost's favorite venue, the empty cellar hole, this "serial ordeal" making one critic think of the trial of an Arthurian knight. But first of all the poet means us to think of Ali Baba and the forty thieves. Though his "adventure" pleases, it doesn't pretend to be more than itself, and we aren't asked to nod gravely, as when reading Jessie Weston or Frazer.

Part of the gauntlet we run, the upstart trees rustle noisily, alarmed like the bird in "The Wood-Pile," or self-important like us as we take ourselves to heart. Getting at us, our poet-guide wills us to create a comforting fable about his homegrown Waste Land, home to someone else once, prospectively ours. Lost we are, as he means us to be, but maybe we lose ourselves to find ourselves, the way a man saves his soul. The journey upwards to "the height / Of country" takes in a children's playhouse, like the Chapel Perilous Eliot's pilgrim is bound for. Once a hiding place for treasure, it held a broken drinking cup, likened to the Holy Grail. We find this symbol of our lost faith in the ruins where old cultures have faded. But Frost's poet has pilfered it, a childish thing to do. He hides the cup beneath a tree root, seen as an instep arch. Incongruously humanized, his figure of speech is sinister, in the same company as the abandoned cellar hole, closing "like a dent in dough."

The cup won't be stolen twice: hocus-pocus, laid on by the poet, assures this. More childishness, the muttering of spells is reinforced by St.

Mark's Gospel (4:11–12), a weird and whimsical passage identified by a helpful scholar, Margaret Blum: "Unto you it is given to know the mystery of the kingdom of God" but not "unto them that are without . . . lest at any time they should be converted and their sins should be forgiven them." So we arrive at our goal, just us, privileged or "saved" ones. The goal isn't of our choosing, however, but chosen for us, a brook near its source that supplied the house with water. In this place of dry bones, no commodity is more valued, as Eliot could tell us and does. Possibly restorative and cold in more ways than one, it is like the spring that feeds it but unlike those ardent streams down below in the valley, endlessly willing to hurl themselves against the shore. "Too lofty and original to rage," Frost's brook has nothing in common with rebellious people who kick against the pricks. The poise that eludes them is hopefully ours, and the poem, ending with a summons the way it began, bids us drink. Turning a skeptical eye on Eliot's "formal ending to an Upanishad," Frost might say it does this in plain English, but that is deceptive.

A mysterious poem, "Directive" looks forward to "The Draft Horse," astonishingly, work of Frost's eighties. In this dark parable of the Fall, his Adam and Eve don't reason why but obey. The poem doesn't justify obedience, however, nor do the man and woman dispute it. They make

> The most unquestioning pair
> That ever accepted fate
> And the least disposed to ascribe
> Any more than we had to to hate.

Purpose, if not malign, then inscrutable, drives the scheme of things, and having no recourse, we take its pressure.

Twenty years or so earlier, Frost (in "The Times Table") opened on "a spring with a broken drinking glass," halfway up the mountain. Subsequently, he said how it got there:

> Here further up the mountain slope
> Than there was ever any hope,
> My father built, enclosed a spring.
>
> ("The Birthplace")

Much good it did them, father and son, and the mountain that "made of us a little while" has long since shrugged off the house they were born in. Another thread in the carpet is Wordsworth, not the nature poet, the chronicler of loss. Picking through the ruins, in this case a Ruined Cottage, his traveler stops to drink at water's edge. On the slimy footstone he finds "The useless fragment of a wooden bowl," like the little things in the play-house that could make the children glad. "It moved my very heart," Wordsworth says, and Frost's poem makes room for this too. Like all con-siderable poetry, it covers much of the tonal scale, hopeful, poignant, amus-ing, even bitter. It has a message but the message equals the poem. Not the man they took him for, Frost makes it hard on the old ladies, including men, who sew samplers. "This above all, to thine own self be true." "Put money in thy purse."

Despite the ambiguity, we apply him, and that isn't improper. Squires says he is fruitful of symbolic extensions, or "halos." But he comes closest to truth, that much refracted thing, when the symbol and what it symbolizes don't make a perfect join. What they make is an enlargement, not an infinite enlargement, only a bigger reticule or bigger window on the world. Keats writes from this perspective in the "Grecian Urn," affirming and denying the primacy of art, Shakespeare in his sonnet XVIII, "Shall I Com-pare Thee to a Summer's Day," and Marvell in the "Coy Mistress." Time's progress haunts his poem, but whether he welcomes or fears it or in what proportions is moot.

In poems like "The Ax-Helve," "Unharvested," a sonnet in tetrame-ters, "I Could Give All to Time," Frost keeps up an enigmatical posture. Like Michelangelo's figures struggling to emerge from stone, his truth is only partially realized. "After Apple-Picking," his first great poem, tells of a literal harvest. There is more to say than this, and close readers will point to the ladder sticking through the tree, saying how it points "toward heaven," etc. But if the poem communicates ulterior truth, we see it through a glass darkly. The poet all but says this. Recalling Corinthians (1, 13:12), he skims "a pane of glass," not ice, from the drinking trough. What it shows him isn't plenary nor lasting, however. As he holds it against the world, it melts, and he lets it fall and break.

Speaking of poetry, he put the ear first and thought the sound of a sen-tence often said more than the words. In some poems his sound, more com-prehensively, his affect, picks a quarrel with the grammatical sense. Listen, and you hear beneath the turbid ebb and flow a sensuous strain appealing against it—

> He says the early petal fall is past,
> When pear and cherry bloom went down in showers.

Still there when the poem is finished, an after-vibration qualifies its ostensible meaning. This overplus is the very thing poetry consists of.

In our century, when most credentialed poets speak by indirections and the characteristic voice is muted, his voice often rises to vatic.

> Here are your waters and your watering place.
> Drink and be whole again beyond confusion.

But his affiliation is primarily to the world of sense. "Lord, I have loved your sky," he wrote in his seventies, and the poetry authorizes the passion. From his fifty years' labor, posterity will choose at least forty to fifty poems for safekeeping. Readers with a Mount Rushmore view of poetry may think this number very finite but among makers and shakers in his time, Henry Ford wrote no poems and Mao Tse-tung none worth retrieving. More productive than either, usefully too, Frost will still engage us when all the cars have clapped out and the revolutions run into the sand.

Part II

The Poetry of Inflections

Chapter 6

Jonson's Small Latin and Less Greek

He was Benjamin Johnson, citizen and bricklayer of London, but getting up on "the Poet's horse" changed his Smith/Robinson surname to Jonson. Then, looking at himself, cold, fat, and old, he added an increment: "as *Virgil* cold, / As *Horace* fat, or as *Anacreon* old." Located on his own word in the best company, he presumed beyond presumption but carried it off. "Let me be what I am," he said, and we do this. Belittlers object that the songs we all recognize, like "Drink to me only with thine eyes," while technically perfect, lack passion. Yet passion is his forte and he knew how to electrify readers. Love and Death were on a par, he thought, both potent in killing, but Love's fires could "fright the frost out of the grave."

Like Yeats, who made Ireland and its story everybody's possession, he had the power to breathe life into clay. Inventing a cosmos, he peopled it with "sons" of his, patrons he condescended to, rivals he detested, a few who deserved to be friends. Most of their names wouldn't reverberate except that he touched them with glory. He didn't say his glory was to have such friends, on the contrary. Sometimes, he told the scholar John Selden, he had "praised some names too much, / But 'twas with purpose to have made them such"—i.e. worthy of this consecrating poet.

The best way to take his measure is to read him aloud. Some poems worth saying over include the "Hymn to Diana," ice (like chastity) but just touched with life; the first and fourth of the lyric pieces celebrating Charis; "The Hour Glass"; "My Picture Left in Scotland"; the Pindaric Ode for his young friends Cary and Morison,

> Who, ere the first down bloomèd on the chin,
> Had sowed those fruits and got the harvest in.

Death engaged him again in the epigrams "On My First Son" and "First Daughter" and the boy actor Solomon Pavy. This last poem mingles rue and whimsy—hard to run them together if you mean to be sincere—and among later poets only Ransom in "Bells for John Whiteside's Daughter" has Jonson's absolute tact. Readers who aren't aware that grief needs its proper emphasis will call his poem frigid.

Occasional poetry took a lot of his time but exceeds its occasion, and milking his formal "topos" he handed down the Decalogue, grumbled, sang, edged close to rodomontade.

> Well, with mine own frail pitcher, what to do
> I have decreed; keep it from waves and press,
> Lest it be justled, cracked, made naught, or less;
> Live to that point I will, for which I am man,
> And dwell as in my center, as I can.

If the "furor poeticus" is what you are looking for, there it is in the last two lines.

"Inviting a Friend to Supper," a great occasional poem, fills out the picture of the affable man who won his affability. Summoning a dinner guest to "my poor house," Jonson promises much pleasure, gustatory and bookish. The pleasure isn't unalloyed, though. "Two damned villains" sought to trap this wary poet when the government locked him up in Marshalsea prison, and his topical poem recalls them. These two mean mischief, always biding its time. "Tonight" is Jonson's word, his alpha and omega, in between a time for "liberty," provisional, however, and abridged.

More than once a religious poet but obsessed with dread, he drew his ambiguous portrait in an appeal "To Heaven," showing Augustans what the couplet, heroic and broken, could do:

> I know my state, both full of shame and scorn,
>   Conceived in sin, and unto labor born,
> Standing with fear, and must with horror fall,
>   And destined unto judgment after all.

This is the coercive or declarative mode, one of the great ways English poetry takes, and though it doesn't begin with Jonson—Greville and Ralegh are powerful forebears—he put his imprimatur on it.

The "carpe diem" theme in English is part of his repertory, first heard from in two poems of his after Catullus ("Vivamus, mea Lesbia"). Herrick and Marvell are among his inheritors in this rumination on Time:

> Spend not then thy gifts in vain.
> Suns that set may rise again:
> But if once we lose this light,
> 'Tis with us perpetual night.

You could call this facile and he strove for facility, "ars celare artem," art hiding art. When he meant to be truthful, his art was clamant, though, a paradox and I hope to sustain it.

The common style of the seventeenth century, probably the most successful style in the history of English verse, employs the abbreviated line of his Song to Celia. Jonson, suppler than his predecessors, made it do different things:

> Underneath this stone doth lie
> As much beauty as could die—

also this:

> Still to be neat, still to be drest,
> As you were going to a feast;
> Still to be powdered, still perfumed:
> Lady, it is to be presumed,
> Though art's hid causes are not found,
> All is not sweet, all is not sound.

Shakespeare isn't helpful to lesser lights who follow him, Milton much less, and the Romantic style, needing the divine afflatus, dwindles to bathos without it. Great luck for minor poets when they have a style at hand they can come up to. Jonson begot this style, and the tried-and-true anthology pieces of the seventeenth century say what he gave his Sons.

I wish I could quote at large but essays are tyrannous, so let me name a few of the names: Lovelace, Shirley, Henry King, Browne of Tavistock, Thomas Carew. Like Jonson, they have the plangent tone:

> The glories of our blood and state
> Are shadows, not substantial things—

but can change key when they want to. Waller wants to, in his verses on a girdle. "Narrow compass," he calls it,

            and yet there
Dwelt all that's good and all that's fair;
Give me but what this ribbon bound,
Take all the rest the sun goes round!

The narrow compass is Jonson's preserve, and exploiting it his special achievement.

His own best subject, he comes before us in a self-deprecating epistle "To One That Asked to Be Sealed of the Tribe of Ben." Men like him meet the test of fire, and he "could say more of such, but that I fly / To speak myself out too ambitiously." He was having his little joke, not for the first time at his own expense, and the pretended deprecating disappears in a pair of odes to himself. The first, a transcendent poem, gives his essence:

    But sing high and aloof,
Safe from the wolves' black jaw and the dull asses' hoof.

So it was Jonson against the rest of the world, a familiar role for poets in a drossy age. Aggrandizing this role, however, he shouldered his way into Parnassus, becoming the god of poetry, wisdom too.

Partly the becoming turns on syntax, deliberately ambiguous:

Then take in hand thy lyre,
    Strike in thy proper strain,
With Japhet's line aspire
Sol's chariot for new fire
    To give the world again;
Who aided him will thee, the issue of Jove's brain.

Everybody knew it was the goddess of wisdom, Minerva, sprung from the head of Jove, who helped Japhet's son Prometheus steal fire from Heaven. But the last phrase describes Jonson, "thee, the issue of Jove's brain."

Three collections make up the bulk of his verse, the *Epigrams* and *The Forest*, both published by a self-conscious poet in his lifetime, and *The Underwood,* uncollected poems recovered after his death. In the standard edition (Herford & Simpson, 1947), the poems run to well over 400 pages, some of them pedestrian—poetry was bread-and-butter work—but almost all spontaneous seeming. Jonson has his own inflection, meaning that he knew how to keep the caesura, or voice pause, on the move. His *Epigrams* aren't always "epigrammatic," like Landor's or J. V. Cunningham's, and make room for longish poems. But the tether is short (not much development), the manner not discursive but enunciatory, and the basic unit the distich, two lines. He aimed at providing an English equivalent of Horace's *sermones,* conversation pieces or "talks." (Whatever you do, don't call them "sermons.") The talk is pointed, however, insistently to the center. Most of his work bears out this description.

The age he lived in had a split personality, delighting in "copia," or amplification, but reserving this for virtuoso performance. (Here is where the Spenserians come in.) When truth was in the cards, it ordered up a different style, not simpler, only tightfisted. Byrd in music shows the split, on his serious side the liturgical composer, on his "Italian" the mere technician. (The dichotomy hardly does him justice, of course.) Truth-tellers in poetry cultivated the epigram. Flaunting its art but seldom digressing, it went to the heart of the matter. In Jonson's heyday fifty different collections saw print.

True as the needle to the pole of the time, he called his epigrams "the ripest of my studies." I think he liked them best because they let him digest things, not indigenous things but categories and classes, a Learned Critic or Reformed Gamester, Death or Peace. Many of the epigrams are called for people he knew, like his enemy and coworker Inigo Jones, a poet (Donne in two epigrams), a Court musician, even his own kin. He keeps his distance from all, though, and not describing, signalizes. According to him, the lowercase mode, delimited by particulars, catches only a piece of the truth. He wants it all.

He thinks he can get it too, truth being "plain and open," also "best when naked." The trial of itself, it needs no other "touch" or touchstone. Out of this conviction comes the famous plain style. "No beauty to be had but in wresting and writhing our own tongue?" Jonson, asking the question, sounds like George Herbert. Not just incidentally, neither poet is good at answers.

Freed from the need to sift particular cases, Jonson doesn't amplify but pares down ("all the false values gone"). The motive behind his style, whether cultivated in his time or ours, is that implied by Thoreau in *Walden* when he tells of slaughtering a woodchuck and devouring him whole, beast, hair, and hooves. This effects his absolute transmigration. In the hands of a master, the plain style is enormously persuasive, as if God were creating the world. Hemingway's best prose, imperial like Jonson's poetry, offers a modern version of this style, e.g. in *The Sun Also Rises:*

> It was a beech wood and the trees were very old. Their roots bulked above the ground and the branches were twisted. We walked on the road between the thick trunks of the old beeches and the sunlight came through the leaves in light patches on the grass. The trees were big, and the foliage was thick but it was not gloomy. There was no undergrowth, only the smooth grass, very green and fresh, and the big gray trees well spaced as though it were a park. . . .

Both these writers impute great dignity to the banal fact. Neither ranges widely, though, nor conveys the maximum of information and suggestion. Devoted to the prosaic truth, they go light on its properties. Criticism pigeonholes both as "realistic," a misnomer, and their successes lie elsewhere.

Jonson's career, though it makes good copy, has hurt him, largely crowding out the work. Prudent Shakespeare, who "wouldn't be debauched," was luckier. Toper, faithless husband ("given to venery," his own complacent judgment), dictator in letters and a bully in person, he was "the best of poets but the worst of men," said Jones, who put up with him for years. He killed his man in single combat between the armies, turning this to poetry in a tribute "To True Soldiers":

> I swear by your true friend, my Muse, I love
> Your great profession, which I once did prove;
> And did not shame it.

Essential Jonson speaks in the short line, the more "superb" (in our sense and the old Latin sense) because understated.

Later he killed a fellow actor in a duel, beat a rival playwright and took his pistol from him. Though the age disvalued plays—only entertainment, snobbish writers said—he dared put his plays on a par with poetry and ventured to publish them, inviting the world's ridicule and posterity's thanks. In *Catiline* he wrote himself into the play, appearing as his hero Cicero, "a mere upstart that has no pedigree." But the "talker" or "tongue man," self-ennobled, gets the best of them all. Worse, he had the gall to fault Shakespeare. He said he loved Shakespeare but "this side idolatry," and Bardolaters haven't forgiven the reservation. Around his ponderous vessel, stately but slow, they imagine nimble Shakespeare sailing rings.

Modern critics, the ones who like him, present a "tangible" poet, "primarily pictorial." Or they commend learned Ben, known for pia mater, whose "immediate appeal is to the mind." The other side of this is the "bookworm, a candle waster," who wrote a neat scribe's hand, and meditating poetry wrote it out first in prose. "Solid, sober, humanistic," dread words all, a recent biographer calls him. Swinburne, tempering praise with blame, said his "flowers," though colorful, lacked fragrance. His Ben was "one of the singers who could not sing." A contemporary editor says, however, that "many of the brief epigrams which seem flat to tastes whetted by the Romantics show sound thought and skillful expression." With friends like this, no poet needs enemies.

Most of the friends stress his moralizing side, not meaning to damn with faint praise. Quintilian, a didactic teacher of Romans in the Silver Age, gave him his critical precepts, and for a poet these auspices don't look good. The famous rhetorician wanted to fashion orators, not poets, and to poetry's old function, teaching and delighting, added a third requirement, getting things done. But poetry gets nothing done, its fruit being *gnosis* or knowledge, not *praxis,* and some think Jonson's mistook its proper business. Their satirist, zeroing in on the time's foibles, brought along an agenda, too bad.

But the critics, both defenders and detractors, have sponsored a fictitious Jonson. His great opposite Shakespeare is the intellectual poet, eyes close to the page, Jonson the Romantic who speaks from the heart, and whatever he got from his master Camden he had in his psyche small Latin and less Greek. Often classical in form, rarely this in spirit, he appeals primarily to the viscera. But dreaming of a golden world, he isn't romantic in our pejorative sense (rose-colored glasses), and a masque he wrote for Christmas gives the content of his many-colored vision:

> dreams that have wings,
> And dreams that have honey, and dreams that have stings.

In a mocking self-portrait, he put himself down as "a mere empiric, one that gets what he hath by observation." But his best pictures owe little to nature. "He hath consumed a whole night," said the poet Drummond, "in lying looking to his great toe." About it, "Tartars and Turks, Romans and Carthaginians, fight in his imagination." A useful setoff to the popular image of a very superior journalist in poetry, this reminiscence opens a window on Jonson the fantasist, repopulating our brazen world with forms "more real than living man." The love poems and the social and political poetry support this quotation, unexpectedly Shelley's.

His art, unlike Quintilian's, is short on intention, and means less to correct than clarify, making a luminous whole. (This *claritas* needn't be pretty.) Faithful to his motto, *Tanquam explorator,* he seems to me an ironist, different from a satirist. When lukewarm, the irony is only pettish, and the first-person pronoun summons real-life Jonson, necessarily a disappointment. Turning hot, however, as in the scandalous portraits of Volpone and Sir Epicure Mammon, it mounts to approbation. A great hater, he lashed vice but his scorn was catholic and what he hated most was dullness. This blurs the line between vice and virtue, perhaps redefining them. A winning phrase of his reprehends that "asinine virtue, patience." Energy, neither moral nor immoral, gets first place in the plays, in the poetry too. Jonson, stirring up the world, made it much livelier. His enterprise is therapeutic but not as moralists understand this.

He had genius but lacked conspicuous intelligence. In *Timber, or Discoveries,* random observations left behind in his desk, he is apt to tell us that silence is golden, style shows the man, and beauty is only skin-deep. Sometimes, deeply felt emotion, not the same as intellecting, transmutes his commonplaces. Embellishing a Latin tag, *iactura vitae* (throwing away of life), he converts sententious matter to gold. "What a deal of cold business doth a man misspend the better part of life in! in scattering compliments, tendering visits, gathering or venting news, following feasts and plays, making a little winter love in a dark corner." With this last phrase we come close to "rare Ben."

His much trumpeted learning, though real, is an autodidact's, missing in the assurance of a genuine scholar like Camden, his teacher at Westminster School. Writing a marriage masque ("grounded upon antiquity and solid learnings"), he begins with a canvass of Roman marriage customs. They weren't on the point but he had to establish credentials. His *Forest* was also *Silva,* so-called because "the ancients called that kind of body *Silva*." *Sejanus,* his failed tragedy, comes complete with more than three hundred marginal notes, "all in the learned tongues, save one." The bricklayer's stepson who paid his respects to Oxbridge and the learned gentlemen of the London law schools reminds you of T. S. Eliot, a provincial from St. Louis, but *The Waste Land* denies where he came from.

Jonson differs in kind from academic professionals—though, dismaying us, he craved their approval—also from Metaphysical poets. "These fencers in religion I like not," he said. Dialectics was never for him. He wrote an English grammar but came down hard on "those extreme anxieties and foolish cavils of grammarians." Caviling is the sinews of one kind of poetry—much of Donne's, Shakespeare's too—but he didn't know this. At his highest pitch he is a singer, among our greatest. He doesn't always sing of love and often his subjects are public. But whatever the subject, reason gets the back of his hand. This poet is opinionated, touchingly, sometimes absurdly himself, and after four hundred years his poetry is still quick with emotion.

In tune with the age on its intellectualizing side, he legislated for poetry, and his critical "theory" leaves telltales. He drew an equation between "art" and "dressing," risky for poets. He isn't finicking but downright, not wanting to bedizen truth, and gains us by imposing on us. (When charm fails, brow-beating takes over.) He won't let his Muse be brought up "by commission," so keeps his distance from the ancients, "guides, not commanders." He steers clear of allusions to myth, divinity, and science. "Old mythologies," when noticed, are generally spoofed. "All this while" he has forgot "some god / Or goddess to invoke, to stuff my verse." Yeats, Jonson's scholar about 1912, picks up on this derisory habit: something ails his "colt," never Pegasus.

In the critical prose, Jonson opens a gulf between poetry's surface, titi-vated with "colors," and its "matter and foundation." One was good because "hid" but the other, being "seen," raised his hackles. "Stand for truth," he told himself, "and 'tis enough." Artistry comes to the front in his epigrams, though, and his well-known lines for Shakespeare praise the man who knew how to sweat and "strike the second heat / Upon the Muse's anvil." The prose tugging one way, the poetry another, perhaps we should trust the tale, not the obiter dicta. But this poet and his poems aren't so eas-ily parted as that.

Realists in poetry—the time called them "empirics"—preferred little truths to big ones. (Jonson's phrase, "a mere empiric," says what he thought of their poking and prying.) He gets up into the watchtower where the light is unrefracted. But as he sails by thorny integers and recondite things, he runs on stereotypes. They don't supply much food for thought and he doesn't excel as a writer of discursive poetry. His métier is the poetry of celebration, faith, or invective. Being heartfelt, it sticks to the surface.

The question-posing style organizes many poems in his time, and many of his accommodate this tradition. He wants to know "what kind of crea-ture I could most desire," or he worries that old topic, Woman's Incon-stancy: "Was it my fate to prove it full in you?" Different from Donne, however, Jonson raises questions to beg them. Usually rhetorical—for instance, in "An Epistle to a Friend to Persuade Him to the Wars"—his can be answered with a yea or nay. He "meant to feign and wished to see" but answers come by fiat. Intellectual pressure doesn't govern, so the poems don't resolve a question posed. His dialogues are monophonic and that is how he wants it, poetry irradiated by what he called his own true fire. Sometimes the fire scorches, but not feeding on particulars, throws only a modest light.

Skimping on analysis, Jonson enjoins or intuits, like his heroine in the long poem, "Eupheme": "All this by faith she saw, and framed a plea, / In manner of a daily apostrophe." God, equipped with X-ray vision, "can dissect / The smallest fiber of our flesh; He can / Find all our atoms from a point to a span!" and so on. Some poets hope to copy Him—in the analytic kind, chiefly Donne—but Jonson lays imperatives on us. "Do this," says his lady to one of her people,

> he did it; So,
> To another; Move; he went; To a third, Go,
> He run; and all did strive with diligence
> To obey and serve her sweet commandments.

The kind of obedience this lady commits us to needs uncommon powers of persuasion.

Jonson looks jealously on poetry's formal requirements, mindful of old Procrustes, a type of the arbitrary poet who lops or stretches his victims to make them fit his tyrant's bed. "Exigent" constructions where recurrence dictates design aren't for him. In his notorious mock-epic, "On the Famous Voyage," progress is like a royal progress from one place to another. Continuity is spatial or chronological, tomorrow following today, not that "propter hoc" kind where things happen "on account of" things. Sonnets obligate the poet to a preordained pattern, and three epigrams in his first book (nos. CXXVIII, CXXXI, CXXXII) show him addressing the form. He wanted to see what he could do with it. But each poem makes seven couplets and might make more or less. If you are looking for progression or development, you don't find it. Where the Shakespeare kind of sonnet asserts sequence, Jonson wonders if its structure isn't merely asserted. Three quatrains plus a couplet frustrate his search for truth, a casualty of lopping and chopping.

This criticism is cogent. Shakespeare evades it because his truth, unlike Jonson's, emerges from the poem and is limited by it, a product of his opportunistic deploying of words and forms. Shakespeare's ad hoc truth is the only one he knows. Jonson is more ambitious, not necessarily more hopeful, however, and who can say if he believed in his truth at the bottom of the well. Sometimes his assurance seems hectic.

He said he didn't dare discriminate our virtues (and we can add vices), "mysteries" that fame's fingers were too foul to touch. If he won't, who will? Abiding the question, he works out a so-to-say answer. Though a friend lacks the pedigree of "our great ones," his "fact" makes up for this. Other friends die young, not much in the way of annals giving their likeness. But what is a man "if valued by his face, / Above his fact?" Surprisingly, this fact "needs naught to clothe it but the air." So let us accept the fact without the witnessing that is "works." Jonson is the Protestant poet.

"I do but name thee," he told a patron, who might have felt short-changed. But "being named, how little doth that name / Need any Muse's praise to give it fame?" Sufficient to "say you are / A Sidney," etc. This is pretty barefaced. "Nothing can illustrate" his wedded couple in a marriage hymn, only the pair themselves. Directing attention to them, he lets it go at that. Meanwhile, spendthrift poets, "loudest praisers," assign a "character" for every part. Jonson means they go in for circumstantial description. He claims he doesn't have to.

In a panegyric to Horace Vere—his "Roman" name punning on virtue or truth—Jonson says easily: "I leave thy acts." To "prosecute" or follow them up "might flattery seem," and he strokes or flatters no man. But more than pride approves his conduct of poems. Like a new cabalist or old Gnostic, he isn't put to corroborating, the name doing the job for him. Evidently a talisman, not an arbitrary symbol, it possesses some charismatic power. This poet has his kinship to Adam in the Garden, naming each creature for its essence. "I named them as they passed" (Milton makes him say), "and understood their nature." All right for Adam, this is hard for others. "I cannot tell who loves the skeleton / Of a poor marmoset"—monkey or courtesan—says Jonson's disciple Lovelace, "naught but bone, bone."

Jonson hopes to lay bare the skeleton or ghostly paradigm. Concrete he isn't, and seems indifferent to Nature in its various guises. Like Bacon, he doesn't want "pictures" to detain him, only "carcasses," he calls them, "tailor's blocks" or dummies, "empty molds." Shakespeare's eye is to the matter; Jonson's looks through it, looking for the quiddity, not the trees but the forest. If you describe a woman's body, you will want to keep "at such distance, as the eye / May rather yet adore, than spy." But the long view, though courteous, is synoptic.

Willing to judge (but like draconian Draco), Jonson isn't nice or precise. In his language, mostly spare and often metonymic, a conventionalized part does duty for the whole. An acquaintance who honors reason (our affections' "king") reduces to abstract value words, "the grave, the wise, the great, the good." Escaping from "proud porches" and their "gilded roofs," another gentleman he knows lives among "lowing herds" in "curlèd woods and painted meads." (Tufthunters, on the other hand, "ride in purple, eat in plate.") Through this generalized landscape, a "serpent river" brings him to "some cool courteous shade." These descriptions that don't dilate much seem decorous to Jonson. Strumpets wear good clothes, he says in his *Discoveries,* but virtuous women don't need them. Though anciently, Truth goes naked (*nuda veritas*), this whimsical idea must raise eyebrows.

Comparisons are odious, but not demeaning: gratuitous. When travelers, drawn by a footpath or the freshness of the fields, "turn out of the highway," they give the likeness of "figured language." It doesn't much absorb Jonson and his comparisons are grudged. Wanting to suggest the spring, he represents it, tersely, as having "got proud earth with child." Shakespeare, describing a ship crowding on sail, thinks of the same figure, but is more taken with the analogy. His sails (in *A Midsummer Night's Dream*) "conceive / And grow big-bellied with the wanton wind." Sublimating carnality, Jonson writes a purged or enameled poetry. His "painted partridge" in the Penshurst Ode, like Pope's "whirring pheasant" in *Windsor Forest,* isn't a real bird caught as it rises but an artifact for the Emperor's palace.

Anticipating the "new philosophers" of the Royal Society, promoters of *res,* not *verba,* he aims to render so many things in so many words. By and large, his things aren't "reified," though. In his poetry, qualification is slighted and often the basic nouns stand alone. Inviting a Friend to Supper, he promises this friend "an olive, capers, or some better salad," maybe a "short-legged hen, / If we can get her" (there is the qualifier, important but barely conceded), "lemons, and wine for sauce . . . partridge, pheasant, wood cock," more of the same.

The blank verse of the plays, enumerative like the rhyming poetry, isn't much given to expanding comparisons or much marked by speculative interstices between, above, and under the words. Mammon (in *The Alchemist,* 2.2), who wants his beds blown up, not stuffed, and imagines how this would be, sounds like declarative Jonson. Words are exclusive, rarely squinting in different directions. Connotation tends to be exhausted in denotation. The result is a style, not centrifugal, like Shakespeare's, but centripetal, the style of the Age of Reason, less reasonable, after all, than pronouncing. Hostile to tangents, it postulates truth hid "within the center." Jonson, like Polonius, locates it there, and thinks that to find it, you have only to point. Maybe no better way offers.

But theory, though often pernicious for poetry, never yet made a poem, and Jonson wrote some great ones. This suggests that a proper audit will put appreciation first, followed by the reasons that support it. "Here is the opinion," says Chief Justice Marshall. "Brother Storey will furnish the precedents."

Seeking to avoid the mendacities of art, the plain stylist gives a lot away. Poems that mean to cohere need their lodestone, however, and the poet who won't investigate must find his attractive force elsewhere. Jonson finds it by cultivating highly formal syntactical relations. In his poetry at its most persuasive, a sophisticated rhetorician has the manage of the poem. Paradoxically, his "plain style" is the most artificial style.

For the poetry of asseveration—a phrase for Jonson's—the great man's ipse dixit makes the difference. "Thus he said." This voice you don't argue with doesn't always cheer us up, like Robert Browning's, locating God in His Heaven. It isn't spontaneous either, no poetry in English paying closer attention to form. The most sincere-seeming of the great poets before Yeats, personal Jonson wins our agreement by asserting impersonal orders.

> Thy praise or dispraise is to me alike,
> One doth not stroke me nor the other strike.

Greeks and Latins had a name for his rhetorical figures, once part of poetry's arsenal, no more. His artful juxtaposing, praise . . . dispraise, stroke . . . strike, defines itself, however, so absolves us of the need to rehearse them.

Insistent parallelism intimates what he meant to do: "I meant to make her fair and free and wise . . . / I meant she should be courteous, facile, sweet." He doesn't carry through on this intention, almost always disappointing us, and I think we conclude that in his disclaimer-poems the occulted point is to frustrated purpose. The frustration, a given, turns on what we are, benevolent, perhaps, not beneficent, and the rhetoric, fierce and poignant, underlines this. An epigram depicting Lucy, Countess of Bedford—Donne, with more assurance, wrote about her too—ends with an injunction: "My Muse bade, Bedford write, and that was she." Just here, Donne's poem begins.

Some poems of Jonson's are gnomic, precluding discussion, some almost mnemonic, aids to memory. Sound chimes with sense, maybe standing in for it. Couplets, ascending to triplets, frame but also require his compendious sayings, less thoughtful than apothegmatic. Blank verse makes you think things over, and in the nondramatic poetry he goes instead to shortened tetrameter lines or elects pentameter couplets. Or he gets his effects by varying the tally from one line to the next—now three feet, now four, then five—or truncating his lines, creating hypnotic melodies that turn dissent aside. Aggressive rhyme has this function, and feminine endings in sequence augment it. Calling attention to themselves, they heighten our sense of prayerful recitation.

Jonson has more than one string to his bow, and sometimes this modulates to banter, both itself and deeply sincere.

> But the language and the truth,
> With the ardor and the passion,
> Gives the lover weight and fashion.
> If you then will read the story,
> First, prepare you to be sorry . . . .

He knows what he is up to, confessing (in his "Fit" against rhyme) how he cozens judgment and brings words to heel. The plain stylist shouldn't do that, accounting for the irascible tone.

The emergence of the ode, its successes depending on this musical up-and-down, coincides with the waning of the more discursive forms, and Jonson, like Milton, finds it congenial. No one ever coped more nobly with the blighting of young hope than he does, in the first Pindaric ode in English:

> A lily of a day
> Is fairer far in May,
> Although it fall and die that night;
> It was the plant and flower of light.
> In small proportions we just beauty see:
> And in short measures life may perfect be.

Priority in this suasive art belongs to the "change of notes, the flat, the mean, the sharp." Efficient "to show the rites and t'usher forth the way"—Jonson claims this in a New Year's poem—they lift the heart or nourish spleen where mere ideas are helpless.

Charming or coercing us, he doesn't make us rack our brains. But though ideas don't mandate his conclusions, this doesn't mean that conclusions are wanting. The harmony he achieves is the inflectional harmony of music, its allegiance going less to words in their reverberant quality than number. You could call this the last resort of a humble man (humble under the skin) who knew himself for a provincial creature, bitten with concupiscence, darkened in his reason, and not capable, unaided, of ascending to the ultimate heights. His mundane endeavors only stain and don't pierce or resolve the white radiance of eternity. But on this middle earth there is much that a man can do and delight in.

In the great Penshurst poem, the poet, like the deity on the first day, summons a new world, superior to our old one. But his "ancient pile" is vague and numinous, its reality established by diction you can see through, the repetition of words and phrases, overbearing rhymes, or the pairing of complementary structures. The mistress of Penshurst, a "good lady . . . noble, fruitful, chaste," lives beneath "the broad beech and the chestnut shade." On her estate "fat agèd carps" come in nets to the hand, also "pikes" and "bright eels." Fantastic Jonson says the pikes betray themselves, tired of cannibalizing, and the eels "leap on land" before the fisherman can take them. Never closing with the golden world as it really is, he implies its difference from proud heaps reared with groaning—they stand around the countryside—but reserves important description to negation. Penshurst is not, cannot, has not. Though it joys in "better marks," they aren't substantial but distanced, versions of the four elements, soil, air, wood (for burning), and water. Surveying his mythic kingdom, he says flatly, i.e. grandly, "All is there."

The fruit that grows on Penshurst's garden walls—"blushing apricot and wooly peach"—though growing nowhere else, looks like the child that covets it, and plum and pear are like "ripe daughters," all fruitful in their time. In this ideal commonwealth, the land, a dutiful subject, "bends" to the river. Not always dutiful, sometimes "high-swollen," the river forgets itself, but ponds on the estate, paying tribute, make good its remissness. So Penshurst has its hierarchies, not conventionally hierarchical, however. "Chaste" is better than "noble," and in another triad the last is the best, "arts" taking precedence over both "manners" and "arms."

Unwilling, perhaps unable, to body things forth, Jonson pays a price for this in poetry some readers find thin. Here the unwillingness cashes for him. His rival creation—house, natural surround, and the people who merge with it—never existed yet, or if it did, went down with Eden. "Outside," a predatory world, ours as it actually consists, denies this civilized place. Marxist critics, missing the denial, read a sentimental poem, not Jonson's. Approving King James and his son, the Prince, he sees these two approaching Penshurst's hearth fires, bright "Penates" set aflame to entertain them. In one possible scenario, he might be the sovereign, "as if" reigning there himself. He doesn't reign there, though, and knows it; the virtues he celebrates are "rarely known" in his age; and the fires, only fires, not Roman deities, aren't lit to welcome the King.

This feckless sovereign, dying in plague time, left a mutinous country on the verge of civil war. (His brave son, struck down by typhus, died before him.) Jonson, living on, knew failing health and penury, worst of all indifference. He kept writing, however—it was what he could do—and the stunning tribute to love these observations lead off with likely dates from the last year of his life. A few years before, he presented the King's Men, once Shakespeare's company, with still another play. This startled them in London, one reporter taking notice of the old poet, "who I thought had been dead."

Chapter 7

Sidney for Moderns

Modern poetry in English gets off the mark with Sidney, the first major poet to write in our vernacular tongue. Wyatt, older by a generation, wrote some memorable poems, and Ralegh and Fulke Greville, Sidney's contemporaries, sometimes match him, perhaps they surpass him. Neither keeps as high a level so consistently, though, nor speaks with such authority to poets in times to come. Partly, this is why Sidney is major.

Readers today are apt to find him conventional—"Sir Philip Sidney and other poets of that kidney"—or "cumbered with good manners," his phrase for himself. But he has a sharper profile than courtly poets in the century before him, most of them subdued to convention, a second nature. Stephen Hawes is one, "magister ludi" to the first Tudor king. Facile in poetry that might be anyone's or no one's, Hawes survives in a couplet:

> For though the day be never so long,
> At last the bells ringeth to evensong.

Skelton, bad for other reasons, drenches his poems with personality, so dies "of his own too much." Sidney breaks with these predecessors, artificial or naively sincere. "I am not I," he tells his mistress (in *Astrophil & Stella*, XLV), knowing how even love poets are most themselves as they go out of themselves.

But he doesn't hide his light under a bushel, and the light takes color, also intensity, from the "persona" that refracts it. Jonson, he of the rocky face and mountain belly, stands on Sidney's shoulders, like Donne, though often vulgar to Sidney's polite. Though most of his poems are conventional in matter, they freshen as the manner redeems them. Literature, someone said, is the orchestration of platitudes, and Sidney's achieved poetry suggests what that means. Brimming with the ardors of convention, two opposed terms adding up to a mysterious third, it validates its claim on the future. Questions of sincerity, originality too, don't arise.

But I have to qualify a little. Sidney's best-known role is Astrophil, hero of the sonnet cycle his reputation depends on. All for sincerity, this star-lover wants us to look into our hearts. But his footprints are plain to see in other poets' snows, and readers can track him, pinpointing the indebtedness, in William Ringler's standard edition (Oxford, 1962). Still, the role-player looks a lot like Sidney. Up-to-date in political matters, a jouster in tournaments and cupbearer to the Queen, he wears the Sidney arms and loves a real-life woman, Penelope Rich, born Devereux, whose arms are glanced at too. This woman's brother was the Earl of Essex, famous, soon to be notorious. Her husband, Lord Rich, appears to disadvantage in three of the sonnets, and "brother Philip" or "Phip" in another. Beginning in hope but ending in despair, the cycle tells Sidney's story or seems to.

But the "tragicomedy of love" plays out on the other side of the footlights. Penelope is herself, also Petrarch's Laura. Stereotypes, lifted from Italian poetry in translation, define her, a "sweet enemy" (*dolce nemica*) who fires off her "sweet cruel shot" (*dolce amaro colpo*), laying a well-read lover in the dust. Getting up in a hurry, he steals a kiss (in half a dozen "baiser" poems that stick close to convention), and remembering old French poets, apostrophizes the bed. Their idea is that beds are for sleeping on. Sidney has another idea, and entertaining it, puts a spin on conventions. His lively meter, inflecting the argument, defines a sophisticated man. Opera bouffe on his comic side ("What, have I thus betrayed my liberty?" XLVII), he means to take himself in hand:

> I may, I must, I can, I will, I do
> Leave following that which it is gain to miss.

But his histrionic order—"*auxesis,*" the textbooks call it—seems less true than its artless opposite, "*catacosmesis.*" Charlie Chaplin's Great Dictator, complimenting an ungainly partner, gives the sense of this outlandish rhetorical term: "Your dancing was superb, excellent, very good, good."

"Cruel chastity," left over from Petrarch's lumberyard, gives Sidney his argument. But romantic love seems a stalking horse in many of his love poems, and taking cover behind it, he shoots his arrows at other targets than the one he points at. Disingenuous, like the baseball pitcher in the poem by Robert Francis, "He / Throws to be a moment misunderstood." Perhaps his real target is the star-lover's life, "coltish," "mad," he calls it, without doubt attractive (XXI). The hardhearted mistress who makes all the trouble isn't always front and center, and though her image shines through sleep in a well-known apostrophe (XXXIX), the poem, replete with other business, is less about her than him. Alert in his springtime, not anymore, Sidney's lover plus other things has come down in the world. Maybe study is the culprit, or serving a prince who kept him in leading strings. Or ambition holds him captive, "still climbing slippery place" (XXIII). All this he denies, blame going to Stella. But assigning it waits on the couplet. If he intends to convince us, that seems very late.

Vamping till ready, he raises / lowers his eyes, asking how Ireland, once half-tamed by "my father," likes its golden bit, or how "Holland hearts"—Dutch but glazed with translucent cloth, so partly hidden—carry on their up-and-down war against Spain (XXX). Matter-of-state, all this pales beside the romantic interest, at least Sidney says so. Often, however, the official interest looks like an epicenter, removed from the true center of disturbance. A great vexed poem beginning, "Though dusty wits dare scorn astrology" (XXVI), proposes that life gets meaning and direction from "those two stars in Stella's face." But Sidney's astrologer wonders if the stars only spangle night's black "weeds" or light some "brawl" or dance in heaven's chamber. Amatory in a pinch, otherwise self-regarding, he lives in a colder universe than Petrarch's.

Wilde, who sometimes nods, said that Sidney's best poem was his life. But the life, ending in his early thirties, is mostly preliminaries to a main event that never happened. Real-life Sidney seems less heroic than vainglorious, shading to priggish. On his shield he wrote in Latin: "These things"—patents of nobility—"I hardly call our own." He was great Leicester's nephew, though—"my chiefest honor," he said proudly—and wanted the world to take notice. Everybody knows the "verray parfit gentil knyght" who, wounded on the field at Zutphen, gave his water bottle to a common soldier. "Thy need is greater than mine," Greville, his first biographer, has him saying. Dying of his wound—and why did he strip off the leg armor that might have saved him?—he rose from the dead and lives a vigorous afterlife in popular esteem. England needed this Protestant hero, so overlooked his poetry, often profane.

Prone to grace notes, the poetry makes an odd setoff to the nonfiction prose, most of it intentional, including the famous "Defense." Reflections on the Queen's marriage to a slippery Frenchman—better break it off, Sidney tells her—go with a tract on the Christian religion, a defense of his uncle Leicester, another of his father, Ireland's Lord Deputy. Irish rebels, he thinks, will come to themselves as they "find the sweetness of due subjection." Easily said! Sidney's prose polemics vociferate a lot but aren't convincing. Even the *Defense of Poetry,* though memorable for eloquence, seems less convincing than suave.

He had his Polonius side, daunting in one so young, and the correspondence gives it scope. "One error is the mother of a thousand," etc. Commending moral philosophy ("the proper study"), he wants his brother Robert to taste its preceptors well before drinking too much of their doctrine. Exercise often, this junior is instructed, learn music and better penmanship, also the "mathematicals," "have a care of your diet and consequently of your complexion." Jonson, keen to find fault, said Sidney's complexion was pimply. Not mature beyond his years but unselfconscious, befitting them, he wrote at twenty-six how he had given up "delight in the world."

His poetry, especially when sad, reports to the contrary. Civilized where the life is callow, it delights in the "manage" of a difficult art. This technical term, from horsemanship (*Astrophil & Stella,* XLIV), suggests how form wars on sadness, converting sobs to "tunes of joy." His own severest critic, he puts himself down, but diction, rhyme, and stress testify against him, and the sad words breed "ravishing delight" (LVII, LVIII).

Most critical writing in our time trains its eye (but not an ear) on what he said, however, leaving how he said it alone. "Vexed issues in Sidney studies," quoting one student, include his ideology, moral, political, or feminist. The feminist side, different from the distaff side, features the Countess of Pembroke, his sister and an early bluestocking. He sat to Veronese for a painting, now lost, and some critics want to know what he looked like. Others explore his debt to Plato, "the wisest scholar of the wight most wise" (XXV). Though the line is a tongue twister, asking attention, they don't ask how its sound might bear on its subject. But ten times out of ten, the right way to approach him is as a technician. Invoking the Muse, he looks into his thesaurus ("dictionary's method," XV), and numbers syllables, keeping his hand in his pocket. What he thinks is ad hoc, coterminous with the poem as he writes it.

He liked to experiment and in poems of his twenties—he called them "Certain Sonnets," a portmanteau term—tried out popular songs (many written "to the tune of"), the villanelle, a first in English, epigrams and impresas, also "quantitative" verse. Modeled on Latin poetry, its organizing principle isn't accent but duration, against the English grain. In the first line of the *Aeneid,* "Arma virumque cano," "Of arms and the man I sing," you must end the verb *cano* with a long, open *o* sound. All these forms, unrelenting in their commitment to the given, work the poet hard, and you can say that he is less a truthteller, canvassing ideas, than an opportunist, trying on different habits. Saying so, I hardly mean to dispraise him.

Pain mingles with pleasure in songs like "The Nightingale," recalling Philomela's rape, or "Ring Out Your Bells," the bells tolling for victims of plague. But Sidney, like Ralegh in most of his poems, personifies reality, so keeps it at a distance. Love is the subject,

> His deathbed, peacock's folly;
> His winding sheet is shame;
> His will, false-seeming holy;
> His sole exec'tor, blame.

In Sidney's psychology, step by step in his poetry, "erected wit" sparkles but "infected will" dims its luster, and we see as through a glass darkly. I think he understood this and rued it.

"Reporting verse," essentially a catalog, is among his familiar strategies. But the items he marshals aren't scrutinized much. Affirmation is by negation, like Jonson's "Thou art not, Penshurst." Though Stella is on his mind, "how clothed, how waited on," whether she sighed or smiled (XCII), he doesn't abide our questions, his either. The name of the mistress, recited often, functions as a talisman. "Now she is named, need more be said?" (XVI). Other poets, Donne and Shakespeare, think there is more to say, but Sidney, keeping mum, leaves his tabernacle empty. Or he ends injunctively: "Stella behold, and then begin to indite" (XV). This is where the poem, if intended for description, might get started.

Characteristic sonnets look like sketches or cartoons for the one he never writes. Claiming for himself a truthteller's role, he lacks an inward "touch," or touchstone, to distinguish true from false (XV). You rubbed this silica-like stone against precious metals to see if they were really precious, but his poetry dispenses with proof and you have to take him at his word. His golden world mostly crowds out the real one, flesh-and-blood reducing to the inert stuff of a blazon. Ivory, rubies, pearl, and gold show "her" skin, lips, teeth, and head, but though a sonnet to Morpheus (XXXII) says they do this well, most moderns are doubtful. If they come clean, they are likely to tell you that his love poems seem more poetry than truth.

The truth they look for in vain is truth-to-nature, however. Sidney's truth is all established on the surface, that is, rhetorically, by wringing tropes

for what he can get out of them or "running in rattling rows" (allitera-
tion). In one of his *baiser* poems, the same word keeps recurring in its
different grammatical kinds: *sweet/sweets/sweetly/sweetness/sweetest/sweetener*
(LXXIX). They all desired, said Lyly the Euphuist, "to hear finer speech
than the language will allow." Poking fun at this mock-elegant speech
("You that do search for every purling spring," XV), Sidney achieves con-
viction in ways he says a poet shouldn't. He sits in Tempe's shade or drinks
from the Muses' well, hoping that something will follow. It does, often
enough to make him a poet worth going back to.

But he isn't a head-scratching kind of poet, and isn't good at working
out answers. What he excels at is handing down the law. In the way of such
truths, his are exhausted in declarative statement, like Ralegh's, though
never as gravid. Problems, often poignant, trouble the surface of his answer
poems, but he doesn't resolve them, preferring to cut the Gordian knot.
What are we but the stars' tennis balls,

>   and thralls to Fortune's reign;
>   Turned from ourselves, infected with their cage . . .
> Like players placed to fill a filthy stage.
>
> (Arcadia, no. 30)

Greville at his most triumphant writes this kind of poetry, e.g. in *Caelica*:

> Fie, foolish earth, think you the heaven wants glory,
> Because your shadows do yourself benight?
> All's dark unto the blind, let them be sorry,
> The heavens in themselves are ever bright.

Downright, not analytic, this is the voice of the greater Augustans. Of
course, its pronouncements are less true or false than majestic, like Dr. John-
son kicking the stone.

Even as a courtly maker, Greville's tone is aphoristic:

> He that lets his Cupid lie,
> Naked on a bed of play,
> To say prayers ere she die,
> Teacheth time to run away.

To "die" is to experience orgasm, and Greville, like Sidney, is powerfully
taken with sexual love. Sidney's change of heart is notorious, however. In

two famous sonnets, both written "in contempt of the world," he renounces/regrets his love poet's role. Though both are earlier work, editors since nineteenth-century Grosart hitch them on to *Astrophil & Stella*. Agreeable to our moral sense at its simplest, they make a neat biographical coda: "Foul vanities to you / Forever more, adieu." The first, "Thou blind man's mark, thou fool's self-chosen snare," looks forward to Spenser, whose insistent rhyme scheme keeps his poems from flying apart. The centripetal impulse nags at Sidney too, and though a couplet ends the poem, his syntax, running over three lines, won't let it stand alone. If it did, he thinks, it might split off from the poem, like a piece of the shoreline falling into the sea. "Desire, desire!" is what we hear as his sonnet concludes. But the important question, "How to kill desire," goes unanswered.

The second poem, "Leave me, O Love, which reachest but to dust," has a rhyme scheme like Shakespeare's. In the final couplet, however, Sidney, recycling a pair of earlier rhymes, withholds that capping *ipse dixit*— "thus he said"—all of us are used to in sonnets. A proverb, admonishing the good man, has it right: "how evil becometh him to slide." But Sidney's poem is substantial—that is, rife with contradictions, or call them countercurrents—and I think he means also that this evil, like loving, becomes him. Conclusions, certified by reason's touchstone, aren't his forte. He seems more involved with the journey than its end.

Like the early sonnets, his prose romance, *Arcadia,* dates from his twenties, though later he went back to it, rationalizing the story. A mirror for magistrates and the rest of us, "degenerate souls made worse by our clayey lodgings," this first modern novel got Shakespeare's attention. But T. S. Eliot dismissed it as a "monument of dullness," and though scholars praise it, only scholars continue to read it. Like a well-formed play, however, it moves toward its "anagnorisis," or revelation of truth. Sidney, revising, meant to cast the truth in relief. This is the didactic writer, driving us on conclusions. He isn't the same as that Sidney who aborts conclusions. So his art makes an agon, if you don't like him you can say it makes a muddle, the moralist with a program versus the poet who didn't have one, except that he liked to be challenged.

Most who wrote fiction when he did follow a linear pattern, their sensational stories having only the unity of whatever comes next. Sidney's are self-conscious, focused not on "vanishing pleasures alone but moral images and examples." He meant them, said Greville, for "directing threads to guide every man through the confused labyrinth of his own desires and life." Faithful to this intention, he enlivened the narrative with pastoral verse, almost three hundred poems in half as many different line and stanza patterns, more than Spenser gives us in the whole of his *Shepherd's Calendar.* Most of Sidney's poetic forms are new in English with him, most he uses only once, and though the poems are bound by context, many, escaping it, survive to the future.

Unlike Italian *intermezzi,* art for the fun of it, all mean to further a preceptorial design. Sidney's quantitative measures argue for this, and though they don't work in English, you feel how he had to attempt them. Rhyme and accent, said theorists like Thomas Campion, stretched the truth or cut it short on their "procrustean" bed. Valuing poetry's good name, Sidney sought to free it from this charge of arbitrariness. But Campion's critique is deeply implicative, and poetry as a kind fails to address it. His disembodied truth (or Truth), uncircumscribed by the definite article or adverbial phrase—and let us add by feet or rhyme—isn't available unless in the perspicuous air of heaven. If Truth and instilling it is your business, you do better leaving poetry alone.

In a black mood, Sidney thought this. But his poems, though they lack "redeeming social value," aren't empty of value, and compose a second nature with its own inner truth or coherence. The coherence is provisional, no help for that, and the poetry, though obedient to the facts as he has them, occupies a narrow ground. He hoped for something better, ascending from particulars to capital-letter statement, but the graven-in-stone truth escaped him and his "there" turned out to be "here." I am quoting Wallace Stevens, who wrestled in many poems with this problem of the plenary Truth and its merely partial exemplifications. Passing through his "crude foyer," ignorant men, poets among them, don't make it through, being "incapable / Of the least, minor, vital metaphor." But though they can't negotiate the jump from here to there, indigenous to catholic, they leave us content with the lower-case world they start out from. This limited achievement is Sidney's.

His fellow poets often give it low marks, valuing poetry only as it diverts idle hours. He himself, the time's bleakness growing on him, settled for this diminished view of his art. But he put it right up there with the divine's and philosopher's when he preached to the "misomousoi." Misogynists hate women and these poet-haters hated the Muse.

Willing the good like religion and philosophy, poetry betters either, having "the more force in teaching." In his prose *Defense* Sidney says so, locating himself firmly in the humanist camp. Convention, seeking to discriminate between science and literature, identifies humanism with a study of the classics, but the fathers of humanism honor the classics from devotion to whatever makes most for "the uses of life." (Bacon, among the fathers of science, is their spokesman.) The devotion to use, rather than beauty as an end in itself, is what humanism means, and Sidney is the humanist *par excellence*.

Promoting the classics, he plays the utilitarian card. E.g. "no philosopher's precepts can sooner make you an honest man than the reading of Virgil." The assertion, while not true, is striking, and gives the *Arcadia* its reason for being. Sidney's purpose, said Greville, was to teach us "how to set a good countenance upon all the discountenances of adversity and a stay upon the exorbitant smilings of chance." This virtue allowed to art is very potent, and all must wish that artists were up to the job.

Leading off our critical tradition in English, Sidney's *Defense* is first of all a job description. (Devotees of *art pour l'art* needn't apply.) He wrote it early in the 1580s, with the other hand writing *Astrophil & Stella*. The right hand didn't know what the left hand was doing, and his ideal poet, indifferent to "gnosis," or knowledge, swears by "praxis," getting things done. Delighting us, he does this only "to move men to take that goodness in hand which, without delight, they would fly as from a stranger." Poetry is a spiritual bolus and the poet a leech or medicine man. Because his patients have weak stomachs or finicking tastes, he wins them to health with "a medicine of cherries." Sidney goes on like that. But he lost his faith in the curative powers of art, or perhaps, talking them up, was never more than half-persuaded: the age, when old verities were shaking, was a great one for hectic avowals like his. At the end of his life, "lifted up to a purer horizon," he discovered the vanity of all artistic enterprise. Greville had second thoughts, Sidney none, and he willed his executor to burn the *Arcadia,* verse and prose together.

Read the verse with the care it merits and you can see why. Simple rhymes weren't taxing enough, so his are often "medial," the last syllable in one line heard again in the fourth syllable of the next. Or he employs triple rhyme, *sig-ni-fy / dig-ni-fy,* after the Italians. "Sdrucciola," they called it, easy for them, harder on English Sidney, and that pleased him. Rime royal pleased him, its returning rhymes grateful to an ear less attuned to matter than interior music. Introducing the sestina to English—six stanzas and a tercet, making do with only six rhyme words—he aggravated its problems a second time round and challenged, wrote a double sestina. The poem's occasion didn't much detain him.

For English poetry's first pastoral elegy, he chose terza rima. Throwing forward endlessly, it recoils on itself, *aba,* then *bcb,* then *c* again, and so on and so on. Sometimes the last word of one line is also the first word of the next, "the redouble." Most of Sidney's verse forms have this reticulating feature. In the radical case, his lines reticulate or "correlate" like lines in a blueprint, resembling him to Spenser, the cranky numerologist. This is how he begins a sonnet in correlative verse (no. 60):

<pre>
     1   2   3   1   2   3
    Virtue, beauty, and speech, did strike, wound, charm,
          1   2   3   1   2   3
    My heart, eyes, ears, with wonder, love, delight—
</pre>

less poetry than child's play. Lynx-eyed scholars look beneath his surface and counting 108 sonnets in *Astrophil & Stella,* discover that the interspersed songs total 108 stanzas. Some point out that Sidney's Penelope recalls the wife of Ulysses, besieged by 108 suitors. What these complementarities mean is less important than the fact that a poet exploits them. Perhaps this clever poet was indulging his cleverness, or on his Calvinist or know-nothing side meant to impose an order the material itself didn't show.

Reworking the same images in the same form, he teases his given until it suggests different conclusions. Let us see, you hear him asking, whether, in his final stanza he can match the first prosodically while turning its point of view upside down. In paired sonnets, and songs like "Ring Out Your Bells," alpha and omega (1) oppose each other, (2) replicate each other, and though mind is at work, seeing to it that Sidney's stanzas cohere, the shift when it comes is more linguistic than thoughtful. Form and content make a tandem, but form is the lead horse, and getting its head achieves a kind of order discursive thought hasn't much part in.

"Bookend" poems in his *Arcadia,* highlighting this order, summon the merchant man, elated, then despairing (nos. 36, 37), or enjoin contrasting modes of behavior. In two terza rima sonnets ("Feed on, my sheep" / "Leave off, my sheep," nos. 23, 24), *Sic* and *Non* go at it hard. Excitement comes from arguing a persuasive case for both. Assessing the possibilities, Sidney fits his words to the music, however. "Dittying," contemporaries called this, pointing an accusing finger at polyphonic composers who swallowed their words. They laid out truth on a tyrant's bed, and Sidney follows suit. The conviction he achieves often seems imposed, as in profane songbooks or some paintings by Van Eyck.

Though his argument poems appear to advance a thesis: "Whom Passion leads unto his death is bent" (no. 27), that is only Reason's plea, promptly controverted for the time being: "And let him die, so that he die content." The controverting is managed in a couplet, and the poem as a whole is cast in that most artificial of forms, old "stichomythia," where I make my point and you trump it. This trumping is essentially rhythmical, though, or say sonantal, as in the echo poem. A musical back-and-forth, it ends by fiat with some such injunction as "Cease, Muse, therefore" (no. 31). Not a QED word, Sidney's "therefore" is a filler, filling out the pentameter line.

Rustic characters in one of his debates, getting beyond themselves, entertain us with a corona of "dizains" (no. 72). Ten stanzas, each ten lines long and each resuming the last line of the previous stanza, end with a four-line crown. Art, not passion, is uppermost in Sidney's debate, or the passion is all gone into art. His Nightingale song, approximating music, highlights feminine rhymes. Trailing off, they muffle meaning, or meaning is sensuous, registered by the ear as it listens without prejudice to the metrical up-and-down.

> But I, who daily craving,
> Cannot have to content me,
> Have more cause to lament me,
> Since wanting is more woe than too much having.

This woe is from life, and the mournful bird sings it, "a thorn her songbook making." But syntax goes both ways, and form itself is the only begetter. Though the song tells of violence, technical commitment inspires the singing. "Form, which is the birth of passion, is the death of pain," says Wilde, this time on target.

Like a good Protestant or monophonic man, Sidney wrote above his lintel: *Nullius in verba,* "Nothing in words." The message was the medium, and he didn't want words and their latencies to hide it. But heightening words, he swears by their magic, trusting often to the primacy of sound. In his double sestina "Ye Goatherd Gods" (no. 71), for example. Exploring all the possibilities latent in his six rhyme words, he sets or scores them but doesn't come to conclusions. His two antagonists only mimic a quarrel (one "writhes," the other "weeps"), and he himself only mimics instruction. Words on their musical side are freed up, and he softpedals the "thought" they embody.

Ye goatherd gods, that love the grassy mountains,
Ye nymphs which haunt the springs in pleasant valleys,
Ye satyrs joyed with free and quiet forests,
Vouchsafe your silent ears to plaining music,
Which to my woes gives still an early morning,
And draws the dolor on till weary evening.

All the major poets, living and dead, confront one another across a gap
in time, and Auden, challenged by Sidney, picks up the gauntlet in his
"Paysage Moralisé." But his sestina is dynamic, his landscape is moralized,
vindicating the title, and the trouble he begins with is mended in his three-
line "collector." Sidney's, a long suspiration mandated by prosody, gets
nothing done, or to say what gets done you need a new terminology. Ask
him for meaning and he refers you, e.g., to the "anaphora." He is writing
what moderns call "poésie pure."

This art that displays itself doesn't conduct to salvation and hooking the
ear, leaves the message to shift for itself. On a dyspeptic view, his, at the end,
"words are but words," tractable at will, and his poetry that chops and
changes them is only a *jeu d'esprit.* "Read it, then, at your idle times," he
said to his sister Mary, "looking for no better stuff than as in a haberdasher's
shop, glasses, or feathers." The year before he died he threw away the sword
upstairs and began his "Metaphrase," a close translation of the Psalms. Tech-
nique still counting for Sidney, each of his psalms employs a different stanza
pattern. But he is dying out of poetry into life. "What" displaces "how" in
this easy-to-manage world, disposing is labor lost, and the sign has priority
over the sound or figure.

But the Social Muse, up front in his theory and certain failed poems, is
sent packing in the poetry he lives by. Carrying water on both shoulders—
both Protestants and new Catholics had to do that in his time—he put his
art in peril, however. For this sprezzatura poet who hankered after salvation,
the fire always waits round the corner. Botticelli, our great celebrant of the
pagan gods and graces, committed his paintings to this fire. Byrd, paying lip
service to the new imperatives, kept one eye on Heaven (his Latin and Eng-
lish church music), the other on earth (his variations for the virginal on sec-
ular song tunes like "O Mistress Mine"). Both needed painstaking and he
honored both kinds. Sidney wasn't up to this, and in the end it cost him.

But the end was a long way down. En route he pleased himself, notably in
Astrophil and Stella. A witty primer, it tilts at sentimentalists like the author

of the Metaphrase, meaning to teach them what poetry is and isn't. They thought it was heart's truth, as when love or nature takes us by the hand (XC), but "ennobling new-found tropes with problems old" (III) is more like it. Though Sidney's poet asks leave to let his passions run their race (LXIV), this leave is never granted, and where matter is most violent, form, anaphoric, buckles it in. Naive poets, oppressed with emotion, let it all hang out; he paints the hell he lives in "with a feeling skill" (II), so renders but also restrains it. Saluting his mistress, he looks like a naif: "Thou art my wit, and thou my virtue art" (LXIV). But look again and you see that his linking verbs are substantives too, declaring his ultimate allegiance.

Rejecting art, he says he copies nature (III). But nature's music is ragged while his obeys the metronome, and adjusting the line is how he achieves the illusion of natural speech. He calls himself "dumb" (LIV), hypothetically a virtue. Silence is best music (LXX), and so forth. But he talks a lot, like Yeats ("Colder and dumber and deafer than a fish"), and like Yeats insists on a hearing. How do we know that he loves "indeed"? I think we know as this lover is artificial, i.e. a poet. Courtly nymphs, liking poets spontaneous, don't regard him:

"What he?" say they of me, "now I dare swear,
He cannot love: no, no, let him alone."

But his speaking voice, manly, volatile, real, that is, composed or tinkered, won't permit this.

A word on that speaking voice: he made it up, of course, intending it to comment on the mellifluous voice all agree to call poetry's. In his vocabulary, however, poetry needs inverted commas. You could say his sonnet cycle is a criticism of poetry itself. Sincere with a difference like all credentialed poets, he speaks what he feels (VI) but doesn't know how he feels until he writes it. As for the "cause" that energizes his poems:

What, is it thus? Fie, no.
Or so? Much less. How then?

(LXXIV)

Propriety demands an answer and he complies. Often, though, the answer seems less compelling than the wordplay that precedes it. Or Sidney's Q. and A. mode is pretty much a simulacrum, the life of the poem being elsewhere.

What can I do with this?—e.g. horse, lance, and hand (XLI)—is a governing question. But any terms will serve as long as he respects them. *On s'engage, puis en voit* is a motto of his. First he gets into things, then looks around, making "speech of speech arise" (XXVII). Unlikely apostrophes furnish him a starting point, and he wonders where the river Thames or the highway he gallops on will take him (CIII, LXXXIV). Biographical critics hope to locate this highway. For sure, it won't take him to London, however, and it isn't the Whitechapel Road.

Out of love with "stepdame Study" (much to-do about this), he has endearing words for "Nature's child," invention (I). But he mines well-worn topics, and like Wyatt in his soul = ship poem, tailors them to personal use. Disposing his material is priority one, the material itself coming second. Critics with a moral bias fault him for this, noting how he flouts the "laws" of rhetorical composition. Sighs ought to come first, breathing out words (VI), but he inverts the conventional order and his words, perused, foster sighing.

Though not much involved with the natural world, he has his touchstone. This is diction, decisive for an artist's handle on things. "Lame" in virtue he is and bogged down in "vain thoughts"—or rather "quick" in them, he says, a different kettle of fish. Reading philosophers like Plato might tame him, but "lame" and "tame" make a rhyme, putting this unhelpful preceptor in his place (XXI). No question, his precepts are approved on the surface. However, "sugared sentence" describes them (XXV), and while all of us honor virtue, its sway seems most fitting in "some old Cato's breast" (IV). Marcus Cato is a moralist but Sidney's qualifiers suggest a fool.

Critical assumptions, often left unsaid and many opposed to orthodox doctrine, underlie his work. This isn't supposition, the work itself makes them vivid. Nourishing my "theory," they give it its empirical ground. (Everybody has a theory, even those, like me, who deny it.) Item one in this Ars Poetica says that for poetry, form is the sine qua non. That doesn't argue black tie, much less petrifaction. It means recurrence.

Sidney's critical prose separates form from content, and the common understanding sees a two-tiered relation. But Sidney's best poetry gives it the lie, not only the sonnets but the songs and *Arcadia* pieces. The future trusts the poems, or ought to, rather than the poet who paid allegiance to his time. Whatever he tells you, content isn't hidden like a pearl within the oyster. When the poem succeeds, the oyster makes the pearl, though the other way round is true too.

Or content is like the soul, i.e. you don't see it unless it takes limbs of flesh. Only a few ideas come down from the past, and if they live to the future, this is thanks to the medium more than the message. Sometimes the medium contradicts the message, for instance in a quatrain from *Astrophil & Stella:*

> Fly, fly, my friends, I have my death wound; fly.
> See there that boy, that murdering boy, I say,
> Who like a thief, hid in dark bush, doth lie,
> Till bloody bullet get him wrongful prey.
>
>   (XX)

Sophisticated readers, sticking with the poem, will ignore the poet's counsel, also his lurid characterizations. Cupid a murderous thief, skulking in darkness? Not likely.

Though love is often the subject, Sidney's poems get their distinctive character less from heart's truth than prosody, including kinds of rhyme, or the absence of rhyme, stress patterns, and rhetorical patterns. Their sum hints at meaning, not denotative, however. You need intelligence to write poems, and some poets are intellectuals, Sidney among them. But intellectualizing belongs to social science, and whatever the poet's meaning, he sings it, literally a hymn in the throat.

His poetry is provisional, setting limits on what he can do. He can't encapsulate truth, or his truths are lower-case. For example, the answer poem ("A satyr did run away for dread," *Certain Sonnets,* 16), responding to his friend and fellow poet Edward Dyer. Too scrupulous to evade the given, not least the sonnet form, he finds himself carried off in directions he can't have foreseen. His matter is the same in poem after poem, and yet he is always at a beginning. Pushing the inkblots around, he keeps at it until they show him a pattern. When this happens, the poem looks preconceived.

Another word for his poetry, as for any poem worth retrieving, is "provincial," a reason why the conceptualizing temperament dislikes it. Though Sidney—and Greville, Ralegh, even Shakespeare—appear to honor the capital-letter truth ("Frailty, thy name is woman," etc.), look closely and you see that the point is to particulars and circumscribed by them. Poetry, different from the Decalogue or Newton's *Principia,* lives on a less efficient plane. In the last analysis, it gets nothing done, hateful to some, agreeable to others, including Sidney on his poet's side.

Debate, good for drama, invigorates his sonnet cycle, a version of the old spirit war between reason and will. But the new mind, contemplating the ancient aspect or "Psychomachia," modifies it in permanent ways. Though virtuous men take the high road to Heaven ("our country," V), appositives and parenthetical clauses impede this forward progress, and the senses, reluctant underlings, struggle like flies in marmalade. In sonnet V, "It is most true that eyes are formed to serve," we know what the senses should do, but subordination and clotted syntax, our clue to meaning, involve us in doubt. Repetition: true, true, most true, begets its opposite, not true after all, but false. Reason comes out on top in its contest with will—sometimes, not always—but its victory looks Pyrrhic or the contest itself is a sham. "Well, Love," says the poet, throwing his hand in, let virtue have the soul, leaving the body to us (LII). This "Well," among other things, is what Sidney brings to poetry.

Chapter 8

Spenser in the Minotaur's Cave

In the well-known Kinnoull portrait Spenser looks like a movie actor, circa 1930s, but frown lines crease the forehead and under the arched eyebrows the anxious eyes don't believe what they see. Service in Ireland with the Queen's Deputy, Grey of Wilton, immersed him in the chaos he never got free of. Lord Grey hanged unruly subjects or he kept them on short rations, notably in Münster, where the poet lived on the spoils of colonization. "Out of every corner of the woods and glens," Spenser saw the Irish come, like skeletons or ghosts from the grave. "They did eat of the dead carrions; happy were they if they could find them." However, said the Deputy, force had to plane the ground for the foundation, and later, in *The Faerie Queene,* Spenser cast him as a type of Justice.

On furlough at the English court with his patron Ralegh, he angled for a sinecure (but philistinish Lord Burghley cared little for poets), then, back on his Kilcolman lands, switched allegiance to the new favorite Essex. Tyrone's rebellion sent him traveling again, with dispatches for the Queen at Westminster. He died at Westminster, January 16, 1599, not yet fifty. For his grave in the Abbey, the Queen ordered a monument, never erected.

Spenser's poetry, "an endless monument," his own hopeful phrase, redeems this lapse. But it doesn't hold the mirror up to nature. Tangled in nature, a Minotaur's cave, he looked for a thread or clue to transact it. Poetry gave him what he was looking for. Most of the popular kinds engaged him and in each he experimented with different rhyme schemes and meters, or made the established forms harder. But the intricate strategies he worked out for himself seem less formal than despotic, like a sanitary cordon fencing round the world he lived in. I don't mean that cordons are bad for poetry, only the sanitary kind.

A bizarre passage in *The Faerie Queene* shows him elaborating his defenses. Harried like the rest of us by the world, flesh, and devil, he takes refuge in a House of Temperance, different from any other in nature. Most houses "turne to earth" again, like the Tower of Babel, and contemplating their wreck, Spenser discovers that "no earthly thing is sure." But he has a hole card, occult mathematics, and it keeps his better habitation from collapsing;

> The frame thereof seemd partly circulare,
> And part triangulare: O worke divine!
> Those two the first and last proportions are;
> The one imperfect, mortall, foeminine,
> Th'other immortall, perfect, masculine:
> And twixt them both a quadrate was the base,
> Proportioned equally by seven and nine;
> Nine was the circle sett in heavens place;
> All which compacted made a goodly diapase.
>
> (bk. 2, canto 9, stanza 22)

Poetry this isn't, but intentional Spenser has higher things in mind, and his House of Temperance suggests the type of a gentleman or noble person. An early commentator, Sir Kenelm Digby, lays out the correspondences, circle for head, triangle for the body's trunk, quadrate for the ground it stands on, etc. Identified with earth, the quadrate or base isn't in plumb, but mystic numbers make this crooked place straight.

The House of Temperance doesn't need jet and marble, though the Irish countryside supplies them, and the man who lives in the house isn't formed from the dust of the earth. All mind, he isn't pestered by sexuality either, being masculine, therefore neuter, like God Himself. This may raise eyebrows, but the sequence isn't mine. Plato in the *Timaeus,* one of Spenser's sacred books, sponsors his reading, a physiology but also prescriptive. Better for us, philosopher and poet think, when the body, known for "misrule and passions bace," takes a back seat to the mind. "Like highest heaven" or the English Deputy inside Dublin's Pale, it keeps a weather eye on our "earthly masse." The twain never meet, however, and "what ligament they have, our author defineth not."

Indebted to books, Spenser's hierarchies owe much to life as well, and "rough rugheaded kerns," Irish rebels, model the body. "Imperfect, mortall, foeminine," that is, sexual (women are centaurs "down from the waist"), it pulls toward earth like Babel's tower. This retrograde motion, promoting disharmony, spoils the "goodly diapase" or compass of the musical notes. Or maybe not: Spenser's psychology isn't everyone's. For other poets in his time, friction in the heavens creates the music of the spheres, and "Empedoclean" Jonson makes Love's triumph depend on the jostling of constituent parts. Maybe these parts or elements are "nicely mixed" when they oppose each other. "This was a man," says Antony in his valedictory for Brutus, not through-and-through perfect but "moulded out of faults." Mingling sweet and sharp, the ambivalent hero cuts a grander figure than Sir Guyon, Redcrosse, and the others.

Tasso in his romantic epic, attractively catholic (lowercase "c") until straitened by the Counter-reformers, says how sweet and sharp "are joined and knit together with a kind of discordant harmony." Spenser, ignoring this ambiguous compound, turns a deaf ear on our "sensible" part, like his Knights of the Everlasting No. The phrase is H. S. V. Jones's, who thinks they might say Yes, except that the moralist, warned off by experience, won't let them. Sometimes, however, Spenser listens to the sirens' singing, and in books 3 and 4 eroticism seems freed to pluck at the senses. This is lucky for us. Discord holds things together, concord, a misnomer, is when they fall apart. Sons of darkness, wiser in their generation than the children of light, understand this.

But Spenser's dual allegiance makes trouble for the poems. In these notes on his poetic, I mean to suggest how he copes with the problem, most poignant when he tells of himself. He does this in *Colin Clout's Come Home Again* (1595), i.e. home to England from self-imposed exile. Though narrative verse, it doesn't progress organically, as when images beget fresh images. Progression is by lockstep, the last rhyme of one quatrain resurfacing in the second line of the next. Spenser's version of old terza rima, like the algebraic curve ascending to infinity, might go on forever. No asymptote breaks the curve, or you could say that this poet's form is uninflected by his content. A Gorgon's head, it petrifies, and he looks the other way.

Tardy praise for dead Sidney, his elegy *Astrophel* (1595) is "seriatim" poetry, structure (such as it is) depending on what comes next. But echoes crisscross the poem, opposing its centrifugal drift. "Reed" in the first stanza is heard as "read" in the second, further on as "feed/breed," etc. Always in Spenser entropy threatens, and perhaps this murmurous consorting of words is a way to hold it in check. The consorting isn't thoughtful, though, only sonantal. James Russell Lowell, an early critic of *The Faerie Queene* and more poetry centered than most, said how Spenser chose its language "for its rich canorousness rather than for intensity of meaning." Words, even when incantatory, have their latencies of meaning, but he doesn't often exploit them.

Civil War rears its head in his *Four Hymns* (1596), where the elements,

like fractious citizens, turn the world upside down. But a mysterious pres-
ence, concealed by "the outward show of things," composes their quarrel.
"Ah! believe me," Spenser says, asking us to take this on faith. He isn't a
reliable witness, however, his credibility impaired by the times that pro-
duced him. Born in the beginning of our modern age, he looks back to the
Middle Ages, when doctrines of expressive form had yet to be heard from.

But the medieval temperament got along equably without them. Its
typical book is "res varias," a hodgepodge. Jean de Meun or John of Salis-
bury, one French, one English but both permissive to a fault, expand their
loose-leaf folders as they need to. The first wrote the age's breviary of love,
The Romance of the Rose, or rather a part of it (no one paying much heed to
unity of composition). English John, clerical administrator and man of let-
ters, helped build Chartres, a miscellany in stone. Neither, coming to con-
clusions, instructs us in the sense of an ending dictated by pressures imma-
nent in the work.

Some medieval poems acknowledge this pressure, *Sir Gawain,* for
instance. Individual tales of Chaucer's, like the Pardoner's or Wife of Bath's,
are artistic in the modern sense. But the work that includes them supports
my generalization, and Chaucer, though greater than Jean de Meun or John
of Salisbury, belongs with them. "Here is ended the book of the tales of
Canterbury," he says laconically, having run out of gas.

In step with modern times, Spenser thinks this indifference to organic
form won't do. But the perception of a shape beneath the skin, characteris-
tic of modern fictions, eludes him. Better than most, he knows how things
fall apart, though, and taking preventive action, imposes control from out-
side. Heavenly Love is his agent, binding, also discriminating, with adaman-
tine chains. Monolithic images, a better bet than philosophy, organize his
hymns. Raised on pillars amidst the sea, earth is like the rock that stands
above the water. Sea and air, girt round with brass or fire, acknowledge
their station, having no choice, and a "mighty shining crystal wall" encloses
the cosmos. Nothing escapes it. Twining fingers must knit the knot that
renders discord helpless, and rime royal, with its chiming sound in the mid-
dle of the stanza, supplies them.

Already in *The Shepherd's Calendar* (1579), the poem that made Spenser
famous, you see him screwing down his refractory material. Alloting a dif-
ferent scheme to successive eclogues, he complicates it with interior music,
rime couée, or tail rhyme, for instance, where two short lines, rhyming
together, serve as "tails" to the longer line that precedes them. Stanza pairs
with stanza, rhyme enforcing the connection, or quatrains fold back on

themselves, *abab* becoming its mirror image, *baba*. One way to see the poet is as a cunning child who creases a piece of paper and pinks it across the fold. An unrhymed sestina, the centerpiece of his August eclogue, recycles the same six words for six stanzas, then runs them all together in a brief envoy. This wheels-within-wheels aspect of the poetry works on us mesmerically, as if Spenser were muttering spells.

In three eclogues, imitating old-fashioned accentual verse he divides his lines with a double caesura, not a voice pause exactly, more like a rest in music: "The keen cold blows [ ] through my beaten hide." Some medieval poems anticipate Spenser's. The famous "Pearl" is one. But the pattern is familiar from children's nursery rhymes, crudely "dipodic." Pairs of feet, combining across a divide, rise, then fall away:

> Sing a song of sixpence / A pocket full of rye,
> Four and twenty blackbirds / Baked in a pie.

This up-and-down pattern isn't naive but deliberate, however. Experience, though it looks recalcitrant, shapes up when the metrist takes it in hand.

In *Daphnaida* (1591), tyrannical form turns into its opposite, and violent emotion runs free. Spenser's elegy plus beast fable reports the death of "a fair young lioness," otherwise Daphne, wife of a friend. Though the poet undertakes to justify her death, unassuaged bitterness is the most of his poem. Meaning to draw its sting, he goes heavy on rhetoric, repeating words and phrases, sometimes the same words, sometimes in their various grammatical permutations. The yield he hopes for is a static or isotropic world, the same (as words forfeit their integrity) in every direction. "A violent order is disorder," though, remembering Wallace Stevens, a modern connoisseur of chaos, and the experience this poem records and means to chasten is less ordered than held in a vise.

Twenty-eight stanzas lead off the poem, each seven lines long, and followed by seven complaints. Each complaint makes seven stanzas, seven lines assigned to each. Introducing the coda (four stanzas), Spenser's word is "Thus," no sequitur more willful. $7 \times 4 = 28$, however, and the coda is 1/7th of the stanzas he begins with. Manipulating tropes and ciphers, he creates his own cosmos. This magus in poetry, admonishing untrammeled nature, is saying, Get thee behind me.

But I have to ask the reader's indulgence. Canvassing technique borders on the incivil, like elevating graphs or tables to the status of text. It seems right, however, for this bedeviled kind of poetry where fettering is the end and arbitrary form the means to achieve it. Let us agree that the figure a poem makes, being up to the poet, is arbitrary per se. More often than you would think, though, form and content, intersecting, reach their term together, in credentialed sonnets after fourteen lines. This point of coincidence is where poets find their limited truth. Spenser can't find it, accounting for his weird conjurations.

A real-life courtship occupies him in the *Amoretti* (1595), eighty-eight sonnets devoted to Irish Elizabeth Boyle. But Spenser's beloved, less a woman than a type, isn't palpably there, and though she plays different roles, nothing special sets them off. Saluting the bride-to-be, he lays her away in his strongbox. Sonnet 15 inventories its contents, "as, item," two lips like rubies, teeth like pearls, locks of finest gold, etc. (Spenser, different from Olivia in *Twelfth Night,* isn't kidding.) Or metonymy describes her, and the part, better because more tractable, does duty for the whole. This lady pleases but gives pain, and her ice is hardened by the fire it kindles.

Spenser's sonnets, as they entertain unlikely truths, verge on life. But though "oxymoronic," i.e. joining discrete things, they rehearse familiar litanies, Petrarch's "long-deceasèd woes." (Sidney, whose phrase this is, means they've begun to smell.) Wit, provoking estimation, isn't part of Spenser's repertory, and while he does the blazon, the anti-blazon is beyond him. His mistress' eyes are like the sun. Declining to assess the formulaic stuff he works with, he keeps reality over there, "behind the shelf."

In sonnet LXXV, "One day I wrote her name upon the strand," he invites comparison to Shakespeare in his no. LX: "Like as the waves make toward the troubled shore." Distressful emotion in Shakespeare's sonnet quarrels with the up-front content, not a fault but a fruitful quarrel, like the Empedoclean clashing of atoms. The young man Shakespeare praises / puts in his place survives as the poetry preserves him. On the other hand, "nothing stands" or survives, a source of satisfaction to a poet with scores to settle. This quarrel between opposites, not smoothed over but channeled, sponsors the tie that binds. Not only in poetry, and Ben Jonson, who knows this, celebrates "All the gain, all the good, of the elements' strife." Spenser won't risk it. His poems aren't tense enough, and when you lean against them, don't lean back.

Structure is a problem, for him the besetting one. Adjusting the Italian sonnet, his "Spenserian" model drops a pair of couplets over the pattern of 4s. One, tucked in deftly at the midpoint, merges octet and sestet. What he doesn't want is a hiatus. Discrimination isn't much, so his sonnets, like

Milton's, look seamless. They have to stop somewhere, and a couplet, decreed, not engendered, puts period to his. More than once he finishes with a hexameter. Perhaps this longer line, superficially a QED, will persuade us.

Petrarch & Co. develop a figure in the octet, then elicit its "sense," not he. Exceptions there are, for example no. LXVII ("Like as a huntsman"), but I am feeling for the normative case. Not stinting on figures, Spenser reserves them for embellishment. If "vermicular" or quick with life, a Baconian coinage and meant in reproof, they might take him in unforeseen directions. Weak or feminine endings function as guidons, or he marshals his words in parallel columns as in the pattern: "Nor . . . Nor . . . Nor" (no. IX and elsewhere). But his "anaphoric" constructions, though bidding for cohesiveness, seem pasted to the poem like bills on a billboard, and the run of weak endings, not suggestive, only fatigues us. "Tired with all these," Shakespeare begins a catalogue of inequities (no. LXVI), going on to list them in paratactic sequence ("And . . . And . . . And"). This is like monotony, not monotonous, however, and Shakespeare's rhetoric creates the poem's soul.

"Correlative" verse augments Spenser's interlocking scheme, and sometimes, positing three terms or figures in his three quatrains, he summons them all at the end. In no. LVI ("Fair be ye sure, but cruel and unkind"), the couplet turns around his 1-2-3 order, revising it to read: 3-2-1. His terms are only counters; never mind how he deploys them. Like the art of the palindrome (verse that reads the same when read backwards or forwards), or the figure poetry newly revived in his time—poems shaped like lozenges, spheres, spires, and rhomboids—his fearful art aims to possess things. Prosecuting this aim, he evacuates them first. Virtuosity is the gain, truth to nature the loss, and his hierarchies don't make us sit up straighter. Decorum at its highest reach—exampled in Shakespeare's no. LXXIII, "That time of year," where the unexpected sequence is the right one—escapes him. No "yellow leaves, or none, or few" in Spenser.

The minor poems "dilate" their being in *The Faerie Queene,* his way of saying (in the last cantos) that things don't change but spread themselves in a new dimension. Spenser's most ambitious poem isn't remembered as he meant it to be, but survives as our greatest romance. Keats, mixing praise with blame, called it a "fair plumèd siren." It still has a following in the universities, one half Chipsian, the other Platonic. The man who first tutored me in its dim splendors brought a dog to class and it slept at his feet while he lectured. Though Jonson complained that Spenser "writ no language," this instructor differed warmly. "*Eftsoons,*" he used to say. "That's a good word and I hope we don't lose it."

Platonist Spenserians don't linger over words but rotate the poem along a horizontal axis, separating the husk from its kernel of sense. E.g. in the Cave of Mammon canto, what do Spenser's apples point to? Related to Eve's apple, they recall the pomegranate, associated with Proserpina, also the golden apples of the Hesperides. This fruit stood for astronomical knowledge. In *The Faerie Queene,* apples are symbolic or nothing. A battle of the books, perhaps still going on, used to controvert these matters. C. G. Osgood—he made the Spenser variorum—kept tabs on the ebb and flow. Vivacious even in his nineties, he set much store by appearance and wasn't dressed for the day without his Borsalino hat. This accommodating scholar let all the symbols in, but Rosemund Tuve, armored like Britomart in her Naugahyde coat, elected only a few. For most, then as now, the poem's superficial truth went unnoticed.

But Spenser's lotus-eaters' form, first the long exhaling, then the intake of breath, isn't a husk and makes a difference for the way we read him. His Garden of Proserpina, while replete with hidden meanings, is first of all a garden and asks attention for itself. This truth that lives in the surface, strictly speaking an overplus, distinguishes poetry from other forms of discourse. Letting down the poets' side, Spenser imitates his critics and doesn't always honor the distinction.

Doggerel verses, heading up his cantos, spell out the meaning, and his stories, "intendments," not "accidents," translate it. Doctrine by "ensample" coming home more efficiently than doctrine by rule, "an historical fiction" colors Spenser's precepts. This is the union of King Arthur and Gloriana, the Faerie Queene. But dealing with character needs a long spoon, so he promotes the indefinite article. His Corceca, an old blind woman, figures Blind Devotion; her daughter's lover—he rapes churches—is Kirkrapine. Faith, Hope, and Charity live in the House of Holiness, where the porter Humilita opens the door to Squire Reverence and Franklin Zeal. Spenser's one-to-one correspondences aim to rid the poem of ambiguity. On his reading, this touchstone of value is foul Error's cousin. Devitalizing content is how he slays it.

Both king and queen have two bodies, public and private, but neither is corporeal and twelve virtues symbolize each. Mustering a gallery of transparent cutouts, Spenser meant to show them all but the death he couldn't anticipate broke off his poem. Injunctions keep *The Faerie Queene* going, and this ultimate enjoining concludes it. Seizing on the number 12, an Ariadne's thread, he hopes it will bring him through the maze. In book 12, the real beginning, also the ending had he ever got there, Gloriana celebrates her yearly feast in 12 days. "Upon which 12 several [separate] days the occasions of the 12 several adventures happened, which, being undertaken by 12 several knights, are in these 12 books severally handled and discoursed." Below the poem's surface, a witches' cauldron is seething. But fetishistic Spenser, asserting authority at a remove, fortifies the surface with uncanny power. That way he keeps the lid on. Recurring rhymes and the cincture-like couplet help him do this.

Strong against dissolution, the Spenserian stanza fuses quatrains with rhyme, and telling of endings, denies them affectively. Ottava rima poems, Byron's, for instance, end each stanza with a whiplash, but Spenser's hexameter line uncoils slowly. J. R. Lowell found analogies in the natural world. Gaining and receding, wave follows wave, "the one sliding back in fluent music to be mingled with and carried forward by the next." This exorcizes the bugaboo, discontinuity.

In the Mutability cantos, the poem's content acts out its form. Fire becomes air and air becomes water, running into the earth. Then the back-and-forth begins again. True, all things hate steadfastness, and a funeral cortege shows them en route to the grave. Marching, they keep step, though. Spenser's fated protagonists seem frozen while moving, figures in a tapestry whose web is always weaving, never wound up. Contrary to Mutability, things changing remain the same, firmly stayed on eternity's pillars.

Mostly, this depends on the poet's ipse dixit. Though sonantal, it isn't heard but overheard, like a tune in the head. Quoting Lowell: "the meaning does not so often modulate the music as the music makes great part of the meaning." Young Shelley, not up to coping with big questions, Life, Truth, and so on, thought that all to the good. Hunting a form for his *Revolt of Islam,* he rejected blank verse—stamped by Shakespeare and Milton, it gave no shelter for mediocrity—but lit gratefully on Spenser's stanza. There, "a just and harmonious arrangement of the pauses" directed attention to "the brilliancy and magnificence of sound." Uncommon learning sets off *The Faerie Queene,* and Neoplatonic Spenser has always been a favorite with critics. But music, not philosophy, is the key to his success. I think we say that his poetry is more sensuous than thoughtful. Few do as much with the available techniques. Like Orpheus, he doesn't rationalize chaos but charms it.

Unluckily, though, antigravity's pull is too strong, and his symmetrical world shows signs of fraying. Though most of Spenser's monsters get their comeuppance, the Blatant Beast, breaking his chain, is still out there. This character from the dark world, "all set with yron teeth," has more to him than "good Sir Pelleas and Sir Lamoracke of yore," and Spenser, aggrandizing the villain at the heroes' expense, has one foot in the enemy's camp. A motto from *The Shepherd's Calendar,* "Vinto non vitto," intimates the problem. "Vanquished, not subdued," the Titans, old troublemakers, dispute their confinement in the underground. Contaminating *The Faerie Queene,* this altercation between artistic purpose and the poet's material jeopardizes his poem's integrity.

Warning signals are flying in the May eclogue of *The Shepherd's Calendar,* where a Catholic antihero delights in idle May games. Full of "jolly chere," they make his heart dance after the pipe, and this is why he is anti-. Spenser's Protestant surrogate pities all that "fondnesse," but affect goes one way, the moral line another. Gained with little "swinck," or toil, sport, not least when sexual, seems more fun than time "sparely spent." Much that matters in Spenser's poetry is morally indifferent, agreeable to easygoing moderns, not him. A fine phrase of Graham Hough's puts this ambiguous poet before us: "His heart was very much in his morality; but it was in other things too."

Not minding their teacher's ferrule, minor characters—a faithful mistress, lascivious wife, and January-like husband—claim "human interest." Some stories, taking on a life of their own, are felt as "accidents" without purpose but themselves. See, for instance, the expensive treatment of the Bower of Bliss or the bathing of the goddess Diana. Why waste "joyous hours in needless pain," seductive Phaedra wants to know. A good question, Spenser thinks, momentarily thrown off his stride. He really did "by Mulla's stream" fondle the maidens with the breasts of cream, and the sensuous face in his portrait might have warned us.

Though *The Faerie Queene* is different things, wherever you drop the lead it brings up the same sediment, and the Mutability cantos, patient of gratuities, mirror the rest of the work. December rides a goat in Spenser's seasonal procession, this zodiacal sign declaring the month of the year. But Spenser's shaggy-bearded goat aspires to autonomy. (Once it suckled "Dan Jove.") Mutability claims preeminence in a world where "short time" cuts down all with his sickle, and Nature, judging this claim, convenes her assizes on Arlo Hill, north of Kilcolman. "Who knows not Arlo Hill?" Anyway, he does, and pleasing himself, zeroes in on this familiar locale. Readers who like personality like him best when he puts himself forward.

Our first wholly competent modern master, he never disserves his craft. Signing up briefly in Sidney's "Areopagus"—reformist poets on Mars's Hill who meant to found English prosody on classical models—he consulted his ear and got out in a hurry. No poet before Milton with a better ear. Though Puritan leaning, he left homiletic verse to homilists like Sternhold and Hopkins. He knew about keeping accent and could weigh and poise syllables, rare among poets in the drab age before him. Also he knew how "duration" might leaven our native accentual verse. His best lines are haunted by the ghost of Latin quantity: "The woods shall to you answer and your echo ring."

But his fluency, a mixed virtue, irons out both peaks and troughs, and "at any moment of reading *The Faerie Queene,* we are ready to go on to the next line, the next stanza" (Paul Alpers). Coleridge, who meant to praise him, remarked in his poem "the true imaginative absence of all particular space and time." Some such comment holds for most of the work. In our parochial world of sharp contours, you are apt to bark your shins, and he prefers a world of ideas. Received opinion, unexamined for a long time, calls him a great poet, but not giving less than good, he seldom gives better. The kingdom of letters needs shaking out now and then, and the next palace revolution will scrutinize his place near the throne.

At least once, however, he showed his back above the element he lived in. The *Epithalamion* (1595) is this dolphin-like poem. My choice for his best poetry, it bristles with defenses, so looks like more of the same. Best to deal with the sameness first, a way of distinguishing difference.

Readers will recognize the anxious eye peeled for number. Joyce needed his electrician's code, Yeats his phases of the moon, and Spenser needs 24 stanzas. Like the Hours that "allot" the seasons, he assigns each its function, 16 going to the day's business, 7 to the night's. A "commiato," or final stanza, resembling the one in *Lycidas* but more than a frame, makes his odd number even. Signalizing the diurnal round isn't enough, and he hitches his fortunes to a greater wheel. In his latitude as the summer solstice began, just so many hours went to light and darkness. The feast of St. Barnabas, July 11, coincides with this turning point, a good day to get married. But he hedged it with placatory gestures. Though short lines—graces he "throws between"—break up his stanzas, long lines predominate, exactly 365. Who would work out their sum? Evidently the poet.

Then—a major surprise—having traced his magic circle against the dark powers, he takes them into the poem. Incomparably the finer of his two marriage hymns, this one isn't frozen but quick with interstitial business, poetry's distinctive overplus. Questions of how, when, and where ask attention, and he wants us to hear the birds' song, "the dewy leaves among." Its provenance seems important. He remembers how the Moon goddess, famous for virginity, took a lover, the Latmian shepherd. Times to come can't believe it but he had his way with her "for a fleece of wool."

"Interstitial" doesn't mean off the point, only between the lines, and what goes on between them is decisive for the health of the poem. Where Spenser in *The Faerie Queene* listens to the sirens' song, in the *Epithalamion* he enlarges the perimeters of the world he lives in, or raising his sights, sees how disjunctive things make a whole. "Endless matrimony" is the wished-for thing but death and fortune's wreck participate in it, and women's "smart," or labor, pairs with sexual delight. Hoping for a wedding "withouten breach or jar," he can't do better than rest "in hope of this." No guarantees in the *Epithalamion.*

Joy comes after dole and the other way round, Spenser's short lines giving priority to one, then the other. Against looming evil, a banning prayer asks the aid of good spirits: "Be also present here." This brief imprecation, acknowledging what it hopes to exclude, may or may not get a hearing. In the darkness where we end, a chastened poet strikes the prayerful note once more. His aggressively ordered syntax, like whistling in the dark, says that spooky "things that be not" really are.

Nymphs and their retainers populate his *canzone* but the real venue is parochial, harder to manage. This poet is up to the task. Fish, excelling all others, swim in his Awbeg River, but the nearby lake is rushy, so locals don't drop a line there. Are these travel tips germane? Spenser thinks so. His Irish scene, mixing profit and loss, is both itself and implicative, and he ventures the particulars that ratify his general truth. Greedy pike prey on the river trout in this sinister/idyllic place; wolves drag down the deer that "tower" on the mountains. A technical word from falconry, "tower" is what predators (like the falcon) ought to do. Spenser, willfully confusing the hunter and its prey, means to assert a different kind of community, however. It isn't petrified like number but all-consuming like life.

The "safety" of his joy promises an enclosed garden but it adjoins our everyday world, boisterous, sometimes vulgar. Sweat and drunken reveling roughen his wedding feast, possibly they grace it, and damsels and boys look on "in amaze," guessing at sexual fulfillment. But their tumult, confused and shrilling, is heard as "one voice," recalling the "sweet consent" of the birds' song. Spenser's ideal woman is well assorted too, that is, a bundle of contradictions. The word becomes flesh in the *Epithalamion* but not because his material beguiles him. Let us say he grows into it. Transformations enliven his poem, the poet's not less than the woman's.

A nonpareil, she puts his damsels in the shade—"merchants' daughters," coarser stuff altogether. But even daughters of the swan share in every "paddler's" heritage, and though known for "goodly modesty," she isn't sugar and spice. Humbling herself, she isn't paying respects to gloomy St. Paul and his man-is-the-head-of-the-woman. Spenser's bride, being human, is properly abased. That doesn't preclude the Saturnalian thing, and "roaring organs" lead on her "trembling steps."

This comprehensive story remembers "pains and sorrows past." But they have their lucky increment, and near the end of the poem, the bride, unexpectedly usurious, collects her debt. The ending isn't foreordained, however. Running a "mighty race," she wears our colors and hopes to win the "guerdon," a large posterity long possessing the earth. But this reward is contingent (though not on desert), and "wretched earthly clods," disabled by their mortality, can't earn it. The gods in their "haughty palaces" favor whom they will, and we wait "in dreadful darkness" on their pleasure.

Other poems of Spenser's stand outside time but the *Epithalamion* feels its pressures. Time to wake, for the Dawn has left Tithonus' bed, "time to sleep" when chaste Diana informs the womb with "timely seed." Spenser, his stiff neck in abeyance, doesn't look askance at the body's "timeless joys." Sexual pleasure has its term, however, and "it will soon be day." Supplicating "this one day"—words that drop like stones in water—he knows how the future is a hazard of untried fortunes, so ends concessively, giving "all the rest" away. Aurora and Diana, deities both and much good it does them, look forward to eternal love. But Tithonus grows old, Endymion dies, and Orpheus, who sang the praises of another bride, loses her forever.

As the poem winds down, "hasty accidents" interrupt it. Someone, jumping the gun, wouldn't wait on "due time," or perhaps the poet rushed his song to completion. Recompensing his bride for the ornaments that should have decked her, he offers a swap, this tribute, an "endless monument," in exchange "for short time." But "for" is ambiguous, telling also of limitation—"just for"—and an unwinking poet entertains its double sense. All we have is abridged, poetry lasting no longer than time does.

A finite journey, not open-ended as often in Spenser's poetry, holds his narrative together, and at its center the sun climbs the heavens. In July it enters Cancer, losing both heat and light. That doesn't happen soon enough for one impatient bridegroom. "How slowly do the hours their numbers spend." Rare when sober Spenser cracks a smile. His little joke is double-edged, though, more and less than ribald. The poem reaching its high point, running down begins. Consummation means declension and "behind his back" he sees the Crab.

Once burned, twice shy, and wary readers suppose that another kind of journey is what they are in for. This expected one, "ascending up" from carnal love, leads to "the inward beauty" of the spirit. Earlier stanzas and Spenser's typical performance intimate this sequence. But a shocking apparition, encountered "in the middle of things" (stanza 11), startles him and us. Though "long loose yellow locks" adorn the bride, analogy suggests her likeness to Medusa. The "mazeful head" of the Gorgon, crowned with serpents, turned men to stone. Athena, goddess of wisdom, rational but including the wisdom of the Furies, wore the Gorgon's head on her breastplate.

In the *Epithalamion,* Spenser makes it his aegis. All seems ordered, even moribund, beside the Awbeg River, but the poet's eye sees farther. Not "deeper," as when we look below the surface, but taking in the whole of things. Contemplating the Furies, no longer under lock and key, he doesn't grudge them their place in the dark, and if they break the poem's surface, this isn't felt as insurrection. "Lightfoot maids" and "wild wolves" vie for his attention, his marriage hymn accommodating both.

Mostly an exclusive poet who opts for either/or, time-honored Spenser sticks close to convention. Or let me put it that his poetry isn't energized enough by the ardors of convention. "Pricking on the plain," he registers to my ear as less urgent than mellifluous. Marriage put him in a whirl, though, and in the *Epithalamion* he stumbled on his own reality. A fortunate fall, it keeps him alive to the future.

Chapter 9

Milton's Two Poets

One is impersonal, honoring his postulates, while the other takes the wish for the deed and evades them. Milton's two poets oppose each other in *Lycidas,* an elegy for Edward King, lost at sea in 1637. A monody, the headnote calls it, clearer by design than old-fashioned polyphony, where different voices compete for attention. Most of the poem bears out this description but intransigent ego pokes up its head near the end, legislating truth like God on Mount Sinai. Readers who consult their ears will wince at this illegal ipse dixit. Coming to himself, Milton hears it too, and in a coda does his best to make amends.

Making amends, etc., sounds like lese majesty, unacceptable to Milton's critics, and the poem they read is seamless. Let us honor their piety and seek to buttress their case. Possibly *Lycidas* is what it is by intention, an imperious regisseur controlling the poem from word one. Staging a debate between opposing points of view, he lends an ear to both, handing down his verdict in the coda. On this reading his famous lyric is also dramatic, assimilating "frail thoughts" in a self-conscious design. So we have a portmanteau *Lycidas,* allowing two different constructions. "Tertium non datur," though, and a third construction isn't given.

Received Milton, a never-less-than-perfect poet, differs from real-life Milton the way despairing Catullus differs from "their Catullus" in Yeats's poem, "The Scholars." "Forgetful of their sins," perhaps innocent of sinning, the scholars cast this Milton in their own image. He wasn't carved in alabaster, however, but had sins on his head, some of them artistic. His schoolmaster God in *Paradise Lost* is at least a bore, possibly a tyrant, the poem showing this when its temperature drops, and he wasn't really sure that you could justify God's ways to men. Raising his voice in *Lycidas,* he shirks a poet's obligation to demonstrate the truth, saying something like Milton knows best.

Naturally, Professor X, famous Miltonist, denied this. Slowly twisting a paper clip in Widener Library's top floor seminar room—above the battle, like a monkish cell on Mount Athos—he spun his tale of the old mossback who stood for Right Reason. A sinister priest in Joyce's *Portrait* gives his likeness, one hand on the window blind, the other looping its cord. Plaiting a noose, he meant to hang us, anyway to string us along. Outside Harvard Yard the tumbrils were rolling—this was in the bad time just after the War, a time for *Areopagitica*—and why weren't we out in the streets? Milton, a contentious spirit, often wrongheaded (like me and friends), would have been out there. Not if you believed Professor X, though.

The impassioned poet, "molded out of faults," is very much to the front in *Lycidas*. Evidently a twice-told tale ("Yet once more"), it resumes the writing of memorial verse, already devoted by the youthful poet to functionaries at Cambridge, a marchioness, a pair of bishops, and a Fair Infant Dying of a Cough. Practice hasn't made him perfect and he glances at his own unreadiness "before the mellowing year," this phrase comprehending also the premature death of a friend. Though knowing how to "build," a powerful word, the friend welters at sea or visits the bottom of its monstrous world, and where is building or purpose in that? Expensive for Lycidas, his elegist too, this "dear" occasion risks self-pity and bathos.

For example, grief-stricken Nature. Putting on mourning, it blots out the world or seems to. "Shall no more be seen," Milton says. Entertaining a shepherd's complaint, "oaks and rills" prick up their ears, and hills, wearied as the day advances, are "stretched out" by the sun. Virgil's First Eclogue, remembered with a difference, says shadows fall from these hills, no heavenly agency needed, and it looks as if Milton is letting us in for the "pathetic fallacy." The "shepherd's trade" being slighted, he thinks about quitting it for sport with ladies of his acquaintance. Not a boastful name dropper, he calls them Amaryllis and Neaera.

Letters to a former schoolmate, Charles Diodati, written only months before he sat down to *Lycidas,* have him growing wings like Pegasus, steed of the Muses. What is he thinking of except "immortal fame"? (Sept. 23, 1637). Self-regard nags at him in the Latin epitaph for "Damon," lamenting Diodati's untimely death a year later. Though Damon is the addressee, Milton can't help asking, "What's to become of me?" Admirers will wish he hadn't.

Most of this, however, *Lycidas* retrieves. The first-person pronoun puts in an appearance but at the remove of art, and as his elegy gets started an impersonal poet has himself firmly in hand. Like Stevens in *Sunday Morning,* where trees evoke "serafin" and hills "choir" among themselves, Milton dresses the world in "our colors." But they aren't fast-dyed or the look of things misleads us. Willows and hazel copses, seeming to commiserate, go on fanning "joyous" leaves, and though "universal Nature" mourns the death of Orpheus, that is only a grace note. Ornamenting the tale, it leaves the outcome unchanged.

Fame still spurs the poet but is felt as "infirmity," perhaps a theme for laughter. Milton, wearing an ass's ears, the first of many transformations, remembers that foolish Midas who backs the wrong singer in a singing match between Apollo and Pan. Touching his "trembling ears," the god of poetry wags a reproving finger. Fame's "meed" (reward or tribute) may or may not await a yearning poet but, as to that, only Heaven knows. Alive, as we should say in Milton's "subconscious," the drowned man won't stay under and in another context rises before the mind's eye, rotting inwardly and swollen with wind. But an unwinking observer confronts this noisome apparition, if not equally, then stoically. The best "meed" he can offer is only a "melodious tear."

The sacred-plus-profane melody, another version of our two poets, offended Dr. Johnson, and he wondered at the reserve, mounting to coldness. Milton's "rural ditties," hardly spontaneous, had to call real grief in question. (No "effusion" of grief where there is leisure for fiction.) "Somewhat loudly sweep the string," the poet instructs his Muses, "allegro energico," decidedly "moderato," though. His music, whatever else it is, is "tempered."

Greatness isn't going off in *Lycidas,* however, and the death of the young hero mustn't shake lions into the streets. Besides, death is "destined" (not only his), so the words that salute it verge on brusqueness. If worth noting, they will have to be "lucky." Milton, like Ben Jonson in his rueful tribute to a boy actor, sees the propriety of composing in a minor key.

The furnishings that go with his elected form—Jove, the springs of Helicon, shepherds with their pipes and lyres—come down from antiquity, and at the end of a long tradition look a little shopworn. They still have their uses, however, submerging the personal voice while giving it a hearing, just sufficient. "I," not real-life Milton but a friend of Greek Bion's, lament my fellow-poet. Maybe a future poet will do the same for me. "And as he passes turn" is how Milton puts it. Diminished from five feet, his abbreviated line says how modest this gesture is.

Matter for biography—but we don't want too much of it—sexuality and its claims flare briefly in Milton's satyrs, dancing "with cloven heel." In old Damoetas, age, sitting on the sidelines, watches their ribald antics. We think about this survivor, long past it. Some suppose he remembers an elderly tutor at Cambridge. But convention when it works inhibits vulgar curiosity, also muting the poet's too importunate business. The pastoral mode does this in *Lycidas* until Milton struggles free of its constraints.

Giving grief a context, the wheel of the seasons constrains and frees him too. "Harsh and crude" at first, the berries he plucks will surely ripen one day—in "season due" is Milton's phrase—and his poem from the beginning intimates this better time. Laurel, myrtle, and ivy, ancient symbols for immortal life, signal it from a distance. Pursued by Apollo, "Daphne with her thighs in bark" becomes a laurel tree in the poem by Ezra Pound, and Milton's transformations are like that. E.g. his Greek Alpheus, transformed to a river, hopes to ravish the wood nymph, herself changed to an underground stream. (Young Milton in *Arcades* didn't mean to be comic when he told how the lustful god "by secret sluice, / Stole under seas to meet his Arethuse.") Coming up for air in *Lycidas,* the two mingle their waters near a famous poet's birthplace. Though Milton's "fountain Arethuse" is only a fountain, at least their waters don't run into the sand.

Melicertes, another "hapless youth," has this qualified luck. His body rescued by dolphins, he changes to the sea god Palaemon. But metamorphosis, the burden of these death-and-transfiguration stories, doesn't include the body's resurrection. Though old typology sees the dolphin as Christ, our hope of life everlasting, Milton leaves the connection unremarked. Melicertes as he was in life is certainly dead, and Daphne and Arethusa have put off the flesh once and for all.

Drowned Edward King, the poem's nominal subject, undergoes this sea change, mixing gain and loss. Struck down by fate, he becomes a local divinity, "the genius of the shore," or returns in the spring as the "sanguine flower" Hyacinth. Natural procession, like the diurnal round, insures his return, as when the evening star or the sun at close of day sinks but rises again the day after. Mythmakers and the natural world, supplying analogies, palliate his hard fate but don't offer to reverse it. The type or avatar survives and this is consolation. All the same, the many change and pass.

Benevolent lookers-on jib at this giving and taking. They want to make the rough places smooth. A tough-minded poet won't accommodate them, however. Justifying God's ways to man is a task he isn't up to, and troubling his poem's sleek surface he raises questions and hints at ellipses. A poet, not a philosopher, he does this in technical ways, stepping up and down the line from longer to shorter, or withholding the chiming sound the ear expects. Technique, said Pound, is the true test of sincerity, and let us add that expectation, frustrated or fulfilled, is another word for convention. Diverging from it is how this poet lets us know what he "means."

In his relatively short poem, ten lines don't rhyme, among them the line he begins with. Fair warning, said John Crowe Ransom, a critic alert to words. But most of the poem's critics, haring after ideas, have ignored it. Modern theorists, a priestly class ideational in its bias, deserve some of the blame for this. Pundits on the Right wonder if they aren't fomenting a conspiracy against the verities we used to live by. But the intellectualizing habit goes with academies, true from time out of mind, and new priest is old pedant writ large. Already Professor X, no conspirator or not that he knew, predicts his successors. All say, sotto voce, let us have theology, biography, philosophy, the cultural background, anything, but spare us the poem.

Omitting to notice the words on the page, this criticism that wants you to call it materialistic is oddly freestanding. Poets see the problem and Yeats prescribes for it. As to "the balloon of the mind," he tells us, bring it into its narrow shed, the constraints of form and language. Milton's innovations depend on these constraints. Without them, his poem bellies and drags in a vacuum.

Taking his own way, he invites comparison to his model text, the Italian canzone. This rhyming stanza, adapted from pastoral poets in the century before him, honors a pattern, the "hendecasyllabic" (eleven-syllable) line, adding to it or subtracting as the poet decides. Mostly, variation isn't haphazard, and having worked out his pattern he stays with it. Scholars find exceptions in the madrigal, *dramma per musica,* etc., but exceptions they are, proving the rule. Impatient of rule, Milton throws the pattern away.

Johnson, observing this, called the rhymes uncertain and the numbers unpleasing. (Though his strictures are less than just, he knew what to look at.) But Milton had an ear. I think his disjunctions mime the poem's failure to cope in last things, so compose a poetic statement. Questions in poetry, different from theology, function as well as answers for the life of the poem, for instance, in Frost's "Design" and Blake's "Tiger."

Some of Milton's questions are rhetorical, implying their answers. "Where were ye, nymphs," more pointedly, where was "the Muse herself" when Lycidas went down? Had they been on the spot, they couldn't have saved him, however. The deep is "remorseless," deaf to poets (old Bards and Druids), even to the prince of poets, "enchanting son" of the Muse. Good hope buoys us, then comes the Fury "and slits the thin spun life." Not long on reasons, Milton won't say more than this.

Destroying us, the Fury isn't malevolent, only "blind." The winds that

batter our vessel aren't "felon" winds, and if rationalizers, making sense of
the world, imagine some great predator marking us down ("rugged wings"
and "beaked promontory"), the poem doesn't support them. On the word
of Aeolus, god of the winds, "the air was calm" the day Lycidas died, no
wrath dwelling in Heaven. No guilty steersman runs his ship on the rocks.
In fact that is what happened, but Milton, aware of the prosaic truth, keeps
it to himself. For Lycidas and the rest of us, "sin" doesn't participate, only
the crack in the bowl. You can call this original sin, though the guilt, if guilt
there is, isn't ours but our first parents'.

Just here, Milton's poem reaches its high point, among the major suc-
cesses in English verse. After all, he has a reading of the evil that dogs us.

> It was that fatal and perfidious bark
> Built in the eclipse, and rigged with curses dark,
> That sunk so low that sacred head of thine.

In this account of inconsolable loss, matter-of-fact turns into metaphor (best
not to translate it, though), and building is posed against building.

Earlier figures for the "tragic flaw" or flaw in the grain include the
canker that blights the rose, the taint worm, or the frost that nips the
flowers. Rejoicing in their "gay wardrobe," like preening youth—but cen-
sure seems off the point—they bloom too early and it costs them. Or the
canker, not waiting for buds or buttons to open, galls these "infants of the
spring." Always in our morning time, contagion lies ready to strike us.
Laertes in *Hamlet* warns Ophelia about this.

Brooding on his friend's "hard mishap," Milton goes back to student
days at Cambridge, looking for clues. Old Camus, the life of learning, wears
a legend in his cap, regretting a favorite "pledge," and perhaps it resolves the
poet's questions. "Inwrought with figures dim," this sybilline inscription
isn't easily deciphered, however, and in the extramural world the mystery
deepens. Corrupted shepherds (clergy and poetasters suited up in one habit)
fumble their art but are "sped" or successful. As to St. Peter, keeper of the
keys of Heaven, all you can say is that his golden key opens while the other,
unlucky, "shuts amain."

Homeliness, rare in a poem that looks away from life to art, puts Mil-
ton's feckless pastors before us, scrambling for a better seat at the table. Their
"lean and flashy songs" contrast painfully with his, and kicking up a storm
like superb Ben Jonson in the Ode to Himself, he threatens his poem with
more reality than it can bear. How they elbow "the worthy bidden guest"!

But the pastoral is from old times a vehicle for social comment, and though this up-to-date aside is introduced "by occasion" of current events, it hitches on to things that outlive them. "Blind mouths," looking back to "blind fury," look ahead to the flowers that strew the dead man's bier. Their "eyes" suck moisture, another startling metonym that tells of impersonal feeding. The "grim wolf," a voracious feeder, belongs in this company. More real than allegorical (like the wolf at the door), it "daily devours," doing its kind. Identifications, as to Roman Church or Anglican episcopate, fill a badly needed gap. If you label this malignant presence, you tame it.

Reality, even an overplus, Milton's poem can cope with, but trouble comes when he drops into fiction. Wheeling on stage a two-handed engine—it stands ready to smite the wicked—a compunctious poet takes violent order with disorder. Commentators have a field day elucidating his famous or notorious lines—Reformation's ax, the sword of the Archangel, the houses of Parliament, and so on. Intervention isn't needed to tell us what Milton means, though. He means poetic justice.

But *Lycidas* recovers strongly. The bones of the dead man, indifferent to our "moist vows," drift aimlessly at sea, their whereabouts unknown. ("Fable," both pagan and Christian, assigns them a resting place.) Summoning vales and flowers to deck the "laureate hearse," a well-meaning Greek poet eases grief with expedients, and Milton knows it. *Et in Arcadia ego,* says this truth-telling witness. Death walks up and down in his idyllic interlude. The pansy, mottled with black, merges with the "swart" star that looks austerely on spring's fresh lap, and the early primrose, dying, recalls the early white thorn, nipped in the blossom. "Purple" is a word for Milton's vernal landscape, lustrous, sanguinary too.

In his catalogue of flowers, the violet stands by itself. Like Shelley's intense atom, it glows briefly, then is quenched. Milton keeps to the level of metaphor, though.

> Bring the rathe primrose that forsaken dies,
> The tufted crow-toe, and pale jessamine,
> The white pink, and the pansy freaked with jet,
> The glowing violet.

Metric makes meaning, and his incandescent trimeter gathers the entire poem in itself.

Hereabouts, *Lycidas,* a lark ascending from sullen earth, might finish. But Milton has something more on his mind, and art deferring to personality, the artist as sleight-of-hand man takes over. Speaking in his own voice, risky business if you mean to be personal, he sponsors another reading of our tragic fate. "Weep no more," the uncouth swain tells a chorus of shepherds, "Lycidas your sorrow" isn't dead. Surprising intelligence, it comes out of the blue, and though meant for comfort ought to deject us. Many are swept along by the rhetoric, however, or like the rhetorician settle for "false surmise." His swain is on to something others aren't aware of, and one scholar points out hopefully that "uncouth" can mean marvelous or strange.

Up to now obedient to the data of the poem and his marshaling of it, Milton hearkens to a new imperative, inner promptings. This loses sincerity, not the common or garden kind but the sense of achieved performance. Poets are most themselves when they go out of themselves, and absorbed in a role have less chance to indulge parti pris. The gain is in disinterestedness, civility too. Looking into his heart, Milton lowers himself to our level. An important question engages him, not what might be, following the given, but what I think should be, where thinking makes it so. Our first modern poet, this subjective reporter is like Wordsworth in "Tintern Abbey" or Arnold in "Dover Beach" where the logic of the poem takes a back seat to desire.

"Sunk though he be beneath the watery floor," Lycidas is only biding his time. Milton knows how to cancel his captivity, but stingy to a fault keeps tight on his instrumental knowledge. Criticism, abdicating its function, does its best to acquit him, however. Superior to "logical or sequential argument," he "simply tells us what he knows to be true." This illustrates the "service" poetry performs, incidentally suggesting why some call it the father of lies. (The critics are assembled by C. A. Patrides, *Milton's "Lycidas": The Tradition and the Poem,* rev. ed. 1983, and a few of them, mostly the "taxonomic" kind, help us get on with our reading.)

One, Holly Hanford, an old-fashioned scholar, does this in a learned essay on the poem's sources, Italian, Latin, and Greek. Charitable in his scholarship, never pedantic, meaning inert, he lets us see that the hood, not least the academic hood, doesn't always make a monk. A generation ago, this lively friend was Milton's best editor and meant to demonstrate where his favorite poet came from. A useful enterprise but fact bound, it wouldn't get a hearing in our new Platonic age.

> "Those Platonists are a curse," he said,
> "God's fire upon the wane,
> A diagram hung there instead,
> More women born than men."

Yeats's women are "the old women," a familiar term of reproach, and aren't gendered, only generic.

Milton's enjoinings sound dissonant to my ear but don't make the critics sit up straighter. One transfers his lines to the Archangel Michael, taking pity as we would wish; another locates the change from sad to happy in the white space between the words. The general run read the poem as an auto-da-fé, or act of faith, dramatizing "a leap from nature to revelation," or a sudden "infusion of grace." This seems plausible. But it isn't God who does the infusing or jumps us from one place to another.

You don't have to have religion to profit from *Lycidas,* and Milton's religion doesn't need special comment, only his conduct of it, as in the "nice conduct of a clouded cane." Nothing wrong with old morality plays, including their Christian view of the world, that a little avoirdupois wouldn't cure. Many pastoral poets highlight religious faith, others, mostly classical, leaving it alone. In the Epitaph for Damon, Milton, looking beyond our vale of tears, gives his dead friend the freedom of Heaven, sets a crown on his head, and more. The facts of the case, laid out by an "anthropomorphizing" poet, support this happy ending, and the laying out is what I mean by conduct. Christianity in *Lycidas,* entering from the wings at a critical moment, pulls the poet's chestnuts from the fire. If this doesn't raise eyebrows, it ought to.

Under cover of an image from the natural world—the sun "new-spangling" its beams—Milton's mortified man finds new life in the world over yonder. Donne in his "Nocturnal upon St. Lucy's Day," lamenting a dead lover and his own evacuated state, has a similar figure. The sun being spent, its "flasks," depleted powder flasks, send forth only squibs, "no constant rays." On the year's shortest day, this enervated sun enters Capricorn, though, forecasting its renewal. Meanwhile, the poet is as he was, still an "elixir" of nothing. "Nor will my sun renew," Donne tells us, pointing the contrast.

Milton, suppressing it, wrests the analogy or fortifies it with supernatural power. (He hopes we aren't looking when he does this.) Lycidas, like the sun, (1) flames again in the heavens, but (2) "through the dear might of him that walked the waves." In this resolution, the harsh forebodings of St. Peter, step by step the venal clergy, are "forgotten," critics think, and the poem, passing through troubled waters, "is piloted to its peace." Anyway, "piloted" gets it right.

The Heaven Lycidas goes to is "unexpressive," meaning that you can't apprehend it. We can thank the pronouncing voice, "thus he said."

Milton's "blest kingdoms meek," like his disembodied saints, don't make it, and though the saints are said to "move" us, we have to take this activity on faith. If they wipe away tears, that is by fiat. Unless by fiat, nothing gets done in *Lycidas*. It isn't kinetic, only a poem. Some, dissatisfied with poetry (but they would go to the stake rather than admit this), propose a threefold structure, yielding results you can point to. Thesis meeting antithesis begets a third state, "one of mystic certainty," and a "worthy Christian poet-priest" discovers that what seems defeat is actually immortal triumph. Christianity doesn't seem to me a term of reproach, so I wouldn't call this discovery Christian.

Extending protection to those who wander on the flood, Milton's efficient hero does what he does by ordinance ("shalt be good") and under his protection "all" prosper. We remember the drowned man, still out there, but never mind. The important lapse is from consistency. Death, up to now our portion, has become the evil we shun.

The coda, an ottava rima stanza cinched by its required couplet, is for damage control. "Thus sang the uncouth swain," says a disapproving poet, moving his chair to a distance. Milton, surprising us—but his poem is full of surprises—reinvigorates the natural round, displaced a few lines back by leger-demain. Morning, announced by the grayfly, enters as the poem begins, going out at the end on gray sandals. An involuntary sequence like the ebb and flow of tides, it gives the hopeful swain his quietus.

The swain's song is "Doric," right for pastoral, also in the triad of architectural orders much the simplest. This singer is a novice, "eager" and "rude" (not illmannered but unpracticed), and "uncouth," describing him, means what we think it means. Just at present he isn't up to his part, and in the couplet Milton dismisses him. Maybe a poet with his hands on the ropes meant to do that all along. But his last two lines are only formally conclusive and suggest a different poet, still at odds with his material. Maybe at the end, breaking off the quarrel, he settles for exigent form. For better or worse, the sense of an imperfect or elliptical ending is among the poem's chief distinctions.

Chapter 10

Rationalism and the Discursive Style

Poetry and prose of high quality are written in the eighteenth century but their range is remarkably narrow. I attribute the narrowness to the generalizing psychology of the Age of Reason. The rationalist prefers a synoptic view of things to the close scrutiny of particulars. One result of his preference is that intellectual poetry, which aims at convincing the understanding, is unsatisfactory. This is true across the spectrum of kinds, whether philosophic, political, or encomiastic.

Writers out to gain your intellectual agreement (not the same as beating you down) will want to analyze like cases. But the rationalist, if he cultivates analogy, is mostly satisfied to affirm or negate. He isn't much given to pursuing ramifications, and in making general statements, doesn't ascend from the particulars they ought to depend on. Let me support this by going first to the prose, some of it still familiar today. At its best and worst, it mirrors the poetry, and seeking to reason with you, shows the same loss in close-up seeing.

For instance, Pope's contemporary George Lillo. Famous in his day but overtaken by time, he wrote *The London Merchant* (1731), the most popular tragedy of the first half of the eighteenth century. In Lillo's play, mind reduces to stereotypes:

> A dismal gloom obscures the face of day; either the sun has slipped behind a cloud, or journeys down the west of heaven with more than common speed to avoid the sight of what I'm doomed to act. Since I set forth on this accursed design, where'er I tread, methinks the solid earth trembles beneath my feet. Yonder limpid stream, whose hoary fall has made a natural cascade, as I passed by, in doleful accents seemed to murmur, "Murder." (3.3)

Nobody mistakes Lillo for Johnson, Burke, and Gibbon, among writers of nonfiction prose the best the eighteenth century offers. But the style they share has consequences for the century's verse forms. Like the prose of *The*

London Merchant, it can't grapple intellectually with the nature of man or man's business. Gibbon, mournful, fleering, and stately, asks a lot of questions but most are rhetorical. His truth is imposed, depending on balance and complementarity, and stereotypes that pretend to clarify hang a curtain between us and the world they describe. We hear of Cicero who, "after saving his country from the designs of Catiline, enabled her to contend with Athens for the palm of eloquence." But "she" isn't visibly contending, and the "palm" is a frigid notation. Following the fortunes of the Second Rome (near the end of the *Decline and Fall*), Mehmet II gives thanks for the conquest of Constantinople:

> From St. Sophia he proceeded to the august but desolate mansion of a hundred successors of the great Constantine, but which in a few hours had been stripped of the pomp of royalty. A melancholy reflection on the vicissitudes of human greatness forced itself on his mind, and he repeated an elegant distich of Persian poetry: "The spider has woven his net in the imperial palace, and the owl hath sung his watch-song on the towers of Afrasiab."

Both splendid and static, this set piece is like early opera.

The Augustans in top form are majestic naysayers and skeptics. Burke corroborates this description, comparing his contemporaries with a more philosophic (meaning more foolish) people. Unlike the French, "We know that *we* have made no discoveries, and we think that no discoveries are to be made, in morality; nor many in the great principles of government, nor in the ideas of liberty, which were understood long before we were born, altogether as well as they will be after the grave has heaped its mould upon our presumption, and the silent tomb shall have imposed its law on our pert loquacity." Aggressively humble, men like him identify discussion and investigation with loquacity, and are unexcelled in announcing that history is "little more than the register of the crimes, follies, and misfortunes of mankind." The Revolution in France consists of the miseries brought on the world by "pride, ambition, avarice, revenge, lust, sedition, hypocrisy, ungoverned zeal," other abstractions.

Burke's style, though magnificent, is less in debt to cerebration than vigorous assertion. In the eighteenth century, cerebration becomes a superior kind of amusement. Hume, the most audacious thinker among the Augustans, treats intellectual speculation as a game. Arriving at his approximation of truth, he doesn't discover but declares it. Some are outraged by what he tells them, needlessly, though. The opinions of philosophy "seldom go so far as to interrupt the course of our natural propensities," and if mistaken aren't dangerous, "only ridiculous" (*Treatise of Human Nature,* 1739). This is like Oscar Wilde: "The intellect is not a serious thing, and never has been. It is an instrument on which one plays, that is all."

Hobbled by human nature, human understanding is a contradiction in terms. If you follow it up to its first principles, you find that it leads us "into such sentiments as seem to turn into ridicule all our past pains and industry, and to discourage us from further inquiries." This dumbfounder of the orthodox made a lot of enemies. Once at Princeton University where Scots are thick on the ground, I knew a David Hume in the Maintenance Department. "Same name as the famous philosopher," I told him. "That damned atheist," he said. One shouldn't condescend to a Scot.

But the nonbeliever resembles the orthodox in appealing to faith against reason. Though common wisdom supposes that motion in one body is the cause of motion in another, consideration reveals "only that the one body approaches the other"—then, "without any sensible interval," the billiard balls click. In vain, says Hume, "to rack ourselves with further thought and reflection upon this subject." His happiness is to demonstrate "that there is nothing in any object, considered in itself, which can afford us a reason for drawing a conclusion beyond it." Like Gibbon, he realizes himself as he demolishes, and like Dr. Johnson doesn't bolster his argument but raises his voice. "Sir," says Johnson, "we *know* our will is free, and there's an end on't!"

Hume abandons the direction his conclusions tend to, and in place of reason exalts an act of will. "Reason is, and ought only to be, the slave of the passions, and can never pretend to any other office than to serve and obey them." Like his skeptical predecessors in the seventeenth century and most of his contemporaries in the eighteenth, he settles for an unsupported ipse dixit. He is good at knocking down badly built structures, not so good at building better ones in which the mind can live as respectably as the heart. How he disappoints us in his *History of England* (1761)! Having got through the Middle Ages (barbarous centuries that go by in a hurry), he or rather "we have at last reached the dawn of civility and science, and have the prospect, both of greater certainty in our historical narrations, and of being able to present to the reader a spectacle more worthy of his attention." This worthier spectacle, though taking, fails of intellectual endorsement.

It couldn't well succeed. The Augustans aren't notable for the sort of affirming that rises from particular cases. Their affirmations are no more involved with intellect than the memorable pieties of Isaac Watts. In discursive prose, their best is *Rasselas,* not cogent but declarative and apothegmatic.

This is characteristic. Burke, in a moving passage, remembers Marie Antoinette, "glittering like the morning-star, full of life, and splendor, and joy." He had "thought ten thousand swords must have leaped from their scabbards to avenge even a look that threatened her with insult."

> But the age of chivalry is gone. That of sophisters, economists, and calculators, has succeeded; and the glory of Europe is extinguished forever. Never, never more shall we behold that generous loyalty to rank and sex, that proud submission, that dignified obedience, that subordination of the heart, which kept alive, even in servitude itself, the spirit of an exalted freedom. The unbought grace of life, the cheap defence of nations, the nurse of manly sentiment and heroic enterprise, is gone! It is gone, that sensibility of principle, that chastity of honor, which felt a stain like a wound, which inspired courage whilst it mitigated ferocity, which ennobled whatever it touched, and under which vice itself lost half its evil, by losing all its grossness.

Whether or not Burke's periods command agreement intellectually, they win you in the deep heart's core.

Johnson, a man you don't reason with, dramatizes the virtues and infers the limitation of this enunciatory style, as when he observes, of the American colonists: "Sir, they are a race of convicts, and ought to be thankful for any thing we allow them short of hanging"; or, of the topography of Scotland, that there is not a tree between Edinburgh and the English border older than himself, a statement more striking than either true or false. But questions of truth and falsity aren't at issue. The wit is so trenchant, the rhetoric so overmastering, as to put rational argument out of court. If you reply, you have to reply in kind. But this is to abdicate (however cheerfully) the possibility of intellectual discourse.

The best poetry of Dryden and Pope bears out the proposition. Its greatness is not only independent of intellectual greatness but rests on the willing suspension of intellect. The repudiating of the investigatory method isn't altogether unlucky, and if some doors are closed, others are opened. If blank verse and kindred forms whose tendency is discursive are weakened, other kinds of verse whose appeal is primarily to emotion become more vital. E.g. the successful cultivating of tetrameters by Prior and Swift, and the couplet by Dryden and Pope. In the negative as in the positive case, the anti-intellectuality of Augustanism governs.

Pope is the heir to several generations of poets who have grown more and more impatient of analysis as a means of ascertaining truth. The bringing to perfection of the heroic couplet is a product of that impatience. The sustained figure, whose job is to explore, is given away. Extreme compression becomes possible, a single value word doing duty for an extensive similitude. The gain is in immediate impact, also in suavity, the loss in real sophistication and ultimate conviction.

Romantic poets, blessed or vexed with an analytic temperament (not all of them, some of them), don't handle the couplet idiomatically. But the poet who acquiesces in the limitations of the form can write more forcibly than ever before. Only what he writes won't bear such close inspection. He has suppressed the proof, everything antecedent to his conclusion. Where Pope, managing a powerful antithesis, praises the virgin,

> How happy is the blameless Vestal's lot!
> The world forgetting, by the world forgot,
>
> *(Eloisa to Abelard)*

another poet, manipulating the value words, might write as powerfully in her dispraise:

> How hapless is the sullied Vestal's lot!
> The world forgetting, by the world forgot.

Sheffield, celebrating the triumph of rationalism, an easy triumph by which

> plain Reason's Light
> Put such fantastick Forms to shameful Flight,
> ("On Mr. Hobbs, and His Writings")

is neither more nor less persuasive than Rochester, who scorns the reason:

> 'Tis this exalted Pow'r, whose Business lies
> In Nonsense and Impossibilities—
>
> *(A Satyr against Mankind)*

or Dryden, who promotes the papacy instead of reason:

> Then granting that unerring guide we want,
> That such there is you stand obliged to grant.
> *(The Hind and the Panther,* pt. 2)

But the reader who takes counsel is obliged to grant nothing. Metric and rhetoric make the conclusion.

One way for the poet to insure that his conclusion won't be disputed because uttered ex cathedra is to urge that the truth is easily come by. If all of us possess the seeds of judgment in our minds, we don't need to go outside ourselves but only to look within. That is the Augustan resolution. Already the vanity of philosophizing has been suggested by Milton's philosopher demons, who found no end in wandering mazes lost. We don't need philosophizing, if only they knew it. Go into the self, says Herbert of Cherbury. Though a question-moving poet, he applies to the heart, after that to the mind, when "universal and eternal truths" are wanted (*De Veritate,* 1624). The eighteenth century picks up on his priorities.

Now the contempt for cerebration, proclaimed inferentially in the poetry of Milton but building long before, becomes an article of faith. "What is the use of discussing a man's abstract right to food or medicine?" It is the discussing Burke won't tolerate. "We know," he says, "and what is better, we feel inwardly, that religion is the basis of civil society, and the source of all good and of all comfort." But the "professor of metaphysics" who likes to discuss is not only useless but vicious. His theories, "in proportion as they are metaphysically true . . . are morally and politically false. The rights of men are in a sort of middle, incapable of definition, but not impossible to be discerned."

I vote yes to this, anyway a partial yes, but what follows is certainly doubtful. Speculation (as in "playing the game of") involves mankind in chaos. "Massacre, torture, hanging!" are the result of the Frenchman's loquacity. "These are your rights of men! These are the fruits of metaphysic declarations . . . !" A thousand years of intellectual activity dies at a word.

Dryden, like Burke, sees no point in haggling over definitions. He is astonished that anyone could misapply the Church's canons, finding "their sense so obvious, and their words so plain" (*Hind and the Panther,* II). He doesn't concede that there are difficult questions and is unwilling to labor at answers. In his poetry, rhetoric stands for argument:

> Shall she command who has herself rebell'd?
> Is Antichrist by Antichrist expell'd?
>
> (II)

The poetry, aphoristic by intention (the better to beguile you with), bears the look of caviling and close debate. Actually, it is mostly courteous and of the surface, no probing, as in Shakespeare or Donne. Genuine argument, always empirical and ad hoc, is grudged. In its place, as a means of finding out what we want to know, Dryden relies on tradition. But if truth isn't slippery, tradition looks superfluous. You waste time and effort, going to your father or bishop. Better and less circuitous to look in your heart. That is what the eighteenth century has taken to doing, well before it turns into the nineteenth. In this manner Augustanism begets the Romantic Age, and Dryden's and Pope's chariness of self-reliance begets the exalting of self-reliance in Emerson, Carlyle, and D.H. Lawrence.

I am being synoptic, like the eighteenth century on its careless side, and had better slow down: Emerson, at least, is a great man, and like Lawrence, sometimes a great writer. But none of these writers sees any necessity for what the last of them called "the fribbling intervention of mind." Going wrong, they take a lead from predecessors like Addison, who thinks "Musick, Architecture, and Painting, as well as Poetry, and Oratory, are to deduce their Laws and Rules from the general Sense and Taste of Mankind" (*Spectator,* no. 29). Perhaps the framing of the laws and rules needs a preciseness of mind above the general sense and taste? But the question doesn't arise. Subtlety and exility, snares that don't catch the truth, catch the subtle man, who falls like a woodcock in his own "springe." In their concern with "nicety of distinction," the Metaphysicals seem ignorant of the fact that "great things cannot have escaped former observation" (*Life of Cowley*). Johnson's dictum isn't true but very close to truth, as when we hear that there is nothing new beneath the sun. The nicety that can pin down the difference seems worth having.

But the new kind of poet doesn't spend himself in nice distinctions. He sees that people may differ on minor issues, but fails to see how they could differ about right or wrong. Right is right, he says, with Stephen Undershaft in the play, "Right is right; and wrong is wrong; and if a man cannot distinguish them properly, he is either a fool or a rascal." The poet himself is neither, and yet he cannot distinguish. He would say complacently that he can't split hairs. I suppose his contempt to have begot his incapacity.

Abraham Cowley, a characteristic figure in the middle years of the seventeenth century, exhibits that contempt, and pays for it in his inferior verse. Ruminating "On the Death of Mr. Crashaw," he decides that religious differences are unimportant. Here, the expected word is "casuistry." That Crashaw was a Catholic signifies nothing, unless to the dead poet:

> For even in error sure no danger is
> When joined with so much piety as his.

Cowley doesn't infer a relation between pious behavior and a faith that rests on lucid thinking.

> His faith perhaps in some nice tenets might
> Be wrong; his life, I'm sure, was in the right.

"Nice tenets" is good: men used to die rather than blur them. But now scrupulosity is taken for quibbling. Disputing is the sterile preoccupation of "subtle schoolmen." The jibing phrase is Pope's, who sees no use in splitting hairs.

> For forms of Government let fools contest . . .
> For Modes of Faith let graceless zealots fight.
> <div align="right">(<i>An Essay on Man,</i> 11.303, 305)</div>

Pope doesn't want to know how many angels can dance on the head of a pin. For that reason his poetry is intellectually shallow. Dryden doesn't want to know either, and with similar results.

> For priests of all religions are the same:
> Of whatsoe'er descent their godhead be,
> Stock, stone, or other homely pedigree.
> <div align="right">(<i>Absalom and Achitophel,</i> 11.99–101)</div>

Though Pope professed Catholicism and Dryden did sometimes, this super-subtle religion died at the Council of Trent.

To Swift, the difference between High Church and Low, between Catholic and Protestant—in terms of *Gulliver's Travels,* between Trameck-san and Slamecksan, Big-Endian and Little-Endian—is the difference between high and low heels. It doesn't matter how you break your egg—or worship, or apprehend the Deity, or interpret the Constitution. The super-subtle intelligence busies itself with strawmen. Of course the Lilliputians disown it. "In choosing persons for all employments, they have more regard to good morals than to great abilities." They do not need great abilities. "We preserve the whole of our feelings still native and entire, unsophisticated by pedantry and infidelity," says Burke. Like Stephen Undershaft, age twenty-four, English may have no capacity for business, no knowledge of law, no sympathy with art, no pretension to philosophy; but they can tell you the difference between right and wrong. "They suppose truth, justice, temperance, and the like"—how cavalier, that final phrase!—"to be in every man's power." Swift supposes this. So does Fielding, jeering at the intellectual pretensions of Squire Western's sister, in *Tom Jones.* His sort of reasonable man is unwilling to carry reason to extremes.

The synthesizers, straining to glimpse the Pisgah-sight, don't attend much to details in the middle distance, or don't much exercise the reason as they move from the definite article to the indefinite. But such exercise is the sinews of poetry as well as political freedom. Omit to practice it, and the reason grows flabby; at last it is held in contempt. Because Dryden has little faith in ratiocination, he thinks "Fallacies in Universals live" (*Hind and the Panther,* II). But whoever visits contempt on the reason must exalt an alternative: instinct, or political or religious dictation. Dryden isn't hostile to conclusions that come from an oracular and arbitrary source: "The church alone can certainly explain" (II). Paradoxically, the issue of rationalism is a weakening of man's faith in reason.

Augustan poetry illustrates the paradox. Dr. Johnson tells us in the *Life of Cowley* that "Sublimity is produced by aggregation, and littleness by dispersion. Great thoughts are always general, and consist in positions not limited by exceptions, and in descriptions not descending to minuteness." Rationalism sponsors this aversion to minuteness, creating a poetry in which emotion has free play but not reason. In Pope the discursive intelligence pretty much ceases to function. It can't sustain itself on phantoms, on naked groves and rugged rocks and tinkling rills, on scornful virgins and ardent lovers and tyrants fierce.

Not that man ceases to believe he can know. Only now the truth isn't achieved either deductively or inductively. Now the making of grandiose systems is out of bounds as much as the hocus-pocus of the mean empiric, busy with his stinks and cracked retorts. Now truth is divined: the poetry and philosophy of the Augustans. But its nature is just as impalpable, subjective, and imprecise as the intuited truths of the mystic.

Bacon, who sets the general truth above the particular, begins the denigrating of words as slippery counters. Locke follows in the *Essay on Human Understanding* (1690), warning us not to bend our thoughts "more on words than things" (3.2.7). He wants us to fly past the nets of language, but not because they beget system making. On the contrary, they spoil it. Commencing a series of *Spectator* papers on *Paradise Lost,* Addison insists that "There is nothing in nature more irksome than general discourses, especially when they turn chiefly upon words" (no. 267, 1712). This running down to anti-intellectualism is inherent in the separating of intellect from its nutriment, the fascination with particular things.

God loves from Whole to Parts: but human soul
Must Rise from Individual to the Whole—

quoting Pope, a great poet who speaks out of both sides of his mouth.

Swift in *Gulliver,* mocking the scientific projectors, meaning, to him, the empirics ("A Voyage to Laputa," chap. 5), is very much of the party and in the original spirit of Bacon, the father of science. Mocking the Scholastics, Bacon merges them with the empirics. But Swift makes fun impartially not only of "Aristotle" but "Plato." He derides the wordmongers, also those who want to get rid of words. The empiric is a fool, but so is the synthesizer. "The learning of this people," he writes, in "A Voyage to Brobdingnag" (chap. 7)—and what he writes is meant, of course, to be inverted—

> The learning of this people is very defective, consisting only in morality, history, poetry, and mathematics, wherein they must be allowed to excel. But the last of these is wholly applied to what may be useful to life, to the improvement of agriculture, and all mechanical arts; so that among us it would be little esteemed. And as to ideas, entities, abstractions, and transcendentals, I could never drive the least conception into their heads.

Baconianism, which begins with the idolatrous worship of reason, turns from reason, in the eighteenth century, as from a heathenish god. Putting away the husk, the particular, in favor of the kernel, the general truth, is injurious by-and-by of the chance for grasping the general truth.

What is left is the original inspiration, Swift's criterion of "what may be useful to life." But finding out the useful is no longer the job of the experimenter or metaphysician. The laws of the Brobdingnagians "are expressed in the most plain and simple terms, wherein those people are not mercurial enough to discover above one interpretation." Swift and the others are imagining how things were with us before the Fall.

Common sense, everybody's possession, will always arrive at the one right interpretation. To read life's riddle, aloof from "ideas, entities, abstractions, and transcendentals," we don't need priest or adept. Disqualifying the hands-on man and the metaphysician as detectors of truth, Swift supplants them with the man of intuitive wisdom. As the eighteenth century yields to the nineteenth, the old objections to the poet, in any case to a kind of poet, fall away. He is able to intuit, to do the vatical thing, as well as anyone. Increasingly, that is what he does do, neither deduces nor investigates but divines and proclaims.

Chapter 11

What Is Augustan Poetry?

"Augustan" is from Augustus Caesar, who gave Rome peace after the Civil Wars and began a Golden Age in the arts. English in 1660 when the King came back thought they saw a likeness, so called themselves Augustans too. This label is useful, linking similar poets who lived at different times. Dryden in the seventeenth century and Pope in the eighteenth are both Augustan.

People who don't like Augustan poetry say it is too intellectual, while people who like it praise its mental toughness. These positions are of course the same, discriminated only by an estimate of value. How you estimate what I call the great poetry of Pope and the lesser but considerable poetry of Dryden and Dr. Johnson is personal to you. It seems on the point to say, however, that its successes are remote from intellectual conviction. Augustan poetry differs in kind from Romantic and Metaphysical poetry. Its means are affective and declarative, not rational but rhetorical and not persuasive but coercive. Augustan poetry is primarily the poetry of emotion.

Arnold called Augustan poets reasonable to a fault ("classics of our prose"), but actually they are retreating pell-mell from the deifying of reason in the seventeenth century. Almost any page of Dryden, Swift, Pope, or Johnson will confirm this. Writers who don't court the reason, they take another road, faith, tradition, or dogmatic assertion. Nature abhors a vacuum and that is how they fill it. Little men, myopic or incomprehending, deride what they lack in themselves. Great men—the great Augustans—have something in them that their wisdoms ought to fear. It isn't to be confused with timidity but resembles the fear Hamlet has of himself when he grapples with Laertes over the grave. Fearing pride of intellect or powerfully persuaded of their sinful earth, the Augustans make a poetry of question begging. They are too proud in their humility to make poetry of answers to a question posed.

You see this fear in Dryden, mutable in his ideas but always disinclined to use the intellect to establish conviction. His poetry, ostensibly argumentative, is more supple than meticulous. The kind of assent it wins depends on the apothegm, not on cogency but comeliness, where the latter is involved with the aggressive use of rhyme:

> Because *Philosophers* may disagree,
> If sight b'emission or reception be,
> Shall it be thence infer'd I do not see?

There is plenty of emotion in this poetry, more than the poet can handle, so he screws it down in an unyielding matrix, generally the couplet. The rigorous form, controlling excessive feeling, helps him hold himself together. Efficient in other ways, this constraint creates great poetry or it allows the chance. Powerful emotion is forced through a narrow channel, and the narrowness of the channel augments the force.

Because of the plenitude of emotion in himself, the Augustan poet repudiates idiosyncrasy (what I "think"). Giving reason low marks, he ought to write a sans-cullottish kind of poetry, but Augustan poetry is aggressively kempt, and typical poems of the period have the look of close-order drill. Poems that aren't typical, like some of Dryden's, help define the convention by their departure from it. In his entertainments like *The Conquest of Granada,* Dryden hides his artful tracks by varying line length from three feet to five to four, etc. Musicians, exploiting the full range of the voice, call this back-and-forth the diapason. In poetry, it means diminishing then augmenting the line. Either way, the psychology seems anti-Augustan.

> Beneath a Myrtle shade
> Which Love for none but happy Lovers made . . .
> [Came] *Phillis* the object of my waking thought;
> Undress'd she came my flames to meet—

and so on.

Dryden, as in this song from *The Conquest of Granada,* is prone, unlike Pope, to freewheeling. At the beginning of the Augustan period, he looks forward but backward too. The more characteristic fun is to run out the tether while remaining faithful to it, and Pope generally sticks to a single verse line. Untethered freedom is a luxury most of these poets don't think they can afford. Often their stinginess works out for the best, as when ill crossing good converts to good.

Matthew Prior as a ballad maker, making his free and easy octosyllab-
ics, presents the Augustan out-at-doors. This mode isn't freedom—my
judgment of Prior says that the word is license. Unbuttoned, the Augustans
aren't easy but disheveled. But Prior's splendidly gravid couplets in the long
poem *Solomon and the Vanity of the World* suggest that as the poet takes him-
self in hand he goes out of himself, so enlarges his stature:

> Dye and be lost, corrupt and be forgot;
> While still another, and another Race
> Shall now supply, and now give up the Place.
> From Earth all came, to Earth must all return;
> Frail as the Cord, and brittle as the Urn.

Structure in this poem is insistently parallel. Reticulation isn't by thought
running free, so finding a pattern, rather by the saying over of words, an
imposed or incantatory pattern. The rhyme, endlessly recurring, beats like
waves against the pebbled shore, defining waves and shore and composing
both. Wallace Stevens gives the sense of poetry like this. Augustan only in
his dandyism, he doesn't know which to prefer, the beauty of inflections or
the beauty of innuendoes, the blackbird whistling or just after. Augustan
poets prefer the beauty of inflections. They write rhetorical poetry.

All poetry is rhetorical to a degree, i.e. acknowledging an arbitrary pat-
tern, and that is why intellectuals are apt to dislike it. Augustan poetry raises
rhetoric to the *n*th power. The figure the poem makes sponsors generalized
maledictions—Swift on our sorry state—or the unsupported *ipse dixit*—
Pope or Dryden handing down the law. You don't see where they come
from, not with your mind's eye, nor why you ought to accept them. You
do, though, if you have an iota of feeling.

Swift, downgrading the analytical method, wants to know (in his rhap-
sody "On Poetry")

> What reason can there be assign'd
> For this Perverseness in the Mind?

The reason he assigns is reason itself, but rhetoric begets and enforces his
conclusion:

> A Dog by Instinct turns aside,
> Who sees the Ditch too deep and wide,

But Man we find the only Creature,
Who, led by Folly, fights with Nature;
Who, when she loudly cries, Forbear,
With Obstinacy fixes there;
And, where his Genius least inclines,
Absurdly bends his whole Designs.

The poem goes on like this, "magically," taking its unity and credibility from verbal and syntactic repetition. Rhetoric doing duty for progression by thought, we believe only as far as the passage makes a formal coherence.

In Augustan poetry when it works, this leaning on rhetoric is all to the good. The rhetorical mode heightens whatever it touches, a gain when you want all your cards on the table, unlucky, though, when you want to conceal them. Pope in *Eloisa to Abelard* is unlucky.

For her th' unfading rose of Eden blooms,
And wings of Seraphs shed divine perfumes;
For her the Spouse prepares the bridal ring,
For her white virgins Hymeneals sing.

In this hypothetically sincere poem, the rhetorical pattern and the artificial diction are at odds with the feeling intended. To a state of less-than-usual emotion, Pope supplies more than the usual order. He gives us the heightening that belongs to art when really what we want, as near as may be, is silence.

Pope's failure is, however, Dr. Johnson's success. In Johnson's ironical "Short Song of Congratulations," antitheses and complements make a formal parade to which the unqualified value words muster:

Long-expected one and twenty
Ling'ring year at last is flown,
Pomp and Pleasure, Pride and Plenty,
Great Sir John, are all your own.
Loosen'd from the Minor's tether,
Free to mortgage or to sell,
Wild as wind, and light as feather,
Bid the slaves of thrift farewell.

Nothing impedes the march of the syntax, the poet having got rid of flesh and blood. If Johnson's hero has a surname, he keeps it to himself. Knowing where he comes from might mitigate the force of our contempt, as when Shakespeare's character says: "This gentleman had a most noble father." Particulars are slighted in favor of personified abstractions. Pride (or Pomp or Pleasure) moralizes, so displaces the one prideful man whose like we won't see again. We don't want to think about his person or peculiar situation. Johnson makes sure we don't have to.

Everyone agrees that the Augustans excel at satire. But Pope and Dryden don't practice the intentional kind. Pope (in a dialogue added to the Satires) thinks his ridicule is cleansing, meant "To rouse the Watchmen of the public Weal," etc., and most of his critics fall in with this view. But stand back from the superbly malignant portrait of Sporus and you see that reformation is no part of his design:

> Fop at the toilet, flatt'rer at the board,
> Now trips a Lady, and now struts a Lord . . .
> Beauty that shocks you, parts that none will trust,
> Wit that can creep, and pride that licks the dust.

Sporus execrated is a thing of beauty. The world of Pope's imagining, filled with creatures like this, isn't made for our scandal (though alive with scandalous business) but for our approbation.

Pope doesn't often involve himself with his victims, so the sharp edge of his animosity is rarely furred. Dryden's best satire, "Absalom and Achitophel," is much less fastidious and resembles the hybrid kind you associate with older poets like Chaucer or later poets like Yeats. (It's poor Paudeen who keeps the till.) In Dryden's version of Achitophel, the eye that looks all round jeopardizes the polemical function. But putting-in-jeopardy is his poem's saving grace and chief distinction. This suggests that satire at its highest pitch turns into something different. "Simply the thing I am shall make me live," says Shakespeare's comic villain, more substantial than villainous. A great satirist plus other things, Dryden spikes his own guns, both his weakness and success.

Whatever form they elect, Augustan poets are generalizers. Understanding that the special is the enemy of the general, they prefer the capital letter to the lowercase. Like classical scientists, they don't want to contaminate their conceptual truth. The abstractions they favor will strike you as pallid only if you fail to grasp the end in view. Gray in his anthology pieces suggests it.

> The boast of heraldry, the pomp of pow'r,
> And all that beauty, all that wealth e'er gave,
> Awaits alike th' inevitable hour.
> The paths of glory lead but to the grave.

Having quoted these famous lines, epigrammatic but not ruminative, you have done your duty by them. Thought is exhausted in memorable statement, it being the virtue of the epigram to preclude consideration pro or con. The poet has said for you what there is to say and doesn't need or want your afterthoughts. This is the blackbird whistling.

You hear his inflected music in the devotional poetry of the eighteenth century, in Charles Wesley's "Morning Hymn," or William Cowper's "Light Shining Out of Darkness."

> Judge not the Lord by feeble sense,
>   But trust Him for His grace;
> Behind a frowning providence
>   He hides a smiling face.

In this poetry the imperative voice anticipates objection, and the rhetorician takes precedence of the intellecting man. Augustans call him a hole-and-corner empiric.

"The rhetorician deceives others," anyway he overcomes them, not aiming to persuade but compel. I think we feel how this is so in the poetry of Christopher Smart. Convention calls him outlandish but his psychological affinities with the age are strong, and such power as he communicates is emotive, not ratiocinative. The imperative mode helps supply it, also the formal apostrophe. In his most famous poem, the "Jubilate Agno," sequence isn't logical but antiphonal, or moves by arithmetic progression. Poems like his might keep going forever. But look at it and see if you don't think so.

Should the Augustan poet put questions, they are generally rhetorical in the sense of implying their answers. It isn't the poet's business to tease you out of thought (like Keats in the "Grecian Urn"), but to convince you—as they used to put it—in your bowels and reins. He knows how to do this. If Addison's octosyllabic couplets add up to poetry, that is because they are witty (incisive, not thoughtful), or naively pious. It is true, as this poet says, that reality has no corner in his "Spacious Firmament on High":

> What tho', no real Voice, no Sound,
> Amidst their radiant Orbs be found:
> In Reason's Ear they all rejoice,
> And utter forth a glorious Voice;
> For ever Singing as they Shine,
> The Hand that made us is Divine.

The rejoicing has its integrity, and sounds or resounds a little, but not in reason's ear.

The rhetorical mode defeats the wild surmise, and in the eighteenth century a whole range of poetry falls out of favor. The long philosophical poem is a casualty of the putting away of intellection—I call this the investigatory mode—in favor of the trenchant expression of heart's desire. The heart has its reasons, also its splendors, but you can't travel with it for long. So, many of the poetic forms and strategies cultivated in other periods don't get much of a hearing, or it isn't successful. Ottava rima, for instance, much in vogue in the sixteenth century, again in the nineteenth and twentieth (Yeats in some impressive poems). This poetic form doesn't drop from favor in the eighteenth century but poets understand that its uses are limited, no good for "major" business, okay for a polite *causerie*. Gay illustrates, welcoming his friend Pope home from Greece—that is, saluting the completion of Pope's *Iliad*. The tone is easy and affectionate, and the fillip each stanza ends with suits it nicely. Later, Byron, mocking the heroic style, put his mark on this stanza but you can't imagine Pope employing it for his version of Homer.

James Thomson, an ambitious poet, hopes to please with different "effects" and sees how the couplet can't manage them all. In his "Castle of Indolence," Thomson is making a conscious archaism ("*Caliphs* old, who on the *Tygris'* Shore," etc.), so resumes the Spenserian stanza. But discontinuity characterizes his treatment of the form: his long hexameter closes turn successive stanzas into little islands, "in the sea of life enisled." An early editor of Spenser's thought that happened in *The Faerie Queene* where "every stanza made as it were a distinct paragraph," and repetition, grown tiresome, frequently broke the sense "when it ought to be carried on without interruption." Disabling in a long poem (said John Hughes in 1715), the effect was languorous, even discrete. But Keats in "St. Agnes' Eve," employing Spenser's stanza, puts it to different uses, and his poem, profoundly sensuous, is at the same time discursive. Unlike Thomson (unlike Spenser, come to that), he cultivates with precision, so with great resonance, the investigatory mode. This is the life of the poem, not linear progression, and says why the form works for him.

Poets who want to spread themselves still think of blank verse, but it isn't propitious for Augustans. Dyer's blank verse poem, "The Fleece," recalls early "essays" in this kind, like blank verse poems by Surrey or Gascoigne. For these sixteenth-century makers, the unit isn't the paragraph but the distich (two lines) or single line. In Dyer or Thomson, unrhymed iambic pentameter looks insistently for repetitive devices, rhyme, assonance, alliteration. I attribute this to a failure of nerve or an access of humility.

The blank verse of the Augustans isn't always centripetal. But its rarefied diction cancels the chance for ruminative poetry or the poetry of nature. Blank verse demands "reality" and the evacuated state of the language forbids it. Milton is the exception, the great poet who empties out the language, preferring his own, and is great enough to make the substitution pass. Though Joseph Warton in "The Enthusiast, or the Lover of Nature" is superficially Romantic, the quality of his vision, like the language that conveys it, turns the subject matter to paste. Thomson has more continuity than Dyer—in *The Seasons,* for instance, where you get the effect of extended verse paragraphs. But the attenuated language—babbling brooks, plaintive streams, unfrequented glooms—contends against nature, so against the fluency that goes with being natural. The woodland creatures Thomson memorializes—like the plover that "in long Excursion skims the level Lawn"—belong in an artificial cosmos. It remains for Pope to certify this cosmos.

Dryden, inattentive to minute detail, can't discriminate in venturing praise, and most of his successors are like that. The formal panegyric under their hand is more embarrassing than mournful, e.g. Dryden's in memory of Anne Killigrew. Johnson, always worth taking seriously, called it the best funerary ode in the language. Maybe he meant that Dryden, strewing the bier with artificial palms, sought to assimilate mortality in art. In Swift the elegiac manner is less embarrassing than frigid. Trying it on in his "Verses on the Death of Dr. Swift," he reminds you of those toga-draped statues that began to clutter St. Paul's in his lifetime:

> Fair LIBERTY was all his Cry;
> For her he stood prepar'd to die;
> For her he boldly stood alone;
> For her he oft expos'd his own.

Praising isn't congenial to the Augustans, Sheffield thinks:

> Yet whatsoe'er is by vain Criticks thought,
> Praising is harder much than finding Fault.

Swift excels in finding fault, as when he censures the poetasters in his own time:

All Human Race wou'd fain be Wits,
And Millions miss, for one that hits.

He doesn't let us look at the true poet, though. Delineating the one that hits is beyond him.

The Augustan style in poetry from Dryden through Johnson is balanced, suasive in the sense of exhorting, grateful to the ear. You achieve this style by getting rid of intellectual complication, like Dryden in a panegyric to his friend Congreve:

In him all Beauties of this Age we see,
Etherege his Courtship, *Southern's* Purity,
The Satyre, Wit, and Strength of Manly *Wycherly*.

But you don't really see. Wycherly is what he is because the hexameter says so. Trouble comes when the metrist isn't sufficiently accomplished. Then the paucity of his thought stands naked.

Pope's manner in *An Essay on Criticism* is legislative or catechistic. Like Solon, he has figured things out. For instance:

Be silent always, when you doubt your sense;
And speak, tho' sure, with seeming diffidence.

Why should we do this? Sometimes speaking (or writing) is how you find your sense. Pope inspires visceral conviction, but the only ground of intellectual agreement is the appeal to matter-of-fact. Psychological realism depends on it, too. Augustan poets don't see that, not that their sensibilities are thin, only that what engages them is elsewhere. Pope's successes, most of them a priori, don't rely on consecutive thought or empirical analysis. Handsomeness is the proof of his pudding, nothing wrong with that when thought isn't at issue. But taking thought is the death of this declarative poetry. The handsomeness the form achieves is felt as shocking—"Beauty that shocks you," remembering the portrait of Sporus—when our intellectual agreement is asked for. The *Essay on Man* and *Essay on Criticism* show what happens to Pope on his yea-saying side.

When Augustan poets turn philosophical or ask you to believe that they are dealing with real men and women, the clamorous form combines with the cursory eye to detail and credibility goes out the window. Impatient of particulars, they fail to catch the living manners as they rise. Argument ad hoc isn't part of their humbler (or haughtier) purpose, so coming to conclusions, they don't catch your agreement. Quibbling fatigues them—"The scholiast's learning, sophist's cant . . . The monk's philosophy." That is Mark Akenside in his "Hymn to Science," a synoptic kind of science that won't ever "dive too deep, nor soar too high." But quibbling is the nerve and muscle of thought.

Pope makes it synonymous with the exalting of personality. Like his century, he comes down hard on intellectual address, preferring nature's glimmering light. A triplet clinches his argument:

> But as the slightest sketch, if justly trac'd,
> Is by ill-colouring but the more disgrac'd,
> So by false learning is good sense defac'd.

This sounds like bad Romantic ideology. The result isn't unruliness or Romantic wildness, however, rather a confining tidiness when thought is in the cards.

> Nature to all things fix'd the limits fit,
> And wisely curb'd proud man's pretending wit.
> As on the land, while here the ocean gains,
> In other parts it leaves wide sandy plains.

But this curbing and snaffling nature is like nothing in nature. The best Augustan poetry being by choice at a remove from nature, that is sometimes a good.

Pope's official commitment isn't to tidiness but catholicity. He is the fiery soul that frets and crowds the pigmy body. The form he employs, cabined, cribbed, and confined, makes against the commitment, though. Putting before us a vision of the immense and daunting store of knowledge, he calls it in question by the couplet form and the figure of speech or the way he applies it:

> So pleas'd at first the tow'ring Alps we try,
> Mount o'er the vales, and seem to tread the sky.
> Th'eternal snows appear already past,
> And the first clouds and mountains seem the last:
> But, those attain'd, we tremble to survey
> The growing labours of the lengthen'd way.
> Th'increasing prospect tires our wand'ring eyes,
> Hills peep o'er hills, and Alps on Alps arise!

What the passage presents isn't so much immensity as nice gradation. Not vast and resisting confinement, the matter is fixed and confined.

This means that Pope's aesthetic doesn't do him justice. He wants us to believe that true wit is nature to advantage dressed, or that true expression, being the dress of thought, adorns what it expresses. But the conjunction of form and content isn't like clothes on a clothes horse, and the artful carapace supplied by the couplet doesn't cover the thought but transforms it.

For Pope (in his *Essay on Criticism*) the Greeks are the exemplary writers:

> Hear how learn'd Greece her useful rules indites,
> When to repress, and when indulge our flights.

Put the Greek tragic poets against this description and you feel at once how they beggar the psychology of the couplet. Not attending much to the *je ne sais quoi*—the time's escape hatch, intimating untrammeled freedom—Pope is uneasy about this. A little heatedly, he wants it understood that "there's a happiness as well as care." But the whole tendency of his poetry is to assimilate the happiness, the unassayable thing, to the studious practice or care. As the former is merged in the latter, the former is denied, not least by the swing and poise of the line, the caesura. "License is a rule." Only fix the deviation and there isn't any.

The reliance on rhetoric, the great hallmark of the Augustan style, takes order with aberration, even when the point is to the aberrant thing:

> In prospects thus, some objects please our eyes,
> Which out of nature's common order rise,
> The shapeless rock, or hanging precipice.

Faintly jarring on the ear, the rhymes hint at shapelessness. But this window on the wilderness is only opened a crack, and the triplet, closing the window, brings shapelessness to heel. It isn't the rock or precipice that the form declares. It isn't anything that out of nature's order rises. It is nature's order.

When alfresco nature gets canonized in the next age, the inhibiting of reality seems fraudulent, maybe squeamish, and modern readers of poetry prefer the windswept lyre. Augustan poetry, displacing reality, entertains a different kind of vision, not euphemistic (mendacious) only "improved,"

improved like Baroque churches where the light of day is excluded and a better world built up inside. The imposition of order, improving on chaos, isn't a tyranny, and though the proverbial wisdom argues to the contrary, gilding the lily doesn't always debase it. This is especially true if you care less for nature than art.

Purging the world of grossness, Pope vindicates art against nature. The heroic couplet makes his achievement possible, and, though he himself thought his chosen form a vehicle setting off the content, it seems truer to say that the content depends on the form. Architects with a moral bias like to say that form follows function. In poetry, however, form creates function, obligating the poet. Some balk at the willfulness of this but Pope isn't one of them. His departures from the given are modest, and warranted, also aggrandized, by the pressure of the form at every point.

Augustan poetry reaches its apogee with Pope but it took the Augustans a long time to get round to him—roughly a half-century after the Restoration—longer than it took Elizabethans to get to Shakespeare. The age's progress to perfection is often broken by false starts and meanders. But as you look at the long period from, say, Samuel Butler ("Hudibras" Butler, who died in Charles's reign) to Joseph and Thomas Warton, who lived into the Romantic Age, you get the sense of a "teleological" progress, Augustan poetry throwing forward inevitably, like history according to Marx. The goal it aspires to is the heroic couplet, just the form for the highest truth these poets had it in them to convey.

Butler's ragged tetrameter rhymes offer one illustration of a false start. Less fluent than garrulous, like the bad political poetry of Andrew Marvell in the Restoration years, they suggest that constraint is the way to expressiveness. Other poets of the later seventeenth century look forward more surely to the century to come. Charles Cotton, the famous book collector, is one. His rhyming tercets almost crave the couplet, as when maids-turned-bottles cry aloud for corks.

> She finds Virginity a kind of ware
> That's very very troublesome to bear,
> And being gone, she thinks will ne'er be mist:
>
> And yet withall the Girl has so much grace,
> To call for help I know she wants the face,
> Though ask'd, I know not how she would resist.

This bantering is just as good when Cotton tries the four-foot couplet. But his lines, missing something, seem imperfect or unachieved.

Pope's mastery of the heroic couplet supplies what is missing and defines the achievement. Blank verse waits on Shakespeare, and Pope evidently needs the unique dependency of line length and rhyme scheme and syntactic closure. The chink and fall of the couplet convinces the ear of a finality of utterance that tercets and quatrains will always reach for in vain. (They have their own decorum.) Five feet are better than four feet when the poem goes on for long. For want of an extra foot, Charles Churchill is unread.

The subject the poet chooses seems not to matter. Gray is whimsical, lamenting the death of his cat, or sententious in his ode on Eton College. He doesn't tarry, however, so the short line works for him. But it puts you to sleep—like the abnormally long line, the hexameter in English, or septenary verse—as it keeps returning on itself. Swift's mordant verses on his own death show this. The epigrammatic richness, good for a hundred lines, surfeits after two hundred. This isn't true of the pentameter couplet. Add one more foot, however, and a radical fissure will likely open in the line. Physiology, something like that, is the culprit.

This is another way of saying that long lines and short lines, resolving themselves, tend to discreteness. John Dyer's tetrameter couplets in "Grongar Hill" won't do for a longish poem. What the form can do, the seventeenth century has already shown. The potential is still there in the middle of the eighteenth century:

A little rule, a little sway,
A sunbeam in a winter's day,
Is all the proud and mighty have
Between the cradle and the grave.

But Dyer isn't making an epigram or an epitaph. For the suggestion of air about the poem, you have to have the pentameter line. Isaac Watts has his impressive quality and like Dryden and Pope, controls the legislative voice. But his short line, whether aggregating to couplets or quatrains, denies the chance for modulation.

This modulating power is Pope's special distinction. Partly it comes from the discreet indulging of the run-on line, partly from the contention of voice stress and metrical pattern. It goes without saying that the contention is always polite. The occasional tinkering of the prosodic norm is influential too, as when Pope prefers the reversed foot to the iamb. Mostly, however, credit goes to the spontaneous dance of the caesura. "Spontaneous" means that this absolute regisseur has his hands on all the ropes. Pope says to his lawyer-friend Fortescue:

> Yes, I am proud; I must be proud to see
> Men not afraid of God, afraid of me.

In this quotation from the epilogue to the Satires, Pope is speaking from the heart. I find the effect deeply stirring.

Not that the personal voice doesn't intervene in eighteenth-century poets. It is rare enough, though—from proclivity, also artistic tact—to make you sit up straight when you hear it. My illustration is from "The Vanity of Human Wishes":

> There mark what ills the scholar's life assail,
> Toil, envy, want, the patron, and the jail.
> See nations slowly wise, and meanly just,
> To buried merit raise the tardy bust.

With these gloomy enjoinings, Johnson the neglected scribbler enters the poem. You wouldn't say he barges in, like Shelley falling on the thorns of life. The convention he owes allegiance to forbids this. Also he is redacting an older poet who wrote in an alien tongue, so what he says in his own voice is muffled.

But Johnson's appearance-at-one-remove makes all the difference between inert convention and convention turned to personal, hence permanent, account. You want the ancient aspect—this is the convention, or, from the side of prosody, the highly circumscribed form; and you want the "modern" poet adjusting his given. The adjustment or variation is perceptible but not surprising, as when the Red Sea parts or the magician pulls his rabbits from a hat. These events are prodigious, therefore discordant. Variation makes a harmony only when predicable of what goes before. If the variation is to tell, the last thing you want is surprise.

Pope acts out this proposition from the side of prosody. The medium he works in is the opposite of unconfined. Going with the heroic couplet where he might have picked a quarrel, he creates the illusion of infinite riches in his little room. Pope is the complete Trimmer as Lord Halifax presents him, i.e. an opportunist like every writer of parts, and the assent he commands in a hundred passages attests his lively prudence in varying the form to which he has made his commitment. Failing the commitment, variation is nothing, or like untethered freedom works out to chaos.

The excitment for Pope, the shrewdness also, consists in living comfortably within his poetic means. His lines are crowded, more precisely they seem to be, but he has no thought of breaking them up. Felt agitation depends on their integrity. If you feel how his lines are often not of a length, that is contrivance and matter for praise. Mostly, he declines to call in the hexameter or to step down the poem from long lines to short. The effect of the "diapason" is make-believe in his poetry. He thinks that is what artistry means.

In *The Rape of the Lock* he deals with society, but this doesn't mean he has "views." What he says is not so much as the tact he says it with.

> The hungry Judges soon the sentence sign,
> And Wretches hang that Jury-men may dine.

The illusion is of varying line length, the rush of the sibillants hurrying the first line to its end, the weighty pause in the second line dramatizing the verb. We take all its painful force, the caesura having stopped us, then, gathering momentum, go on again. No doubt the effect is to rouse our indignation. This effect is contingent, however. The substantial content Pope disposes is generated by the form, or his imperious form allows and enables the content. If the content impinges powerfully, that isn't from humanitarian fervor. The multitude has fervor. The poet is singular, and feeling, has the wit to dispose.

Not able to prevent the rape of the lock, one of Pope's spirits is punished for this:

> . . . as Ixion fix'd, the Wretch shall feel
> The giddy Motion of the whirling Mill.

Ixion, fettered to the wheel, disputes his confinement. The off-rhyme says this, and the couplet trembles with giddy motion. But that is only as the fetters hold. Dryden's couplets, on the other hand, are almost never wholly fettered and sound to my ear less close to Pope or Johnson than to Marlowe (e.g. in *Hero and Leander*), a hundred years before. You recognize the sound of Dryden in the conspicuous presence of run-on lines, the resort to the hexameter, the frequent expanding of couplets to triplets. Whether you call this generosity or fudging comes down to personal taste. I think Pope's is the more difficult and more rewarding kind of art.

Dryden's long poems are marked by great narrative fluency but in the service of a mistaken impulse. His basic impulse is to use the couplet as a vehicle for philosophic debate. Freeing up his lines and the units they compose, he hopes to beguile us with the effect of interior movement, mimetic of thought. This poet is working against the heroic couplet and what it can do at its best.

Eighteenth-century poets don't make their best things through dilating but reining in, their characteristic virtue. Swift envies it, knowing how he falls short:

> In Pope, I cannot read a Line,
> But with a Sigh, I wish it mine;
> When he can in one Couplet fix
> More Sense than I can do in Six.

The desired thing is to fix or anneal, so perhaps to exorcize chaos. Later poets live on better terms with themselves, or they wonder what the trouble is. Thomas Warton, who thinks that truth's "universal pattern strikes mankind" when it is "by no peculiar taste confined," is an unselfconscious harbinger of the age to come. But never mind the Romantics, who have their different truth. Warton at any rate has got it backward. The want of fit confinement engenders a mortifying confinement.

The late Augustan poet who gives his pentameter couplets free rein can't tell the difference between promiscuity and freedom. Oliver Goldsmith, a genuine poet writing when the great style has begun to reach its term, wants to resuscitate the couplet. But he likes to amplify and its narrow compass goes against his grain. Though you remember the quotable bits—

> Truth from his lips prevailed with double sway,
> And fools who came to scoff, remained to pray—

the cinching apothegm meets you less often than it used to. Reading "The Deserted Village," you want to say: let the heroic couplet do what it can do, or find another form.

As the first-person pronoun gains on the age, a new form is required to entertain it. (The couplet can't accommodate the dreadful "I" of "The

Castaway.") Cowper addresses the requirement and in "The Poplar Field" goes back to the anapest. (Prior, for quotidian matters, does this too). The longer foot is artless—but not spontaneous, only ingenuous—and Cowper thinks it enforces his more natural subject. His poplars are felled:

> Twelve years have elapsed since I first took a view
> Of my favourite field, and the bank where they grew;
> And now in the grass behold they are laid,
> And the tree is my seat that once lent me a shade!

This is superior as a comic version of "Tintern Abbey."

Blank verse is wanted, a less emphatic rhythm contingent on natural piety. The Augustans find what they are looking for as they repudiate truth to nature and the prosodic structure that declares it. Dryden in *The Hind and the Panther,* turning his back on the Metaphysical mode, courts a different kind of truth. Even when he drops the couplet, as in his "Song for St. Cecilia's Day," art still takes first place. He doesn't want to come to intellectual conclusions, and the experience he evokes is outside a merely thoughtful man's ken. Declining to negotiate an intellectual progress, he offers us instead a world aloof from rational inspection:

> *Orpheus* cou'd lead the savage race,
> And Trees uprooted left their Place,
>   Sequacious of the Lyre.

Dryden is Orpheus transforming the world, and his high-toned diction meets and effects this uncanny business. Dryden's readers are "sequacious," following their leader. Volition isn't in it and they have forfeited the chance for disbelief.

This applies more powerfully to Pope, whose power isn't from ratiocination but feeling:

> Why did I write? what sin to me unknown
> Dipt me in ink, my parents', or my own?
> As yet a child, nor yet a fool to fame,
> I lisp'd in numbers, for the numbers came.
> I left no calling for this idle trade,
> No duty broke, no Father disobey'd.
> The Muse but serv'd to ease some friend, not Wife,
> To help me thro' this long disease, my Life.

On the etiology of the disease, Pope has nothing to say, no strictures on pride or presumption, etc. That is just as well. Great Augustan poetry is generalized pessimism, melancholy feeling as never before.

> Year chases year, decay pursues decay,
> Still drops some joy from with'ring life away:
> New forms arise, and diff'rent views engage,
> Superfluous lags the vet'ran on the stage.

And that is where Dr. Johnson, having summoned this metonymic figure, is satisfied to leave him, on the other side of the proscenium arch.

The cursory eye of Augustan poets is often taken for careless. But Pope isn't out to render flesh-and-blood. Like Gwendolen Fairfax, he looks at truth and nature through a lorgnette. This is no bad thing: a real fish, a real bird aren't better, necessarily, than his version of them as "the life that fills the Flood . . . [and] warbles thro' the vernal wood." In *An Essay on Man* he presents the ample range of creation:

> Mark how it mounts, to Man's imperial race,
> From the green myriads in the peopled grass:
> What mode of sight betwixt each wide extreme,
> The mole's dim curtain, and the lynx's beam:
> Of smell, the headlong lioness between,
> And hound sagacious on the tainted green.

Blood isn't what we get here but ichor, the nectareous substance that flows in the veins of the gods.

In *Windsor Forest* the matter is nature, but the denizens of Pope's world have put off mortality—the pheasant clothed in its glossy, varying dyes, the well-breathed beagles, the exiguous hunter who raises his tube (never his shotgun). When living nature infiltrates the golden world, the fall is from decorum, not lapsing into the artificial style but from it. Gay in "Pope's Welcome" lapses from this style, so recalls at a distance the lively but congested world of *The Dunciad*.

> I see the friendly Carylls come by dozens,
> Their wives, their uncles, daughters, sons, and cousins.

This isn't company but a crowd. Pope, declining to enumerate or particularize, shows you how the yield of cursoriness, anyway for him, isn't thinness but veneer, by design hard, in effect beautiful:

> . . . happy Convents, bosom'd deep in vines,
> Where slumber Abbots, purple as their wines:
> . . . Isles of fragrance, lilly-silver'd vales,
> Diffusing languor in the panting gales.

In *The Dunciad,* however, the myriad of particulars rarely ascends beyond the lowercase. Asked to bear too much reality, the world this poem composes isn't golden but brazen.

Not so *The Rape of the Lock.* The great decorous poem of the Augustans, it shows the poet absorbed by a higher reality. But don't call it "Platonic"—it has its own substantial character, proof against time:

> With hairy springes we the Birds betray,
> Slight Lines of Hair surprize the finny Prey.

With Belinda's spirits we are up in a high place, "distilling o'er the Glebe the kindly Rain." Pope fills his cosmos with ill-assorted couples, but not "him" and "her":

> Whether the Nymph shall break Diana's Law,
> Or some frail China Jar receive a Flaw;
> Or stain her Honour, or her new Brocade,
> Forget her Pray'rs, or miss a Masquerade.

These pairings, though disjunctive, cohere to make a rival creation. Forcing us to salute it is Pope's nearly unique success. The coherences have always been there but latent, and his genius is to make them emerge. All great poets do this, converting the oxymoron (eccentric pairing) to common coin.

> Not louder Shrieks to pitying Heav'n are cast,
> When Husbands or when Lapdogs breathe their last.

To our mortification but in the event to our credit (where comeliness is credit), husbands and lapdogs announce their affinity.

Appealing from reality, Pope's couplets open on a world where we have put off corruption. This is the better world of *The Rape of the Lock.* Mortality—all that deliquescing stuff—is vitrified in art.

> For lo! the Board with Cups and Spoons is crown'd,
> The Berries crackle, and the Mill turns round.
> On shining Altars of Japan they raise

The silver Lamp; the fiery Spirits blaze.
From silver Spouts the grateful Liquors glide,
While China's Earth receives the smoking Tide.

Pope isn't willing to remain in his high place or enameled place for long, and *The Rape of the Lock* is his one ambitious poem that makes a perfect whole. He has an impulse, not easily quelled, to take violent order with disorder. On this rock, much of his poetic enterprise founders. But though his hectoring manner dejects us, the handing-down-the-Decalogue manner persuades. Heaven is ordinant,

Who sees with equal eye, as God of all,
A hero perish, or a sparrow fall,
Atoms or systems into ruin hurl'd,
And now a bubble burst, and now a world.

Marshaling tropes or rhetorical questions, Pope gains our assent by letting eloquence stand in for niggling consideration. The best of him is interstitial:

Let us (since Life can little more supply
Than just to look about us and to die)
Expatiate free o'er all this scene of Man:
A mighty maze! but not without a plan.

The parenthetical phrase is what we remember. It isn't a contemptible yield.

When reality, our common clay, engages this poet, the heroic couplet fails him. The form cries out for art, and the presentation of reality demands that art be hid. Or perhaps it is Pope and his mastery-beyond-appeal who is enforcing my definitions here. More than any other poet, he alters once and for all the nature of his chosen form. Looking back, I am tempted to say how the heroic couplet can do only this thing, not another, as if it had inherently a limitation and a power. That can hardly be. Drayton, in his *Endimion and Phoebe,* does things with the form that are alien to Pope's practice. But when Keats resumes it for his *Endymion,* it seems he isn't writing couplets at all. Pope stands before him, warning him off. What Pope does to the form effects, in T. S. Eliot's sense, a permanent adjustment to the whole history of poetry. After him, the heroic couplet engenders expectation.

Chapter 12

Remembering Shelley

Shelley, who never got old, was the poet I cared about most in my youth. His watercolor likeness, once owned by his biographer, Newman Ivey White, still hangs on the wall in my study. But I haven't often reread him, and wonder if he isn't a poet for the young, his appeal fading as the shades of the prisonhouse close upon us. They were all so young, Shelley and friends, collectively the Pisa Gang, Trelawny, Jane and Ned Williams—he did the watercolor with the mad electric eyes—Mary Shelley and Clare Claremont, half-sisters by Godwin's two wives, Byron, the only one over thirty. Trelawny, a real Byronic hero, living into great old age, at the end came back to die in Rome. For half a year, no more, he saw Shelley plain and wanted to be buried beside him. Browning's poem gives the sense, the eagle-feather picked up on the moor, a hand's-breadth amid the blank miles.

Heir to a great estate, among the largest in England's southern counties, Shelley did what he could to throw this inheritance away. The man who scorned religions was a fool for Christ's sake. Once, meeting a barefoot woman hobbling over rough stones, he came home without his shoes. A nerve, he called himself, "o'er which do creep / The else unfelt oppressions of the earth." This sounds a little like the Sensitive Plant, not the poem, the poet, known for shrinking. He surprises you, though. "I go on until I am stopped," he said, adding, "and I am never stopped."

A boyhood friend, Thomas Jefferson Hogg, remembered him reading "for 16 out of every 24 hours." He read Homer in Greek, Lucretius in Latin, Calderón in Spanish, Goethe in German, Tasso in Italian. Living in the Italian countryside in his last years, he read Herodotus. He sat naked on the rocks beside a forest pool, then, folding back the page, dropped into the fountain. When he drowned at sea it was like that, his reading, Sophocles and the poems of Keats, thrust into his jacket as he got ready to die.

He and Keats always go together, as in the old Modern Library edition, a Bible for many. But other than dying young, they have little in common. Shelley's commitment, vowed early and poles apart from Keats's, was to Intellectual Beauty. Later he asked rhetorically: "Have I not kept the vow?" But it thinned his poetry, not provincial enough. Like his Witch of Atlas, "a sexless bee," he tasted all blossoms, confining himself to none. Other poets make abstract things substantial; he turns this around, hard on those who loved him. "Don't be like your brother," said his father the baronet to a younger son. "Take care that you don't learn too much." The father is a heavy, but his conventional wisdom has its corner of truth. Shelley, soaring above the earth, didn't see that.

Expelled from Oxford for an atheistical pamphlet, he took lodgings in London on Poland Street. It brought to mind Thaddeus of Warsaw and freedom. But he didn't stay in London or any place for long, bitten by discontent, divine and other. In Dublin at age nineteen—having gone there, he said, to forward the cause of Catholic emancipation—he stood on the balcony of his hotel, showering passersby with an *Address to the Irish People.* "O IRISHMEN, REFORM YOURSELVES!" he told them. From Lynmouth on the Bristol Channel, he issued a *Declaration of Rights.* Like a castaway's message in a bottle, it went out in homemade boats on the water, or floated aloft tied to balloons.

Stories like these endear him, anyway to me, but send up danger signals. Shelley talks too much and the talk is too declarative, the product of a mind often violated by ideas. He wrote quickly and carelessly, not always bothering to make his details square, even antecedent and pronoun. Like many poets of the last two hundred years, he puts his cards on the table, a fault. It seems a bizarre complaint to make of "modern" poetry, generally faulted for being obscure. But great poetry gives you the sense of meaning more than it says, and clamorous poetry like Shelley's says at least as much as it means. *Prometheus Unbound,* often called his greatest poem, is pitched very high, a strain on the reader. Interspersed rhyming songs do what they can to lower the pitch, but nag at us all the same.

Though he tries out different verse forms, his experiments are more Swinburne than Sidney, like the spun glass of Murano, less impressive than the skill that went to make it. In "The Sensitive Plant" and "The Cloud," the relentless beat tells of "poetry," and it wearies. Sound is mesmeric and incantation does duty for thought. Matter goes one way, manner another, not a deliberate disjunction. See, for instance, his lines on the Euganean Hills, where the intellectualizing cast seems blurred by the meter, lulling intellect to sleep.

In the threnody for Keats, political asides vie for attention with the dead poet. This matter between the lines doesn't function, as with Shakespeare, to intimate a greater world, only a special bias. A brief dirge shows nature storm tossed and sounding like it ought to, but he himself hears it wailing "for the world's wrong." Paradoxically, this peg is too slight to hang his poem on. The wrong will be rectified someday, not yet, and "the world's great age" is always about to begin. Always tomorrow, never today, seems a bad recipe for poetry and life. Raising their eyes, writers like Shelley leave the foreground untended. But it isn't the politics of his vision that fatigues us. He isn't enough convicted of sin.

In his "Mont Blanc" he celebrates a "universe of things," but things don't crop up in the poetry much. Exceptions confirm the rule, like the song from his unfinished drama, *Charles the First:* a bird on a wintry bough, frozen wind, freezing stream, leafless forest, the sound of a millwheel. Auden and Pearson, liking Shelley best when least typical, make room for this poem in their Viking Portable Poets, regrettably no longer in print. Mostly, however, his ideal poet reserves attention to the noumenal world. Our physical world—the "painted veil"—was raw materials, and from them he created "forms more real than living man." Anyone could make the word flesh.

When Mary complained that one of the poems lacked "human interest," he agreed it was so. "You might as well go to a gin-shop for a leg of mutton," he said, "as expect anything human or earthly from me." But the poetry quivers with erotic feeling. A rose is like a nymph stepping into her bath, disrobing all the way (in "The Sensitive Plant"), a woman, when her lover's being overflows, is a chalice receiving his wine (in *Prometheus Unbound*). Sexuality itches at him in "Epipsychidion," among other things a defense of free love. (Scholars heatedly deny this.) Heaping praises on a young Italian girl, Emilia Viviani ("Seraph of Heaven!" etc.), he composes a litany better suited to the Virgin. He isn't a through-and-through Platonist, however, and the animal in him smells his heroine's "loose hair." It gives off a "wild odor," invading him, he says, to the soul. Others would say, "to the skin."

Both cranks and eleemosynary men line up beneath his standard. Newman White, his best scholar and a man of feeling, chaired the Socialist Party of North Carolina. His Shelley is a man worth knowing. Dinosaur Marxists, on the other hand, sponsor a professor of political science. Christopher Caudwell, who wrote nonsense but died bravely in the Spanish War, saw in Prometheus the bourgeois capitalist "trameled by the restraints of the era of mercantilism" (*Illusion and Reality,* 1936). Shelley, though never so crude, makes love to this trivializing employment.

Keats criticized his "magnanimity," just the right tactful word for political zeal when it seeks to take over the poem. Curb it, he said, "and be more of an artist." But doing that would have warped the grain of his genius. In 1817, the publishers C. and J. Ollier brought out "A Proposal for Putting Reform to the Vote throughout the Kingdom," signed by "the Hermit of Marlowe." Up river on the Thames, Marlowe was one of his many way stations. In the same year the same firm published *Poems, by John Keats,* a conjunction that might have distressed him. Loving art, however, he loved humanity more.

But love of the world begins with love of self, and of that he had too little. Trelawny said he "loved everything better than himself." This accounts for his abjectness, the other side of the blithe spirit. In his imagination, he was Actaeon, savaged by the world or his own thoughts. Bowed by "a heavy weight," he envied the wind that blows where it wants to, and the skylark's unmeditated gladness. Ill health tormented him, and like Coleridge he shook with spasms of pain, but no one has ever said why. His grief bears such an emphasis—too many tears for the man "whom men love not"—that we wince when we don't turn away.

I am quoting from his "Stanzas Written in Dejection," a poem that lives up to its title. In the last stanza, however, he seems to judge himself, condemned, like Dante's sinners, for melancholy in the light of the sun. "When the Lamp Is Shattered," a sentimental lyric, often anthologized, continues the self-regarding strain. But like the Dejection poem, it pulls itself together, and the ending redeems many sins:

>   every rafter
> Will rot, and thine eagle home
>   Leave thee naked to laughter,
> When leaves fall and cold winds come.

This impersonal voice that makes little of palliatives isn't often Shelley's. Uneven in quality, he is a poet of peaks and troughs.

Admirers, lavishing praise, don't discriminate between them, and most critics in our time haven't given the former their due. The machinery of the elegiac poem—winds sobbing in their dismay, etc., etc.—nearly does for *Adonais.* But Shelley, though much falling, reaches heights unequaled since the greater Jacobeans. E.g. the "leprous" corpse that turns into flowers and mocks "the merry worm that wakes beneath." Sorrow is the meat he feeds on, but accommodating its opposite, he sets against death's pallor the color of sky and earth. Hecticity all gone, the note of quiet seems a throwback to earlier times, before poetry began raising its voice:

> Great and mean
> Meet massed in death, who lends what life must borrow.
> As long as skies are blue, and fields are green,
> Evening must usher night, night urge the morrow,
> Month follow month with woe, and year wake year to sorrow.

Shelley isn't invariably Romantic, pejorative sense. *Adonais,* the bleakest of funerary poems, offers for consolation only "shelter in the shadow of the tomb." In "The Sensitive Plant," truth, crushed to earth, stays there, while the wicked rise up from their charnels. Purposive Shelley takes a holiday in the "Letter to Maria Gisborne," suiting his informal couplets to a polite occasion. Civilized discourse is the stuff of "Julian and Maddalo," a.k.a. Shelley and Byron under Italian skies. Berlioz sets the scene in his "Harold in Italy"—you can hear the two of them galloping across the Lido—and in the viola part captures all Romanticism's sweetness and yearning. For once, Shelley leaves this alone. He wants a different voice, fluent, masculine, urbane.

Couplets, fitted to a shorter line, surface again in a sexy "Invitation," meant for Jane Williams, his friend's pretty wife. A virile seduction piece, his makes no bones about it.

> "I am gone into the fields
> To take what this sweet hour yields;—
> Reflection, you may come to-morrow,
> Sit by the fireside with Sorrow.—
> You with the unpaid bill, Despair,—
> You, tiresome verse-reciter, Care,—
> I will pay you in the grave."

This sophisticated Shelley harks back to Restoration poets. But I mustn't make exceptions the norm.

Essential Shelley is the one who agonizes at every pore, attuned, like his Witch of Atlas, to inchoate feelings and thrilling sounds we hear in our youth. Both are gone soon enough, but his poems record their pressure. Some of the poems suggest a neurasthenic who lacked male robustness.

Byron called him the Snake, tall beyond the average and leaning forward when he walked. Perhaps he intended a lamia-like Shelley, beautiful but sinister, even demonic. In person he was tense, in sensibility morbid. These case-history terms say too little, however. In *Prometheus Unbound,* he is the lonely man who drinks oracular vapor from the dark underworld, or drains to the dregs the maddening wine of life. Ideas, his fatal chimera, led him to elaborate a world where men have quit being wicked, "women too, frank, beautiful, and kind." But he lives with an intensity few can support, knowing "the pain of bliss / To move, to breathe, to be."

He isn't that perfect Shelley convention used to insist on, and misses the mark as often as he hits it. Living in a high place, he has a long way to fall. But his ardor is enormously taking. Emotion, no doubt excessive, belongs to his youthful time, when "tears throng to the horny eyes, / And beatings haunt the desolated heart." It should have learnt repose, he says, and with the coming of age this happens. An ambiguous privilege, it wasn't his.

Part III

The Hymn in the Throat

Chapter 13

Herbert at Play in the Fields of the Lord

Herbert's peers, among makers of the short poem, are Yeats, Frost, Donne, and Jonson, and Shakespeare at sonnets. Keats belongs in this company but left a smaller body of permanent poetry. Donne, notorious for his difficulty, actually gives less trouble than Herbert, and much of the hermetic syntax and recondite learning are easily elucidated by footnotes. Yeats has his private system, obtrusive in a few poems, for example, "Byzantium" and "Ego Dominus Tuus." Mostly, however, the system is absorbed in the poems, and this poet, handled with the care he merits, is plain sailing. Shakespeare, offering insistently the negative of his positive, is the poet who comes closest to Herbert. Like a fabulous beast that ate its own paws without knowing it, Renan said, assessing Shakespeare. This is Herbert too.

In his "Holy Scriptures I," he seems to tells us that Scripture is the sum of perfection. Devout readers take strength from this, and meaning to strengthen them Herbert writes his poem. A Christian poet whatever else, he isn't out to fool us. But like certain of Shakespeare's sonnets the poem includes a counterstatement, disputing its up-front content. This skeptical-irreverent poem doesn't cancel the panegyric, though, Herbert liking to have it both ways.

His title, typically humdrum, begets expectations, not fulfilled or possibly exceeded. Scripture is a vade mecum (so far, what we expect) but also too good to be true:

> Precious for any grief in any part;
> To clear the breast, to mollify all pain—

i.e. one size fits all. A mirror or looking glass, Scripture is agreeable to the ladies who consult it. But the ladies are vain and the looking glass fools them, "mending" their eyes. Scripture, also a well, "washes what it shows," cleansing, at the same time sprucing up the (doubtful) image in the water.

In this truth-telling ledger "heaven lies flat," open to inspection. But "flat" is also insipid, and says that Scripture's truth, not nourishing much, is jejune. Like a staff "subject to every mounter's bended knee," it helps the reader on his way to heaven. But this supporting function, suggesting abasement, suggests complaisance too, Scripture telling the reader what he wants to hear. The poem goes on like this, exasperating point of view.

Some other poets, even great ones, running together negative and positive, do so ironically, and the negative voice mocks the official poem. Herbert, not an ironic poet except at his own expense, sponsors a partnership of lion and lamb. Another way to put it is to say that his poems, rough and troubled with contrary movement, throw back against the current like Frost's West-Running Brook. This is a natural movement. Herbert has a phrase for his art that resembles nature: "My crooked winding ways" ("A Wreath"). In "Church-lock and Key" the poet's sins, "out-crying" his plea for mercy, are so many stones in the stream bed. Interrupting the current that sets toward heaven, they imperil his salvation. But like stones they make the current "much more loud to be." This boosts the chance for salvation, an eccentric reading of our lapsed condition. Most older readers of Herbert missed the eccentricity, and Frost is widely admired for his natural piety and shock of white hair.

Herbert the devotional poet, growing in a straight line, is "still upwards bent" ("The Flower"): always on the way to heaven and determined to get there. He sets the word against itself, however, his "bent" meaning both "determined" and "deflected," and he hopes all his dyings "may be life in death" ("Mortification"). That is inconsequent but Herbert has no option, harboring in himself two contentious persons. They go their separate ways, one touching heaven, the other holding tight to earth ("Man's Medley"). Sometimes the hand that touches heaven makes a fist.

Herbert's biography, like his best poetry, declares the inconsequent man. Or you can call him many sided, fish and flesh by turns. Izaak Walton, looking back in old age, wrote the biography, meaning to spread on the record a "great example of holiness." Uncomplicated Herbert under his hand turns into a simple parson, the type of the Protestant saint. He was saintly, among other things. Modern biographers, scrutinizing the record (meager, when all is said), call Walton in question, but I don't want to quarrel with this friendly hagiographer. He meant his old friend well and meant to do him justice. Better to say that Walton's ear was imperfect. Like many of Herbert's readers, riffling pages in *The Temple,* he heard what he wanted to hear.

Walton's Herbert takes after his pious mother, who would "often say 'that ignorance of vice was the best preservation of virtue, and that the very knowledge of wickedness was as tinder to inflame and kindle sin and keep it burning.'" This is true for Herbert, the second clause, not the first. Lady Magdalen Herbert, a prodigious bluestocking, is celebrated by Donne in "The Autumnal": "In all her words, to every hearer fit, / You may at revels, or at council sit." Herbert, taking counsel, looks like an apt pupil. Writing to his mother, he says how a "late ague" in him has "dried up those springs" where the Muses live. No matter, though: "I need not their help to reprove the vanity of those many love-poems that are daily writ and consecrated to Venus." Then he breaks into poetry, anxious with questions.

The questions are rhetorical, standard for a poet who doesn't have any answers except as the answers are given. (Here he shows his connection to Jonson, unpersuaded by reason, so laying it all to faith.) The poem, a sonnet, is untitled, and God is the addressee:

> Doth poetry
> Wear Venus' livery? only serve her turn?
> Why are not sonnets made of Thee? and lays
> Upon Thine altar burnt?

These questions have their answers but the answers are "antiphonal," Hic countering Ille with no intermission or conclusion unless the poet decrees it. ("Decreeing" is when he says simply, like Ovid in his *Amores, Hoc opus exegi,* "I have ended the work.") For instance in "The Pearl," where the pious refrain disputes the ways of Pleasure:

> the sweet strains,
> The lullings and the relishes of it;
> The propositions of hot blood and brains;
> What mirth and music mean; what love and wit
> Have done these twenty hundred years.

Much to ponder in that last phrase, gravid when you say it over. And still the refrain has its unimpaired vigor: "Yet I love Thee."

The ways of Pleasure or "way that takes the town" are carnal and powerfully attractive. Recited, they jeopardize the goal of salvation. Spiritual things, the stuff of religion, get Herbert's suffrage but that is largely by fiat, and the capitulating when it comes seems ungrateful:

Yet, for I threatened oft the siege to raise,
   Not simpering all mine age,
Thou often didst with academic praise
   Melt and dissolve my rage,
I took Thy sweetened pill . . . .

("Affliction I")

In superb reversal of convention, "simpering," equated by pious poets with profane love poems, "Venus' lays," must characterize religious devotion.

Herbert was born in a castle in 1593, very different from Shakespeare, busy at this time pulling himself up by his bootstraps. His six brothers included Edward Herbert, Lord Cherbury, famous as a diplomat, minor poet, historian, and "atheist" philosopher. Another, Master of the Revels under King James, censored stage plays. There were girls in the family, and Walton musters and dismisses them ("all married to persons of worth and plentiful fortunes"). None of these siblings predicts the poet, and his formal provenance, like Shakespeare's, "butcher boy of Stratford," or Keats's, somebody's by-blow, raises more questions than it answers. At fifteen he entered Cambridge, afterward becoming public orator there. This post was a stepping stone, and two immediate predecessors went on to be Secretaries of State. That looked like Herbert's destiny. Ambitious, he meant to compass it, so learned the modern tongues, also Latin and Greek. This is matter-of-fact but not incidental, and Herbert, playing with words, runs the gamut of their meanings. Altogether Shakespearean in his feeling for innuendo, he isn't vain of language, steering clear of big words, but his alertness to nuance is uncanny. You need a big dictionary to read him.

Bacon, some say, though jealous of words on their slippery side, submitted his writing for Herbert's approval. King James, respectful too, was his patron. Visiting Cambridge, he took Herbert for "the jewel of that university," giving him a sinecure, a religious "cure" where the parishioners got on without the incumbent. This was unscrupulous, but Herbert spoke no regrets. Walton summed him up—well heeled, well connected, a touch sybaritic, something of a toady. "He enjoyed his genteel humor for clothes and court-like company, and seldom looked towards Cambridge unless the king were there, but then he never failed." So he drew his wages in a world of mirth.

Like Shakespeare's Prince Hal, this ur-Herbert functions for his biographer as a marked setoff to the real thing. But Shakespeare's hero learns nothing he didn't know at first, and Herbert in his life and art doesn't put off "the old man" but amalgamates old and new. He saw how the thread of life, "like other threads or skeins of silk," composed a tangled yarn "full of snarls and encumbrances." This tangle yields his unruly likeness. Disaster, predicated of our mingled yarn, came when King James died in 1625, and Bacon, a year after, fell from power. No further advancement opened for Herbert except, as for Donne, through the church. His connections got him the offer of a humble living in Wiltshire, Bemerton parsonage, a mile outside Salisbury. Wilton, the family estate of the Herberts, in other days a rich nunnery, lies just up the road. Herbert at Bemerton epitomizes the conscientious pastor strong for works.

When you read him, however, you feel that works don't avail. His stock lies dead, his husbandry is dull, and increase doesn't improve it ("Grace"). Unexpectedly, though, this incapacity, far from damning him, acquits him. "Antinomian" Herbert, not above slyness, is what he is by virtue of his maker. "The crop is His"—quoting from "The Discharge"—where "His" is the Lord's, and what comes up from the ground, "bent," maybe, is what the Lord has sown. Others grudge at this but Herbert, playful and provident, makes it count for him, a version of the Fortunate Fall. Accepting his "discharge," he isn't a rakehell, never that. Only if he slips, this doesn't put him out. How should he know any better? He hears tell that at Judgment, some mean to plead good works, saying that their lives excel in merit. He means to thrust a testament in the hands of the Judge:

> Let that be scanned.
> There thou shalt find my faults are thine.
>
> ("Judgment")

This is impudent but winning, and other metaphors from other poems suggest that Herbert, having found a handle, is turning it for what it is worth. His God is a tapster, and this delinquent at the bar can't pay what he owes. Insouciant, he isn't cast down, though:

> But all my scores were by another paid,
> Who took the debt upon him.
>
> ("Love Unknown")

Or he is an indentured servant, not to be shuffled off, God being constrained by laws of His own devising ("Artillery"). God's blood, a purge or "physic," washes him clean (his faith understood as all in all enabling), and guilt, a sour prattler, is left without a word ("Conscience"). So Herbert is lucky.

The great house at Wilton, a moral fable in stone, tells of loot and expensive clutter in a world changing for the worse. In remarkable contrast is the church at Bemerton, a pitiful little chapel where Herbert served the locals. He wasn't in a hurry to serve, and this contrast, as with others, is more vivid than illuminating. Like Donne, he hemmed and hawed, bemused by great expectations, then finally in 1630 accepted his vocation. But tuberculosis overtook him, and three years later he died, short of his fortieth birthday. He was like Keats, worn out by the fierce dispute between "damnation and impassioned clay." Or "he had too thoughtful a wit"—this is his self-portrait—"a wit like a penknife in too narrow a sheaf, too sharp for his body."

He left behind that one manuscript book, "Sacred Poems and Private Ejaculations," a hundred and sixty poems, mostly short, all religious, and published by a pious friend soon after his death. The Temple is a Christian church complete with its furniture, physical and spiritual. Describing this furniture, the poems are marked, says my old Oxford Companion, "by quaint and ingenious imagery rather than exaltation, and occasionally marred by extravagant conceits and bathos." Possibly Herbert concurred in this estimate. The friend to whom he left his poetry, Nicholas Ferrar (resurrected by Eliot in the *Four Quartets*), was asked to make it public if he thought it might "turn to the advantage of any dejected poor soul." Otherwise, said Herbert, let him burn the poetry, "for I and it are less than the least of God's mercies." But the poems solaced many, and soon after Herbert's death *The Temple* became a best-seller. Admiring readers took from it what they brought to it.

On that day in 1630 when Herbert was inducted into the priesthood, he looked at the court where his heart was laid up "with an impartial eye." He said he could see plainly how it was all fraud and titles and flattery, "and many other such empty, imaginary, painted pleasures." Against this, God and His service offered "a fullness of all joy and pleasure, and no satiety." That is what he said, bidding ambition good-bye, but the poetry he wrote, by intention instrumental, argues passionately for the glories that swell the heart. He wasn't a hypocrite but like a coat of many colors, one of his analogies, and the passion, not calling the piety in question, kindles and inflames it.

His first sermon at Bemerton, a florid exhibition piece, established his credentials. This out of the way, he looked askance at what he had made. God didn't intend "to lead men to heaven by hard questions," and Herbert vowed to keep future sermons "plain and practical." Complicated diction was out, so were metaphor and multiple meanings. In the poetry too: he wanted shepherds for his auditors, "simple people," and claimed nothing for his art. A peremptory poet, he favored the imperative mode: "Invention rest, / Comparisons go play, wit use thy will," etc. ("The Posy"). So art was gratuitous, and all you had to do was declaim. This is beguiling, though, like the sprinkling of rhetorical questions, meant for sardonic but coming home as something else:

> Is it no verse except enchanted groves
> And sudden arbors shadow coarse-spun lines?
> Must purling streams refresh a lover's loves?
> Must all be veiled, while he that reads, divines,
> Catching the sense at two removes?
>
> ("Jordan I")

The little poem that puts these questions takes its stand against the senses, the intellect too. But Plato's noumena, e.g. the ideal bed, better than the carpenter's, don't shadow his lines. The phenomenal world—"sudden," at that—lies behind them, and the weight is on the side of sense and intellectual address. Who will quarrel with "a lover's loves," all liquidity and easy susurration?

Herbert, even when racking his brains, isn't an intellectual poet, however, and his Antinomian bias, freeing him from responsibility, circumscribes him too. "Follow not truth too near the heels," he says in his Outlandish Proverbs, "lest it dash out thy teeth." Acute, even niggling when it comes to words and nice distinctions, he isn't adept at putting them together, and the truth of his poetry is mostly declared. He goes in for adjuring rather than persuading, the imperative mode being useful as it throws dust in our eyes. (Donne on his rhetorical side is practiced in this mode, as in his hectoring satire "Of Religion.") Necessarily, Herbert's is rhyming poetry. You don't imagine him writing blank verse, properly discursive. He doesn't work out answers, and the investigatory manner functions largely as a blind. (In this he resembles Jonson, for instance in the "Pindarics" for Cary and Morison or in the histrionic "Ode to Himself.") Nervous, self-catechizing, pointed with question marks, Herbert's famous poem "The Collar" looks like anti-poetry bitten by intellect, not made up but "real." The questions beg themselves, though, and in the answers, not detected but affirmed, consecutive thinking doesn't much participate. The poet on his intellectual side is incurious, or being proleptic, like the God of "Redemption," doesn't need to take thought.

"Redemption" is unique, and Herbert at sonnets, declining to investigate, pretty much disuses the form. Progress is merely linear, the poetry of enumeration. Many of his poems are like this—e.g. "Prayer," "Joseph's Coat," "The Answer," "Avarice," "Sin I," "Dotage" (only the last not a sonnet). One poem is called "A Dialogue," but Herbert doesn't give us the strife of *Sic* and *Non,* and resolution is wanting unless he puts his hand on the scales. Riddles fatigue him. Not untieing them or powerless to do this, he settles for cutting the knot ("Home," "Divinity"). Mockers vex him with their questions, implicative ones too, but he answers with an ipse dixit ("The Quip"). Declarative statement can't keep going for long, though, and most of the poems are short. There are exceptions, like "The Church Militant," one of his rare failures. A longish poem, running to 279 lines, it wants to be discursive, but Herbert can't carry this off.

Innocence of organic form characterizes much older poetry in English, for example Spenser's, desperate for guidons. Herbert, different from Spenser and the "superstitious" minor poets who precede him, isn't innocent but profoundly skeptical. His intellect doesn't show him the shape beneath the skin, so he wills its presence, applying this from outside. His words and phrases, mesmeric on his tongue, make a litany, unifying the poem. Or rather they confer the favor of unity, "favor" meaning the face of things. Radical examples are the echo poem "Heaven," "The Call," "A Wreath," "Clasping of Hands," and "Coloss. 3.3," whose motto, italicized, bends obliquely across the poem. Often rhymes are double or medial, or the same rhyme keeps cropping up, giving the effect of a sestina ("Aaron"), most magical, i.e. least rational of verse forms. Or the poet plays with words on their sonantal or superficial side. In Herbert's "Paradise":

> I bless Thee, Lord, because I GROW
> Among the trees, which in a ROW
> To Thee both fruit and order OW.

And so on for five stanzas. Observe his perversity or crookedness, however: the common term in this word game isn't growing but diminishing.

Finding reality intransigent, poets in his time and a little before manipulated ciphers, making poems shaped like lozenges, spheres, spires, and rhomboids. The art that goes into this is cunning but not thoughtful, and most likely defensive. Dryden, Hobbes too, sneered at his figure poetry ("The Altar," "Easter Wings"), saying it lived in "acrostic land" where the poet tortured words, seeking glory from difficulties of his own making. It isn't glory but structure he is after, however, a way to give shape to the void. At its highest pitch, his poetry involves us in doubt, posing questions the intellect can't cope with.

Coleridge, a sympathetic reader of Herbert's, is useful on this point, a hard one. In a famous passage he says that the poet, employing the synthesizing and magical power of imagination, achieves "the balance or reconcilement of opposite or discordant qualities." Herbert doesn't achieve this balance. Jagged with energy, his opposites confront each other but don't effect a reconciliation, only an amalgam. Discords are still audible. Herbert's failure at resolution is also creative, though. Disabled and knowing this, he lands us up in the dark, illumined fitfully. Half-lights, it turns out, are best to see by, and ambiguity is his poetry's saving grace.

The mirror of our equivocal condition, ambiguity doesn't mean confusion but a more nearly comprehensive mode of coming to terms with experience. All poetry that works is clear—at least as well written as prose, Pound said it ought to be—but the clarity isn't limpid, like a shallow stream. In major poetry a myriad of things reticulates to things, making a composed scene, sufficiently ordered. The composition is always aggrandizing, though, as "hills peep o'er hills, and Alps on Alps arise." This constant opening out, darkening perception, warrants its integrity.

In a musical age Herbert, more than most, was master of music, and his poems are like music, polyphonic, however, old-fashioned. Different voices make a medley, but everything is foreground and all the voices get honored, not just the "cantus." Walton, praising "Affliction I," reads this poem as "a pious reflection of God's providence," and so it is. But "Affliction," poem and category, offers something more ample, not monophonic. This musician laments his life-denying commitment:

> Consuming agues dwell in every vein,
>   And tune my breath to groans.
> Sorrow was all my soul.

Sorrow has another face, however, the pain it gives working out to music. But this isn't a happy ending, and the negative and positive coexist all the way through.

Herbert is among lyricists our great ambivalent poet: at any time more than one value occupies or besets him. His soul loves the Lord—that is the melody or cantus—yet "it loves delay" ("Justice I"). Sins shrivel the heart but fecundate too ("The Flower"). Eros, reproved by this priest, is vindicated by him, in "Church-Music," for example, where "heaven's door" opens on the house of spirit, also, confounding us, on the "house of pleasure." Salvation is the end but flesh in its stubborness, not caring to rise at Judgment, reads a lesson to the grave, "possession." The possession is everlasting, anyway in hope, the body liking well enough its imperfect garment ("Doomsday"). Invoking the Lord, flesh prays for salvation. The verse invokes Him too, saying ever "Come." But this imperative, a false rhyme, jars on the ear, making a "broken consort," itself a contradiction in terms.

> Come, dearest Lord, pass not this holy season,
>   My flesh and bones and joints do pray;
> And even my verse, when by the rhyme and reason
>   The word is *Stay,* says ever, *Come.*
>
>   ("Home")

This is inconsequent Herbert to the life, affirming against both rhyme and reason.

Rhyme, giving the effect of cinching, comes in handy to poets at a loss to end their poems. Not inept but open-ended, Herbert often skews his rhymes. Unlike Marvell, a great minor poet with an uncertain ear, he does this deliberately. In "The Collar," for instance, the stance is all bravado for thirty lines or so. Then this truculent poet, wanting an ending, caves in:

> But as I raved and grew more fierce and wild
>   At every word,
> Methoughts I heard one calling, *Child!*
>   And I replied, *My Lord.*

The last rhyming pair is imperfect, however, perhaps like the submission. So this poem is elliptical, and "word" and "Lord" not quite squaring, sound qualifies sense.

In Herbert's lowercase world, rugged particulars clamor for attention, and general statements get qualified out of existence. Where we want the gist, he asks us to pay attention to gratuities, logically off the point. In "The Windows," the glass figures the medium of discourse, but God anneals it (heats it, then cools it), reducing its brittleness. His windows, pestered with imagery, filter the message through a carnal envelope. This means a loss of transparency, and the light—pure naked thinking—comes across as refracted. Oddly that doesn't perturb Him. Unfiltered light, Herbert thinks, lacking texture, confers a specious clarity, "watrish, bleak, and thin."

To render clarity—i.e. truth in its complicatedness—he wills us to suppose a somber moiety of shade. So his way to truth isn't purification but akin to corruption, remembering small beer. His poems make a tangled skein, composition undoing itself, or else an emulsion where nothing precipitates out. ("Nothing" means nothing definitive, as when we look round for the moral.) The second of the "Employment" poems shows him swapping back and forth:

> Man is no star, but a quick coal
>   Of mortal fire:
> Who blows it not, nor doth control
>   A faint desire,
> Lets his own ashes choke his soul.

Here we are asked to damp our passions, controlling desire, at the same time to stoke them. Failing to blow the quick coal of our being, we turn to ashes, not carnal anymore but dead. An unexpected observation coming from a preacher, it denotes this comprehensive poet, scandalously catholic if you read him all the way down.

Lively with carnal life, Herbert's poems give hostages to the world and flesh. In "The Glance," his soul stirs with erotic longing, and God, its object, comes like a female lover "in the midst of youth and night." The adverbial phrase, not inevitable, evokes visions of crimson joy. Sometimes the lover, male and disingenuous, argues the ingenuous poet "into hopes":

> Therefore my sudden soul caught at the place,
> And made her youth and fierceness seek thy face.
>
> ("Affliction I")

His stars in their spheres are whores in a brothel, the elements too, inspected by "the subtle chemic," a prospective customer, sexually on the qui vive ("Vanity I"). When the priest puts off the man, this is matter for regret:

> My mirth and edge was lost; a blunted knife
>   Was of more use than I.
>
> ("Affliction I")

"Edge" is like Hamlet's edge, and to take it off would cost Ophelia a groaning.

But Herbert isn't nudging us, only apprising us: his stuff is flesh, not brass. He isn't Yeats, a wild wicked old man whose body wants a hearing and isn't backward in demanding it, and his sexuality is occulted. You have to look twice to see what he is up to, "catching the sense at two removes." Looking for the second sense in his poetry isn't devious, only an imitation of life. His "sweet strains" or "relishes," recurring like leitmotifs, speak to each other, also to the burden or cantus, promoting a lifelike altercation.

Absolute Herbert, "The Flower" derives its vitality partly from the occulted thing. Acceptance is the poem's burden, as it builds or "glides" to its conclusion. Some, disputing this conclusion, like the poet, are reproved:

> Who would be more,
> Swelling through store,
> Forfeit their Paradise by their pride.

The swelling is puffing up, befitting the prideful man, also tumescence; and "pride," residually, is lust, this man being in heat like Shakespeare's supposed lovers in *Othello,* "salt as wolves in pride." But sonnet 151, where soul sanctions the body's lust, comes closer to Herbert and his "multiplex intelligentia," being all at once comic, sober, lubricious, and moral:

> flesh stays no farther reason,
> But rising at thy name doth point out thee
> As his triumphant prize. Proud of this pride,
> He is contented thy poor drudge to be,
> To stand in thy affairs, fall by thy side.

In "Love III," a shy or impotent man is helped along by a woman, host to his unwilling guest. But Herbert's quick-eyed host is like a wanton, and his suitor's "thing" is "slack" from his first "entrance" in. Offering to "serve," the man who can't "stand" is made to sit and taste Love's "meat," woman's flesh. Though Herbert's language demands these readings, they aren't emphasized, unlike Donne's, who has his *épater-le-bourgeois* side. In Holy Sonnets XIV, God is a rapist, man a deflowered virgin. Sometimes, reading Donne, you wish he would tone it down. Reading Herbert, many readers, unsurprised and unarrested, genuflect and keep going. However, his poems make a large portmanteau, and not to estimate this is privation.

Fortifying general statement, a little practical criticism seems in order. I choose for my exemplum Herbert's "Virtue." An anthology piece and short enough to get by heart, this poem will be familiar to any reader who knows Herbert at all.

Sweet day, so cool, so calm, so bright,
The bridal of the earth and sky:
The dew shall weep thy fall tonight;
        For thou must die.

Sweet rose, whose hue, angry and brave,
Bids the rash gazer wipe his eye:
Thy root is ever in its grave,
        And thou must die.

Sweet spring, full of sweet days and roses,
A box where sweets compacted lie;
My music shows ye have your closes,
        And all must die.

Only a sweet and virtuous soul,
Like seasoned timber, never gives;
But though the whole world turns to coal,
        Then chiefly lives.

"Virtue" reads like a homily, progressing in obvious ways to its point. This poet puts his trust in the world over yonder, a first reading and always tenable, however many times you go back to the poem. But other readings, opposed or complementary, ask for a hearing. If you miss them, you empty out the portmanteau. Eighteenth-century readers do this, chopping Herbert's poems to fit the common meter of evangelical hymns. John and Charles Wesley, founders of Methodism, are conspicuous offenders, and the two of them, revising "Virtue," opt for a monophonic Herbert. They suppose that language is only the dress of thought.

Syntactic order in "Virtue" is patented Herbert, repetition with variation to enforce the idea. Here the scheme is anaphora, a like arrangement in three stanzas, intermitted in the fourth. The formal likeness asserts essential sameness, a dismal community, thrall to death, and the departure from it augurs our hope. Four terms are deployed—day, rose, spring, and soul. The first three are ephemeral, the poet reserving his enthusiasm for the last. Incremental and minatory, the refrain builds in power until the conclusion oversets it: "For thou. And thou. And all." As stanza 4 opens, the oversetting is signaled by a reversed foot: "Only." Mostly, though, this meter-making argument, chary of departures, goes its even way. Diction offers few surprises, predicting the homily. There are no tricks in Herbert, and one mustn't call this a false clue.

For countercurrents wrinkle the poem's placid surface. Soon to go down to night, the day, refreshing, equable, and shining, seems affectively good. Syntax, compelling, requires us to look again at the modifying words. Against the day and not so good is the conflagration of the Last Day, the business of stanza 4, when the world turns to clinker. Sound infiltrates sense, and end rhymes in the last stanza strike the ear as closed or clenched. In the first three stanzas, long vowels compose the rhyme words, telling of duration. Death is uppermost in line 11, but feminine endings, a pair of them in this third stanza, contend against it, and "shows" and "closes" slow the line like a musical retard. (Reading, we don't say this to ourselves but we "hear" it.)

Where the Creator in Genesis I separates earth and sky, the day yokes them together. But first of all this bridle is a bridal or marriage, more poignant for being so brief. Standing in for the rest of us, the dew, personified, bewails the "fall," or setting sun. But "fall" must evoke sinning too, as in the Fall of Man, also slackening, as when things "give," or yield. Music is part of this congeries of meaning. A musical note being lowered, we hear a dying cadence or dying fall (like Orsino's in *Twelfth Night,* 1.1.4). All these meanings speak of loss.

The sweet rose of stanza 2, humanized like the day, is ireful but splendid, and vaunting in the face of death—"braving" him when he takes us hence. Blood, disputing our mortality, mantles the cheeks, or petals. The poet participates in this protest, and his image of the rose, fragile and sensuous, makes a balancing point for the poem. An inductive logician (this is the posture), he moves from particulars to his general statement. But see how he entoils himself, incidentally his readers. Menacing general statement, he puts his vivid particular in the middle of things. What is it we remember when the whole world turns to coal?

Root and grave make a nexus, life in fee to death, and the anguished beholder, cognizant of this, recalls the dew of stanza 1. Looking on beauty, he is like Actaeon looking on Diana naked, or like Keats's venturesome poet in his "Ode to Melancholy" who sees how the veiled goddess has her shrine "in the very temple of delight." This beholder is "rash." Only the quaritied man sees so far, however. Like the thing he contemplates, of great price, he gets our attention.

In Herbert's triad of doomed things, the rose attracts us most but the order of terms is ascending. Day, the shortest term, begets the flower, longer lived, and the spring, living longest, makes room for both. "Full" is the word for spring, like brimming water, an unfailing source, spring or fountain. This is attractive. But spring is also a "box," simultaneously a perfume box, the "sweet coffers" made of alabaster or precious metal where Herbert's people kept rose perfume; a music box, whence this poet's music sounds; a coffin where sweets lie in death. *The Temple* isn't a miscellany but an integer or coherence, and other poems enforce and enrich these meanings. "This verse marks that, and both do make a motion / Unto a third, that ten leaves off doth lie" ("The H. Scriptures II"). In "Sighs and Groans," Herbert's judgmental God puts His hand in "the bitter box," packed with corrosives. Dusted with perfume, swaddling clothes are laid away in a box. But this "chest of sweets" smells of mortality, and the clouts are "Little winding sheets" or grave cloths ("Mortification"). Our alluring flesh is a box, stuffed by God with delights and made in His image and likeness. "All Thy sweets," says Herbert, perhaps admonishing the Creator, "are packed up" in this box ("Ungratefulness").

"Virtue's" *compacted* is better, the great word that says the poem, sweets not huddled up at random but ordered or composed, also thick or solid, compendious too, much richness in a little room. Herbert enlists "my music," his poem or his poetry, in their context. Likened to sweet things, this music isn't like the virtuous soul. Perhaps it has no "virtue"? Dying, it makes a harmony, though. Herbert's linguistic gamut declares this. His "closes" are endings but cadences too, a union or junction, a composition between parties, as when I close with you or agree. Like the conclusion or "fall" of a musical phrase, this closing is felicitous, "sweetest last" (we remember Shakespeare's *Richard II*, 2.1.12–13). So music dies, sweets also, and the root is in its grave. This figure, quickening in context, says different things, among others that dying verifies living, expensive and worth the cost.

A teaching poet, Herbert isn't done with us yet. Erotic intimation suffuses his poem, comprehensive like the life it betokens. Readers of "Virtue," not prudish—only seeing what their conditioning lets them look for—will likely gird at this. Cultural conditioning has promoted a whey-faced Herbert, and only Shakespeare's most recent editors are alive to his range of meanings. The Oxford Dictionary, outsize version, useful for reading Shakespeare, illuminates Herbert too.

In its range of meanings, his "fall" includes detumescence, and "die," three times repeated, has its sexual sense, endlessly available to seventeenth-century readers. Herbert's sweets, "compacted," engage in plots and cherish secrets. Hid from the light, they "lie" together, suggesting sexual play: "Lie with her! Lie on her!" That is fulsome, Othello thinks (4.1.35). Herbert's coffer of sweets, a box, is also a pudend: "also," not "is," no one meaning in his thesaurus suppressing the others. "To the wars, my boy," Shakespeare's comic villain tells a home-keeping hero. "He wears his honor in a box unseen / That hugs his kicky-wicky here at home, / Spending his manly marrow in her arms" (*All's Well That Ends Well,* 2.3.295–98). "Virtue's" *rose,* a flower and palpably itself, suggests pudend too, *root* suggesting penis. He who finds Rosalind, "sweetest rose," or pudend, "Must find love's prick," says Shakespeare's Clown in *As You Like It* (3.2.117–18). Herbert's virtuous soul takes color and substance from these carnal things it might be like and isn't.

Up front and humanized, day, rose, and spring are in the eye of the beholder, while the soul, not apostrophized, not humanized either, is seen from afar. A figure says how this soul is matured, dried, or hardened. Like timber, it never gives: bends or yields or shrinks (OED 1627, activating the "fall" of l. 3). But "gives" has another sense, and readers who read the poem as a homily, no more, will ignore it. The ear ought to cue them, "gives" rhyming with "lives." In its other sense, "gives" means "tenders" or "bequeaths," as when flowers and perfumes, giving freely of themselves, "subdue the smell of sin" ("The Banquet"). Jealous of itself, not magnanimous, the virtuous soul doesn't do this.

Green timber warps; seasoned, it becomes supple. So after all it bends or gives. Not the soul, however. This soul alone, though dry and quick to kindle, survives the flames of Judgment when "the elements shall melt with fervent heat, the earth also, and the works that are therein shall be burned up" (Second General Epistle of Peter, 3:10). But how can it, as the poet is faithful to his analogy? The conjunction "sweet and virtuous," both vital and concessive, provides us with the answer. God, Who might choose to withhold His sweet savor, chooses instead to impart it. (He does this in "The Banquet," "The Odour," "Ungratefulness," "Sighs and Groans.") Behind the scenes or on top of the heavens, He intervenes in "Virtue," and His intervention makes the difference. The soul survives or wins because it is "virtuous," good no doubt and sexually chaste, but also and crucially as it possesses miraculous power, what we can't bid for, something conferred. This victory, in last things, is no thanks to the soul.

Innate or endemic in us, virtue on its technical side comes up often in Herbert—e.g. in "Providence": "Who hath the virtue to express the rare /

And curious virtues both of herbs and stones?" Their virtue is like that unction Laertes daubs on his sword. Only let the sword's point scratch a man's skin, and no poultice so rare,

> Collected from all simples that have virtue
> Under the sun, can save the thing from death.
>
> (*Hamlet,* 4.7.144–46)

But life, not death, is in the cards here, and Herbert's "virtue" is a life-dealing tincture, quintessential like the philosopher's stone ("The Elixir"): "A secret virtue bringing peace and mirth." There was a good man in Salem who lived "sweetly" but foes dogged him to death. Possessing this virtue, he would have escaped them ("Peace"). Sweet and good he was; not "virtuous," though.

So the soul, neither calm nor angry and not quick but inert, lives "chiefly" or most of all when ephemeral things, lacking "virtue," are gone. The "whole world" (heard as spondaic: something to pause on) turns to coal at the end. This burning coal is charcoal, living matter "compacted," and the living is in the burning, unseasoned and sweet. Yeats, absorbing Herbert's poem in a little poem on the illness of Lady Gregory in 1909, catches its residual feeling:

> Why should I be dismayed
> Though flame had burned the whole
> World, as it were a coal,
> Now I have seen it weighed
> Against a soul?
>
> ("A Friend's Illness")

Yeats's soul, a substantial presence like Herbert's day, rose, and spring, isn't wraithlike but incarnate. We won't see its like again. John Unterecker, a gallant poet and critic, used to talk about this.

Against the mutable particular is everything the priest, his eye on heaven, calls important. But in the scale of sickness, which says how quick bright things come to confusion, the immoment thing, dying, asserts its enormous claim. Ross Lee Finney, the composer, hearing me read Herbert's "Virtue," hears the sequence: "Sweet. sweet. sweet. Only a sweet." This is one response to the poem.

Does it mean that the warmth of everyday, so taking, persuades us more than the world over yonder? Perhaps Herbert after all is out to fool us?

Some great poets are ambiguous in the pejorative sense, turbid in spite of themselves. Wordsworth protests too much, contaminating "Tintern Abbey." Some poets put us off in meditated ways—Donne, for instance, in his "Canonization," leading us to suppose that sexual love is puerile. Only a few poets can assimilate, while controlling, different points of view, even antithetical, in a single poem. Keats is one. In his "Grecian Urn," life is short, art long, and who doesn't know it? Marble "brede," not "breed" but sculpture, the folk on the urn are superior to flesh and blood: "all breathing human passion far above." But this radiant positive, meaning to encompass truth, suggests its own gainsaying, and Keats's doomed men and women, all breathing human passion, are far above the frozen figures on the urn.

Unambiguous Herbert, the Protestant saint, despises "honor, riches, or fair eyes." "Dust," he calls them, but that is caricature, offensive to this stickler for nice discriminations. Coming closer, he sees the dust for "dear earth":

> Full of glory and gay weeds,
>   Brave language, braver deeds.
>
> ("Frailty")

The perception is burdensome and most of us slough the burden, turning apostate or sinking the man in the priest. More comprehensive than most, Herbert entertains his antithetical truths. He isn't equable about this, sometimes kicking up a storm. But he carries his baggage with him to eternity.

Chapter 14

Marvell's Tin Ear

Andrew Marvell is the greatest minor poet in the language, praise that points in different directions. Certain Baroque composers are like him, always right around perfection though not often achieving it. We are grateful for a style in which grasp and reach, both of magnitude, come near coinciding. Practitioners of this style value art as an amenity. Pulling back from egoism and the melancholy that goes with it, they don't tug at our heartstrings or stun us with a final crescendo.

Milton, everyone's idea of the great poet, wrote epics, Marvell the four-foot line, but he moved freely within its narrow compass and you still hear his echoing song. The organ tone, invented by Milton, is beyond him, also, though he wrote Latin poems, the resonant latinity. His most ambitious poem, "Upon Appleton House," is bread-and-butter work, paying tribute to a patron at home in Yorkshire. General Fairfax was the patron, and Marvell tutored his daughter. With the left hand he versified, or "languishing with ease," dropped his fisherman's line in the water. But Herbert Grierson, widely traveled in the seventeenth century, called him "at his very best" a finer poet than Donne or Dryden. The delimiting phrase is critical, and only twenty or so of the poems are permanent. Half that many, a prodigious number, tell of his greatness, however. Readers who measure greatness by the yard will want to ponder Jonson's couplet, remembering a friend who died young:

> In small proportions we just beauty see,
> And in short measures life may perfect be.

Mostly, his writing is middle style, decent, not grand. Shakespeare fortifies the common tongue with "aureate" diction, as when a murderer's hand is said to "incarnadine" the "multitudinous seas," but Marvell inclines to native English words (always excepting the famous "annihilating," mind's function in "The Garden"). Decent doesn't mean monotonous, and open vowel sounds, liquids, and sibillants jostle each other in his compacted line:

> Let us roll all our strength, and all
> Our sweetness, up into one ball,
> And tear our pleasures with rough strife
> Thorough the iron gates of life.

More than once in the "Coy Mistress," his pairings (like "rough strife") seem equally weighted but make an iambic foot. The spoken voice, slurring the metrical pattern, obscures this. All the same, the voice remembers the schoolroom, and acknowledging its coercive presence, Marvell runs two horses in tandem. The opposition between the lead or centripetal horse and the off-horse, centrifugal, creates the equilibrium of his few great poems. Poets like Milton demolish and reconstitute the forms they inherit. Marvell accommodates them, and counterpointing is how he wins his successes.

The four-foot line, vitiated by "fatal facility," Byron said, might have turned him into a rhymester. But his music is full of contention, and though he favors short lines, they vary in length. Some poems mix two different feet, others double that number. "Weak" endings elongate his abbreviated lines, or truncated feet cut them shorter. Pierre Legouis, among his best critics and willing to criticize, said they don't do that often enough. But variety in Marvell, as opposed to helter-skelter, is contingent on his largely unruffled order, ruffled only when it has to be.

Sometimes, not often, violence threatens this order. In "The Nymph Complaining for the Death of Her Fawn," "This waxèd tame, while he grew wild," where "this" is the fawn but also the reined-in couplets. "He" is the fickle lover, and growing wild, stands for content. In the fruitful quarrel between them, content, often turbulent, takes a back seat to form but gathers strength from it too. Ameliorating the recurrent rhyme, the caesura makes its own tune, obbligato to the major one. Marvell's "complaint" comes close to bathos, simplicity's unlucky twin, but as is usual in the poems, a living voice, inflecting it, retrieves it. Against the tetrameter bit and bridle in "The Garden," reversed feet, off-rhyme, run-on lines, and crowded lines oppose their contrariness. Varying the metrical commitment (but not much), "stumbling on melons" mimics what it describes, a fall in the garden and another fall of man.

The poetry survives thanks to "Mary Marvell," i.e. his housekeeper

Mary Palmer. She wanted the money he left behind at his death, so pretended to widow's status, and in 1681 published the *Miscellaneous Poems* as work "of my late dear husband." She found the poems ("books and papers of a small value") in Marvell's Covent Garden lodgings, and without her self-serving industry they would have perished, a matter of indifference to him. He really was the Carpe Diem poet who took no thought for tomorrow. People in religious times, thinking only of the other world, found the secret of success in this one, someone said. Marvell, though not religious, is in on the secret. For this reason he lives to posterity when others, preoccupied with after-fame, are forgotten.

The poems are singular but the life lacks glamor, all gone into the art. Sprat, the historian of the Royal Society, approving his friend Cowley, might be giving Marvell's likeness: "You would never guess by his discourse that he was a poet." All the poetry we care about predates the Restoration; after that he fell silent or wrote polemical verse, low-temperature scribbling that doesn't need going back to. You gather his opinions, not synonymous with his thinking, from four prose pamphlets, circumscribed by the time that produced them. Prose was his medium when he stood before the public, poetry what he did in his closet.

His nature allowed of "penetration," that is, two bodies occupying the same space. He uses the word in "An Horatian Ode," saluting Cromwell's return from Ireland, and illustrates what it means in his own person, accommodating a poet and a poetaster. Examples are the ode itself, one of the great poems in English, and "Tom May's Death," a vulgar squib, both work of the same year, 1650. This suggests a bifold personality, "two distincts, division none," like Shakespeare's Phoenix and Turtle. Some other poets wear two faces, one for life, one for art, among them Wallace Stevens, the businessman and elegist of sexual passion, or usurious Shakespeare with his "fines, his double vouchers, his recoveries." Likely, the two faces have their relation, *Hamlet's* misogyny rising from self hatred, and tedium vitae in Stevens begetting the palm at the end of the mind. Marvell hid his light under a bushel where it burned more fiercely, possibly cause and effect.

The son of a reverend, "facetious and yet Calvinistic," he flirted briefly with Catholicism, then quit it for the English Church, everybody's via media. Like his halcyon in "Appleton House"—a type of the opportunist, this fabulous bird followed the prevailing wind or opinion—he smoothed troubled waters. Doing that came naturally, and he never met a point of view he couldn't assimilate. Starting out as a lukewarm Royalist, he became a lukewarm Parliamentarian. The difference was minor but mattered to

him. Milton raised big questions and answered Yea and Nay; he is the poet
of fine calibrations.

Unmarried like Herrick, he hugged himself to himself, but spent himself lavishly on behalf of the public weal. For almost two decades he sat as
MP for Hull, wearing out while still in his fifties. Three hundred years later,
Philip Larkin, poet and public servant, chose this provincial place "by the
tide of Humber" to complain in. Marvell doesn't complain, and though he
left four hundred letters, most are a bureaucrat's, addressed to Hull's mayor
and officials of its Port Authority. Tonnage and Poundage is the theme of
the letters. He rarely let the mask slip, not wanting to make a spectacle of
his botches and blains.

The man of affairs is coarser. Rendering to Caesar, he told them in Parliament that "whatever prince God gives us, we must trust him." Under the
Stuarts, that took a strong stomach, and what he couldn't stomach he turned
away from, leaving England on the outbreak of war. He grew more taciturn
as he got older ("naturally and now more by my age inclined to keep my
thoughts private"). The Crown's despotism provoked this question (in a
rarely candid letter to a nephew he liked): "What probability is there of my
doing anything to the purpose?" Readers of the letters won't hold their
breath on the answer.

But the Member of Parliament had a scurrile tongue and a short fuse,
once putting up his dukes on the floor of the House of Commons. While
others kept their counsel, he argued in the pamphlets for political and religious toleration. He didn't sign the pamphlets but all knew who the author
was, and death stopped his breath just as the government was about to.
Nineteenth-century Romantics, establishing a pedigree, honored the "supporter of free principles" (Thomas Campbell), who upheld them, said
Hazlitt, "not in the best of of times." Leigh Hunt saw an "inflexible
patriot," Whittier "one of the inflexible defenders" of freedom. Each imagined a monolithic man, something like Cromwell in "An Horatian Ode."
Flexible is what he was, though, in and out of office, and it isn't his partisanship that keeps him alive but his gift for hanging fire. Enervating in a
public man, this is the special distinction of the poetry, so nicely balanced
that a hair will tip the scales and isn't allowed to. Glancing at the Civil War
in one of the pamphlets, he has a stunning phrase: " I think the cause was
too good to have been fought for. "

Critics locate him at home in nature, loafing and inviting his soul. He
longed to be free of personality, however, and disappearing into nature

didn't realize but effaced himself. Licked, clasped, and curled by ivy, he stands upside down in "Appleton House," turning into an inverted tree. But the nature he hid out in was also a veil he parted. Behind it lay a better world, Thessalian Tempe or nature "vitrified," as in the incorruptible crystalline sphere, home of the immovable stars. He thought this perfect place worth getting back to. One of the pastoral dialogs says what it wasn't like:

> There's no wolf, no fox, no bear,
> No need of dog to fetch our stray,
> Our Lightfoot we may give away.

At home in this undifferentiated state—"Nature's lap," a periphrasis—nobody bustled, spoke opinions, or inclined to either side of a question. Marvell's shepherds and shepherd girls see it in their mind's eye, like an empty canvas of Lely's, still awaiting the hand of the artist.

But his pastoral poems, imagining the State of Innocence, include the Fall of Man. From travels in Spain, he remembered another version of the tabula rasa. the *toril* or bull ring before the bulls entered, staining the sand. History began with their bloody incursion. Its damage isn't retrievable, and the poetry's wistfulness only underscores this. All is "enforced" in "The Mower against Gardens," the world is no longer "what once it was," and the end of "Appleton House," preserving an artist's copy, lets us feel that the vanished Saturnian Age far surpassed it.

Cloistered nuns in the poem share something of Marvell's skittishness. Shying from the touch of hands, his drop of dew is like a coy novitiate.

> Every way it turns away,
> So the world excluding round,
> Yet receiving in the day.
> Dark beneath but bright above.

In *Ros,* or "Dew," a Latin version, the exiled soul, disentangling itself from the senses, withdraws completely "into the fortress of its own light" (*The Latin Poetry,* trans. W. A. McQueen and K. A. Rockwell, 1964). It has a model in Jonson's "brave infant of Saguntum," born just when Hannibal came down on his birthplace. Not born altogether but half-in, half-out, this considering child didn't like what he saw, and Jonson, keeping a straight face, tells how, retreating hastily, he made his mother's womb his urn. Marvell would like to do that.

But his poise is very rare. Wanting to fly away from our temporal station, he isn't in a hurry, and his comprehensive soul, preening till ready, "whets and combs its silver wings." The light in their plumes is "various," not monochromatic. Distinguishing its different hues sets him apart from poets of last things, like Henry Vaughan, his contemporary:

> I see them walking in an air of glory,
>   Whose light doth trample on my days;
> My days, which are at best both dull and hoary,
>   Mere glimmering and decays.

Vaughan's "mere" could never be Marvell's.

Sometimes his keener eye turns him toward preciosity. For the death of Lord Hastings, he hunted up "a store / Of tears untouched and never wept before," rivaling early Dryden in bathos. He shared a vice with Crashaw, each detecting resemblances not apparent to most. When pointed out, they make us spring to attention, the wrong response to poets whose surprises, said one of them, ought to come naturally the way leaves come on the trees. A stupefying poet, Crashaw illustrates to the contrary. Doing what he can with Mary Magdalene's tears, he has them brim in her eyes,

>   two faithful fountains,
> Two walking baths, two weeping motions,
> Portable & compendious oceans.

Marvell isn't up to that, and his tears, or rather hers, are only liquid chains, fettering the feet of the Redeemer ("Eyes and Tears"). Hoping to clarify, he doesn't mind if he leaves you astonished.

But in another and more persuasive context, he says how tears are waves, far deeper than any the ocean discovers ("Mourning"). Woman's love is his subject and a skeptical reporter surveys it. His next-to-last stanza isn't skeptical, however. "The Indian slaves that sink for pearl" through these waves you can't fathom never sound the bottom of one. Then, following his usage, Marvell backs away. "But sure as oft as women weep, / It is to be supposed they grieve." The conventional judgment, given tongue by J. B. Leishman, calls his poem mock-heroic or satiric. But parts of it exceed the whole, and this judgment misses the heights he climbs up to.

Living between the not-quite-extinguished past and the emerging future, he checked out his surroundings. What he sees has no analogue in nature. New-made hay piled in haycocks looked to him like pyramids rising from the desert sand near Memphis, or tumuli for Roman soldiers, long dead. He says his scene is painted, prompting expectations of Watteau or Fragonard, but we want some eccentric visionary like Hicks of "The Peaceable Kingdom." The Minotaur prowls the maze in his formal gardens, and beneath his "wat'ry maze" huge sea monsters threaten our wrack. Cattle, grazing near Appleton House, seem like a painted landscape reflected in a looking glass, i.e., much diminished in size:

> And shrunk in the huge pasture show
> As spots, so shaped, on faces do.

But another angle of vision inspects them, suggesting the stars in their courses:

> They feed so wide, so slowly move,
> As constellations do above.

Not grasshoppers but giants live in these meadows, and from their green precipices laugh at us mockingly as we walk lower than them.

Diving beneath the surface, he brings up flowers, proof that he's been to the bottom and surveyed it. The lowercase mode was on the way out, and not many in his time took the trouble. He says of himself, in one of the few letters that flag a reader's attention: "I am so subject to be particular." The tendency to particularize implies a willingness to pause, and he has nothing of Milton's brooming-out-the-attic psychology. But the annalist of meadows and gardens doesn't dote on them much, liking some surrogate better. No ripe plum fingers its rosy bloom, no pigeon tumbles in summer air. He wasn't Keats and didn't want to be. Lamb remembered "two honest lines" of his:

> Where every mower's wholesome heat
> Smells like an Alexander's sweat—

but Marvell is quoting some fabulous ancient. Things as they were didn't often engage him.

His descriptions are less parochial than generalized, or like Ben he does without them, saying of an unknown lady that all you needed "to commend her" was to name her. Seen from the windows of Appleton House, his nature is *fragrant, shady, deep, transparent*. Ambition is weeded and Conscience tilled in its emblematic garden, laid out in primary colors like the one in "Eyes and Tears" or "The Unfortunate Lover." In "Damon the

Mower" the day is scorching like his care, the grass is withered like his hopes. Everybody who knows him knows the incandescent passage in "Appleton House" where he glimpses through thick hazels "the hatching throstle's shining eye." This apparition, both real and surreal, might compensate a great naturalist, but the exception proves the rule and the poetry doesn't show another like it. But though partial to abstractions, he was able to taste them, an ability unique to him, and his solitude is "delicious."

Seldom lowering his eyes, he doesn't often raise them, no Pisgah sight out there. Still, he sees a long way, coming at the end of a journey that began ages since. His "Mower to the Glowworms" includes in its circuit the rape of Philomela, while Damon the Mower keeps company with Phaeton, son of Apollo. Meant in jest and earnest, the connections, almost at snapping point, still hold. "Love's whole world" wheels on the lovers in "The Definition of Love," "the greater Heaven" reveals itself in a drop of dew, and the fall of grass in "The Mower's Song" suggests that all flesh is like it. The suggestion isn't belabored. Marvell's poems are generally implicative, but unpointed conclusions muffle the questions they raise. Life, a pilgrimage, is also a player's stage, and his modest truths reflect this.

Deaf to the glories of the sounding cataract, etc., he prefers the world "in more decent order tame." What he misses out on lowers his stature, and he isn't on a level with Wordsworth. But his "tame" doesn't argue insipid. "Unproportioned dwellings" stand in sorry contrast to Appleton House, not diminished, only taken in hand. This describes his natural-plus-domesticated world, like a cultivated Frenchman's in the age of the Sun King. Giving a Gallic spin to the criticism, Legouis reminds us how, in France, "when you leave Paris you go 'aux champs,' or even 'au désert,' words that should not be taken at their face value." Mountains don't rise in these fields or this wilderness. "Hook-shouldered," Marvell calls them, wittily contemptuous.

But the eighteenth century, whose point of view this anticipates, appreciates "the sublime," not to his taste either, and he isn't a precursor of the Augustans. Bilbrough's hill and grove is what he likes:

> See then how courteous it ascends,
> And all the way it rises bends;
> Nor for itself the height does gain,
> But only strives to raise the plain.

This rationalizing of grandeur is serious, at the same time whimsical, not least in the last line, soft-shoeing off like a vaudeville entertainer. His subject matter, resembling his favored verse form, is apt to be slight, eyes and tears, a drop of dew, poems about mowers. But it builds to surprising conclusions, e.g. in "The "Mower against Gardens," pastoral and something more. Taking off from the tulip craze of the 1630s, when hybrid bulbs brought a fortune, he explores the difference between nature and nurture. Without evident strain, he hangs this major topos on the slender peg of his given. Shakespeare, in *The Winter's Tale*, adjudicates it too, over the course of five acts. But "more in less" is a rubric for Marvell.

Amplifying trivial business might provoke ridicule, like "a clown in regal purple dressed," but his comparisons of less to more are self-conscious, marking a civilized man. Our last successful poet in the pastoral tradition, he filters his material through an ironic sieve. This got harder as the seventeenth century waned. Tame and wild cohabit in his "luxurious" garden, begetting "adult'rate" fruit, and his "green seraglio" has its complement of eunuchs, stoneless cherries that procreate without a sex. Bermudas, his earthly paradise, is one part real, two parts painted backcloth. "On daily visits through the air," fowl like English tradesmen crisscross his grassy stage, lit with golden lamps that started out as oranges. Rocks frame a Christian temple, both lowered from the flies.

His poem, furnished with a male chorus, also with winds that prick up their ears, looks doubtfully but with affection at our passage across the waters of life. Its Puritan voyagers, leaning for survival on the everlasting arm, "rather boast" of their faith, and he lets us know that he hears them:

> Thus sang they in the English boat,
> An holy and a cheerful note,
> And all the way, to guide their chime,
> With falling oars they kept the time.

This facile rhythm, like Eliot's "la la" in *The Wasteland,* puts the poem's aggressive piety in perspective. Some modern critics hear in the last lines a celebration of Providence, even a work chant, soberly rendered. But the ingenuous prosody, not thinkable unless deliberate, forbids this.

Seriousness that gets beyond itself transgresses the bounds of civility, and "Appleton House," a serious poem that hopes to be civil, opens with a Clevelandesque stanza.

> Within this sober frame expect
> Work of no foreign architect . . .
> Who of his great design in pain
> Did for a model vault his brain.

Metaphysical poetry at the end of its rope, this sets the tone an urbane man feels at home with. Pictures in "The Gallery" offer aspects of his soul, the more personal, the more "contrived" or "composed." The connoisseur of pictures plays the role of presenter too, asking us to "see how" in "the Nymph Complaining" and elsewhere. Full of brio ("O help! O help!"), his poem is like music, Purcell's for *Dido and Aeneas*.

Keeping his distance, he keeps the footlights between us and him. His Unfortunate Lover, born in a tempest or rather "masque" of elements, owes less to life than heraldry ("In a field sable a lover gules"). Death, ritualized in "An Horatian Ode," loses its sting, at least its grisly aspect, as the royal actor ascends a stage or scaffold. The illusory world of theater, evoked by "scenes and machines," gives a lead to Appleton House and environs. "No scene that turns with engines strange" is stranger. Marvell's reality, though imitation, persuades us, like a trompe l'oeil painter's.

His mowers who look "tawny" thanks to the makeup man "seem like Israelites to be / Walking on foot through a green sea." "Like" is important. In the "Dialogue between the Soul and Body," the tormented soul hangs in chains, only "as 'twere," however, and the heroine in "Mourning" weeps "as if" to strew the ground her lover lies on. Handling metaphor, Marvell moves from less to more, but his self-critiquing wit puts hazards in the way of his progress, and his willful failures announce a skeptic's deep reserve. Old Mayans, who could have rounded off their portals, didn't want to invent the arch. It stood for completeness, and Marvell, psychologically, belongs in their company. Many of his poems don't finish but subside.

He has a given: "Daphnis must from Chloe part." Arrived at the crisis ("Now the latest minute's run"), he looks back to Drayton in a famous sonnet, "Since there's no help, come let us kiss and part." But Drayton turns his poem around, bailing out the hero; Marvell, disappointing us, goes on undeflected. He prefers the reed to flesh-and-blood Syrinx. Fruition is the greedy vulture's prey ("The Gallery"), and ten times out of ten he withholds it. Or nine times out of ten, remembering "To His Coy Mistress." But Marvell's greatest poem doesn't lend itself to summary statement.

Most poets equate fulfillment with maturity, Marvell begging to differ. "More white and sweet" than flesh, his snowy fawn hasn't grown up yet. From the garden it lives in, omnipresent in the poems, sexuality is purged. Trees don't bear twice in this Hortus Inclusus, man walks "without a mate." Part of the furniture, lambs and kids figure childish love, not red-eyed like lust but colored green by a poet who lives most intensely in the prepubescent time. Many poems tell us this, "Young Love" supplying a generic title and "Little T.C." a heroine. Her job, facing down the wilder flowers, is to tame them.

Step by step, however, the definition of adult love is despair. Marvell calls it "magnanimous," meaning that it acquits him of loving. Consummation begets convulsions, as when you flatten the round world into a planisphere. This image for sexual coupling is violent but the polite tetrameters order its unruliness. No doubt his chastened verse form put limits on the ground he could cover. But the greater truth is that he can't address love and heartbreak without qualification. In "The Nymph Complaining," as the ingenue-heroine suffers the "smart" that undoes her, Goldsmithian tremulos manage her distress ("When lovely woman stoops to folly"), and whether she is comic, tragic, or amalgamates both, is hard to say.

"Daphnis and Chloe," ranking with his best, despite its frigid title, verges on tragedy. Before it gets there, however, the unfortunate lover turns into Don Juan:

> But hence virgins all beware:
> Last night he with Phlogis slept;
> This night for Dorinda kept;
> And but rid to take the air.

Only the ungrateful will complain of the witty ending, but achieving it Marvell lets great power leak away. This is the expensive side of his civilized style.

"Daphnis and Chloe," pastoral in the modern vein, is more than usually aphoristic—

> Gentler times for love are meant;
> Who for parting pleasures strain
> Gather roses in the rain,
> Wet themselves and spoil their scent—

but Marvell's mournful trochaics tie up the intellect with their "sweet chordage." It isn't that he disliked ideas, rather that his mind was endlessly receptive. Antinomies, even contradictions, often ignoring what seems proper to either, live side by side in the poems. Soul carries diseases (in the dialogue with the Body)—cramp, shaking palsy, pestilence, and ulcer—but they aren't soulful. "Upwards bent," i.e. bound for, also away from, Marvell's drop of dew looks two ways at once, like Cromwell in his "private gardens." Fated to ruin "the great work of time," he does the job willingly. This equivocal hero differs from / resembles his opposite number Fairfax, who retires to the private life but can't cease from "warlike studies." Marvell's adversaries, partaking of each other, make judgment uneasy.

His dialectical contestants only feign hostility. Fencing partners and much alike, says Harold Toliver shrewdly. The altercation doesn't draw blood. "Chlorinda and Damon" and "Thyrsis and Dorinda," pastoral conversations between him and her, are only formally dialogue, exercise work for Court composers like Henry Lawes. The better-known dialogues between the Soul and Pleasure and the Soul and Body have this copybook character. Soul, in the first of them, comes out ahead, but this is by fiat. Affectively, Pleasure gets most of the kudos. A much finer poem, the second dialogue pairs *Sic* and *Non,* but you look in vain for Ergo ("Thus"). Wit is indispensable but handed round in equal shares; questions are good, but only if rhetorical or left unanswered. Marvell's dialogue form, essentially a blind, doesn't beget conclusions that involve investigation, and for that reason he likes it.

"Ready oft the port to gain" (in the "Dialogue between the Soul and Body"), he runs on the rocks or puts to sea again. Or—another metaphor—he looks like old Sisyphus, pushing conclusions up the hill. Before he gets to the top, the stone rolls down to the bottom. His poetry likes to challenge the poet. Having won our assent to its affirmative case, it wants to see if the negative can match it. Hard-and-fast choices don't let him do that, so he gives us an emulsion where nothing precipitates out.

The distaste for extremes might mark him for oblivion with moderately willing Barkises and moderately improvident Micawbers, but he made the middle way an adventure, traffic to the left and right of him. His salmon fishers in the last stanza of "Appleton House," their leather boats hoisted upside down on their heads, sketch his likeness. "Antipodes in shoes," they grope forward in a hemisphere of darkness. But sooner or later Marvell's "rational amphibii" get where they are going. Not only rational, their natures are also double or dual, at home in and out of the water.

"Amphibious" is one word for him, "androgynous" another, like his heroine in "Mourning," both Danae and the shower of gold. His weirdly inclusive nature, "self delighting, self appeasing," will have made it hard to write poems. All he wanted was to lie still, "settled in some secret nest / In calm leisure." Anyway, he says so in his fragment from Seneca. Saintsbury, wondering why he didn't write more, supposed "a kind of mental effort of gestation," too strenuous to repeat very often. Some poems support this, and "Bermudas" imagines a not especially Puritan God spoon-feeding us with melons and figs. "Uncessant" laborers who labored after the palm, oak, or bays raised his eyebrows. If he had an end in view, it doesn't appear, and all our comings and goings seemed to him merest parade.

But the "mental effort" that taxed him was less the creative act than making a composition where positive and negative lived together on equal terms. This needs an effort of will, agility, and sanity of the order we associate with Shakespeare. The wonder isn't that Marvell wrote so little poetry but that he nerved himself to write it at all.

His impulse is aesthetic, neither moral nor immoral, and resembles his Dutch painter's in "Appleton House." Working on "this naked equal flat," the world, he means to build it up again, more pleasing to the eye. But his poems are sicklied over with sadness, even death. In "Eyes and Tears," weeping and seeing are one and the same. The world's essence is showers, sucked up every day by the alchemic sun and poured back again in pity. None of this seems pleasing. The showers are refreshing, though, like Keats's "April shroud" in the "Ode on Melancholy." Tears, not a source of pain but pleasure, are "made to crystallize into things of beauty" (says Leo Spitzer), a marble nymph, an alabaster fawn. The blood that flows when they kill Marvell's fawn isn't life's blood but dyes what it touches, like "a purple grain."

Don Cameron Allen, an erudite critic with a bump of sensibility, located the story of the murdered fawn in its historical context. Classical, medieval, and Renaissance analogues help us get forward, but in the last analysis "the colors tell the story." Leishman, mulling over the last lines, is good on their predominant impression of whiteness, closer to the poem's quiddity than the crime of the wanton troopers, the grief of the nymph, or the cutting off of innocence. Some, with an eye and ear for political intimation, think Marvell's poem aestheticizes the horrors of Civil War, just as his Drop of Dew, excluding the world, presents a poet who can't endure the Interregnum. But Marvell is himself as he keeps his correspondences to the level of intimation. Uppermost is the kind of vision—decadent, if that is how you see things—that looks at composition rather than behavior. What he wants is handsomeness, more on the point than instruction or ethical content.

He still has a foot in the Metaphysicals' camp, and sometimes like Donne he puts his mind to a problem. But he does this less to philosophize than to display his moral philosopher side, for instance in the commonplaces from Seneca. Mostly in the poetry, apothegms do duty for resolution. In the

"Horatian Ode," we move from thesis through antithesis to synthesis but never land up there. The characteristic strategy is the one old poets call *horismus,* a rhetorical as opposed to a logical definition. Justifying regicide, a special pleader pleads against himself: "'Tis madness to resist or blame / The force of angry Heaven's flame," but Marvell's saying is less logical than trenchant. Poets have to stop somewhere.

A poet of stasis, he suspends "the river's fall," quoting from his "Dialogue between the Soul and Pleasure." (Step by step, when he passes judgment, you wait for the gavel to drop.) The Chorus ending the poem, an exuberant quatrain, puts period arbitrarily to an antiphon or fugue. In Marvell's question-begging poetry, teaching defers to metrical modulation. We are on the way to Verlaine (in the *Art poétique*): "De la musique avant toute chose."

Saying so much, I have to acknowledge that the super-suave poet has a tin ear. Metrical ends meet as he augments the line with an extra syllable, even an extra foot. Apostrophized in "Appleton House," England is a "paradise of four seas," their number dissyllabic like the "four winds" of "The Nymph Complaining." Some poets cultivate off-rhyme deliberately, setting up a faint dissonance between the idea and the verse that embodies it. Yeats is one, George Herbert another. Marvell's discrepant rhymes, a fair number of them, seem inept or impatient: "quills" and "utensils," "flowers" and "yours," "lay" and "Celia," "return" and "Saturn," "I" and "cruelty." His fawn is vanished "to" the place the swans and turtles "go," and its garden so overgrown that "you would it guess / To be a little wilderness." Wrenching idiomatic pronunciation to make the rhymes square, he has his lowbrow side.

The new moral imperative obliges poets to come to conclusions, but he doesn't distinguish good from bad. Though Italian opera, brought to England in his lifetime, assigns musical signatures to the hero and villain (tenor and bass), he fails to hear them. Hostile to polarities, he keeps picking up the Sirens' song, and can't or won't tie himself to the mast. In the best poems this shows as virtue, the other side of his vice. He didn't like Dryden, a poet of sharp antitheses. When he tries for them himself, he blurs them. Satire, teaching us how not to do things, isn't his forte, and the poet's ancient role of moral instructor eludes him. Cicerone is more like what he is. Getting up in the pulpit, a priestly censor

> Sings still of ancient rights and better times,
> Seeks wretched good, arraigns successful crimes.

This is Marvell's obligation (in the Tom May poem, etc.), but he can't discharge it. Disabling for satire, he lacks tunnel vision, and his once-and-for-all pronouncements don't have the air of coming down from Mount Sinai. Nothing he gives us is like these freestanding lines:

The paths of glory lead but to the grave.

True wit is nature to advantage dressed.

To buried merit raise the tardy bust.

In "The Coronet" he notices two kinds of poetry, one finicking and investigative (untieing "slippery knots"), the other declarative and apothegmatic (shattering intricate structures—"my curious frame"—at a blow). He cultivates neither, but a third kind peculiar to him. He can't manage the heroic couplet, and fails at panegyric verse ("The First Anniversary of the Government under O.C."). Knowing what's good for him, he leaves the elegy alone. Like blank verse, it seems outside his scope or not congenial to his temper. Poems like "The Fair Singer" dispose pentameters with workmanlike skill, but mostly the longer line betrays his genius. Dryden sees how it offers the chance for handing down the law, Milton for rationalizing man's first disobedience, but Marvell doesn't codify and doesn't canvass for truth. He isn't going anywhere, and as he says in "The Coronet," his fruits are only flowers.

On the surface, the Horatian Ode controverts this. Reflective or philosophic like certain poems of Horace, it features a tripartite structure, the right form for dialectic. Thesis and Antithesis argue the question for and against, Synthesis choosing the point of view it prefers. Devotees of closure like the eventuating pattern. But Marvell, electing it, distorts it. Diction, prosody, and matter-of-fact query progress and abort resolution. A bleeding head, inauspicious for the future, promises a better future, but brings to mind King Charles's head. Resembling Caesar's, it gets blasted by Cromwell. But Cromwell "ere long" will be Caesar. Clear-cut distinctions are out of place in this truth-telling poem. Life doesn't honor them, Marvell either.

His special talent is for the "diapason," when concord reigns through all the notes of the scale. Narrowing lines of four feet to three feet is how he asserts priorities:

> So restless Cromwell could not cease
> In the inglorious arts of peace,
> >   But through adventrous war
> >   Urged his active star.

"Restless" is posed against "could not," and "urged" against the star that constrains a volitional hero. Perhaps the verb, a reversed foot, suggests what the poet is thinking. The suggestion is veiled, though. In the account of the King's execution—

> *He* nothing common did or mean
> Upon that memorable scene . . .
> >   But bowed his comely head
> >   Down as upon a bed—

"Down," strongly inflected, signals calamity, but though captive to it, the King is free from guilt. "*He,*" taking the stress, declares his difference from the regicides. The trouble is that Marvell has to have it both ways, or rather this is his ode's chief distinction. It looks as if the "royal actor" is a touch histrionic. Clapping bloody hands, the men of Cromwell (1) applaud their own performance, (2) applaud his, despite themselves, (3) hope to drown out a victim, turning his death to farce. But the scene in which he and his enemies posture isn't the same as the shambles or bull ring. Played on a "tragic scaffold," i.e. a stage, this ceremonious occasion acquits both the hero and villain.

As the poem begins, portmanteau words like "forward" and "forsake" build the credit of the forward youth who has to choose what path to follow. Or is it that these words tell against him? No need to review Marvell's two-in-one diction. Cleanth Brooks has done that for us (1946), incidentally clarifying the image of the New Critic as a lexicographer with feeling. Professor X in his rebuttal (1952) asks for more exclusive readings, not "pejorative" but through-and-through approving. Banishing ambiguity, he boils down the ode, less comprehensive when he is done with it than the one Marvell left us.

Unresolved contrasts are of its essence, active against passive, knowing against doing. As it nears its term, these two modes of behavior are said to coexist in the Protector:

> So much one man can do,
> That does both act and know.

But the verbs bristle with difference, and for once the off-rhyme is on target. Or perhaps we are to fault the poet's tin ear. Faced by his poem's structure with the need to pass judgment, he settles for a couplet, never mind that the facts don't sustain it. By fiat, the active man, though superior to morality, becomes its supporter: "How good he is, how just." Holding up his sword hilts, he shows us the Christian cross, and a pious apothegm, commenting on this "effect," tells us how the same arts that gained a power have to maintain it. These arts recall the "wiser art" that wove a net for the King, but Marvell, suppressing irony, is getting out of the poem any way he can. The strain must have been enormous—qualifying point of view until he almost annuls it—and I know no other poem where pro and con divide the honors with so impartial a hand. But this poet of aesthetic Pyrrhonism falters when he comes to conclusions.

Only in the "Coy Mistress" does the triple structure work for him, and then only as it violates Seize the Day conventions. In "The Definition of Love," Fate, a.k.a. the poet, looks jealously at consummation, and "union" and "ruin" make a near homonym. "To His Coy Mistress" follows up on their convergence. But the poem ends happily, or seems to. Anaphora, implacable and suiting the occasion, hurries it along: "Now therefore . . . Now let us sport us . . . And now" take our pleasures, "tear" them, if we must. In the old punctilious world, we might postpone our pleasures, finding time to "complain," indite blazons, so forth. Marvell's world is post-Petrarchan. Time collapses, and a contrary-to-fact clause reports this.

But though poet and mistress can't stop the sun's progress, they have an alternative, reserved to the last line: "yet we will make him run." The conventional seduction piece plucks up courage when it comes to this "yet." Promising fierce delights, it meets and gratifies expectation. Just here, however, Marvell's poem entertains a different conclusion, neither suasive nor ribald but violent. Like the great ode, "To His Coy Mistress" divides in three parts. But the bounding lines aren't fixed, and an undersong unites all three. It has a common term, nastiness. Though the "Lady" is deferred to, ironic courtesy greets her, meant, like the chilly vocative, less to dignify than diminish. Worms will "try" her virginity, no image more horrid, while the glance at her "quaint honor," punning coarsely like Hamlet's "country matters," must shock us.

Stretching out consummation, the Amphitryon story bears comparison to Marvell's. But his "long love's day," monosyllabic, even sinister, doesn't exhilarate as it did for Zeus when he lay with Alcmena. His mistress deserves compliments, but hers are fulsome, mocking themselves, and her desert finds an echo in the deserts that lie before them. "Vast" they are, resembling empires, but also his "vegetable love." This word that "drags its slow length along" needs four syllables.

In convention's poem, death, blocking our path, thwarts fulfillment. But Marvell, seizing the day, tears it "thorough the iron gates of life," not death. Bringing us up short, his penultimate couplet seems thick with impediment, "rough strife," "thorough," longer than need be. Maybe life has lost its savor, and a lethargic poet finds too much time on his hands. Running is what the sun does as his poem gets started. But unlike that Joshua who made it stand still, he engages to speed up its progress. Perhaps all attachments reduce to "vegetable love," and this Petrarchist at the end of the journey can't abide it. Taking order with time, he wants to cut it short, or he wants the piquancy slower hours deny him. Both possibilities seem open.

Chapter 15

Arnold between Worlds

In the Victorian picture gallery, Arnold is the preachy one, wagging his finger. Step closer, however, and the cartoon comes to life, asking affectionate attention. The moralist was a cutup who scandalized his friends. A dandy in youth, his hair guiltless of scissors, he still hints at pretension in age, knowing that we aren't civilized unless we pretend. Charlotte Brontë found him striking, but his "assumed conceit" put her off. He wouldn't be Victorian-pious.

At Rugby, where his father, Thomas Arnold, presided, rigorous teachers seized his youth. That is what he said, but wriggling free, he made antic faces behind his father's back. At Oxford, he skipped chapel, read French novels, wasn't the student they hoped for. He knew what belonged to youth, "Gay raiment, sparkling gauds, elation strong." That he knew other things goes without saying, like the bride of Jacapone in one of his poems, who wore sackcloth next to the skin.

A promoter of abstractions, Hellenism, Philistinism, "the best that is known and thought," he was at the same time intensely parochial. When he traveled abroad, on the Continent or in America, he did his official devoir, but made room for the countryside and catalogued its plant life: sheep's parsley, wild parsley, tansy, pellitory, pennywort, mugwort. He knew the Latin names, too. Nurturing the evergreens that framed his English garden, he shook loose the wet snow that meant to break them in winter. He was a fisherman, he kept domestic animals. A charming long poem eulogizes his dead canary, Matthias, while offering a self-conscious parody of his chief idea, "the severing sea" that divides us.

Born on Christmas Eve in 1822, he died sixty-six years later of the heart disease that killed his father. But he didn't go quietly. The wife of a friend remembered him, waiting at dockside for his daughter's ship from America—she had married a native of that country he had doubts about, and was coming home to England with their child. In his eagerness to see them, he leapt a barrier and fell down dead. "Horrid pains across my chest" forecast his death, but as he prepared to meet it, his face shone with "joy and lightness of heart."

Always in need of money, he lectured in America, 1883–84, a "sixty-year old smiling public man" whose upper-crust "u" would have given offense, except that his audience couldn't hear him. American Redskins, Whitman leading the whoop and holler, knew a paleface when they saw one. "I accept the world," said magnanimous Walt, but drew the line at "fellows" like Arnold. "One of the dudes of literature," he wasn't welcome in the New World, already surfeited with "delicacy, refinement, elegance, prettiness, propriety, criticism, analysis." All these bad things coalesced for Whitman in the vellum binding proposed for a new edition of his poems. He rejected it scornfully, together with "hangings, curtains, finger-bowls, chinaware, Matthew Arnold!"

But the angle Arnold saw things from didn't rule out a social conscience. Taking after his father, he wanted to improve the lot of mankind. Thomas Arnold, dividing the races into those that could help themselves and those that needed help from others, shouldered the White Man's Burden. He thought the Church should be socially useful rather than doctrinally correct, assimilating religion to political parties and the YMCA. Like modern American liberals, he trusted to contractual solutions. But Lytton Strachey's "venom tooth" leaves him still standing, an attractive man of the second order. His son, resembling him in outline, is much larger.

The public man stood with the Hellenes, dedicating art to joy. But Hebraism suits his "sad lucidity of soul." The world was a furnace, consuming us, he said. Eliot, willing poets to see, beneath the beauty and ugliness, "the boredom, and the horror, and the glory," thought Arnold missed the last two but knew something of the first. He is a histrionic poet, however, always on the qui vive, and boredom is outside his ken. (I don't speak of the life, only the art.) With horror and glory he lived on intimate terms, knowing the bugle music "where hunters gather, staghounds bay," and "the unplumb'd, salt, estranging sea."

As Inspector of Schools, then Professor of Poetry at Oxford, he spent his life educating the young. The middle class, his class, knew too little, and correcting that, he told his sister, "is the object of all I do." He took the English-speaking world for his classroom, meaning to endow it with sweetness and light, "the two noblest of things," said Jonathan Swift, like the honey and wax the bee filled its hive with. Splendidly, he thought "the sweetness and light of the few must be imperfect until the raw and unkin-dled masses" possessed it (*Culture and Anarchy*, 1869). In the year of revolu-tions, 1848, he shook out the red flag, another of his surprises.

"Plain and dusty," he called the world's work, but discharged it. Though "we cannot kindle at need," dogged effort did as well, and "tasks in hours of insight will'd / Can be through hours of gloom fulfill'd." Stren-uosity goes with the age. In his notebooks he admonished himself: "read Franklin once a week," or he quoted Proverbs, a favorite text: "Drowsiness shall clothe a man with rags." He made New Year's resolutions, also lists of books to read, and having read one, drew a line through the title. Studying Greek and Hebrew, he rose at dawn to get everything in. But he never pulled a long face, and said his daily regimen that might have killed a horse gave "great pleasure."

England went over Niagara in his time, a revolution he tracked and kept pace with. He had a grand but blighted love affair, at least the poems say so. His buried life, the title of one of them, stayed buried, sparing his friends, and his white hairs were all internal. His three sons died before him, trying his stoic's faith hard. The faith, in its origins Protestant-Evangelical, led him naturally to think of life as warfare. "Onward Christian soldiers, on to the bound of the waste!" He took his lead from Dr. Arnold, who antici-pated "the approach of a greater struggle between good and evil than the world had yet seen." But the father's "buoyant cheerfulness clear" wasn't his, and his father's God died with him. Arnold, acknowledging this, is the coldest Victorian. Jesus is the subject:

> And on his grave, with shining eyes,
> The Syrian stars look down.

Out of the matter-of-fact came the poetry, amalgamating disparate things. Heroic masculinity is one, but Arnold, even while he honored it, celebrated weakness. He covers a wider spectrum than the Protestant hym-nal, and keen for the struggle, is "sick for calm" (*Balder Dead*). "It irk'd him to be here," his judgment of his friend Clough. This friend is also a surro-gate, and "of his own will went away." Other protagonists invite com-ment—his Scholar-Gipsy a truant, Mycerinus an Epicurean—and in poems like "Requiescat," it seems he wants to lay down his arms. That is what the hero does in his retelling of the Edda.

But not Arnold. The metaphor of an army marching as to war is his personal benchmark. In *Rugby Chapel:*

> See! In the rocks of the world
> Marches the host of mankind—

and in the "Epilogue to Lessing's 'Laocoon'":

> But ah! how few, of all that try
> This mighty march, do aught but die!

"Obermann Once More" sets before us the world's "warfare waged with pain," and *Thyrsis* the "unbreachable" fort of the world. Thomas Arnold meant to breach it, though, and wrestling with Satan let friends feel that God fought beside him.

Whether the battle is fought for the Lord, his son the poet doesn't tell us. The armies that conduct it are "ignorant," however. Over the plain, the living still contend where the dead fought before them. An impressive late poem, "Bacchanalia, or The New Age," reports this. But the outcome of the struggle, like its meaning, remains obscure.

Arnold's indispensable poems number roughly a dozen, including four long ones. His output is small but the whole, a real oeuvre, is more than its parts, and the ratio of quality to quantity is high. He was in his twenties when his first volume appeared, and though he kept his hand in for the next thirty years, his energies went increasingly to prose. After the death of Arthur Hugh Clough (1861), once Damon to his Pythias, he composed the monody, *Thyrsis*. The last of his major poems, it dates from his forties. He reminds you of his near-contemporary Manzoni, a great poet in youth, then a famous novelist. Everyone knows *I Promessi Sposi* but Manzoni's poetry is greater than his prose, and this is true of Arnold as well.

He coveted glory, not the crowd's applause but the right, real "Amphictyonic" thing, the suffrage of Greek city-states in council. The high-toned word is his, part of his affectation. While he kept it up, the poetry prospered, but when he got down off his high horse, it died. Other Victorians are themselves in every particle, but Arnold is himself and some other. Eliot, assessing him, blows hot and cold: "the most satisfactory man of letters of his age"; however, he wrote "academic poetry." The two judgments are immiscible unless you write off the age, and disputing the second, I hold with the first. Most readers, when his name comes up, think of the critic. Now that the dust has settled, though, the criticism seems belletristic. But the poetry gives more pleasure than anyone else's between the Romantics and Yeats.

The giant tread of the Romantics is always present to his mind, but he isn't a Romantic. "Why should a man desire in any way / To vary from the kindly race of men?" The question—Tennyson's in "Tithonus"—sounds like Arnold, but as with other things, he splits his vote and admonishing Romantic poets, salutes them. He is the scion of a great house, now fallen, and much of his poetry is "Memorabilia." A half-believer "Who never deeply felt, nor clearly will'd" (his self-portrait in *The Scholar-Gipsy*), he missed seeing life whole, but his piece of the whole is worth having.

Though partial to Wordsworth, he didn't inoculate nature with "healing power." Smoke or what looks like it broods over the water in his *Stanzas from the Grande Chartreuse* but gives no notice, even uncertain, of vagrant dwellers in the woods. "In harmony with nature," the title of an early sonnet, is a Romantic shibboleth, not one of his, and he thinks man begins where nature ends. Optimism, possibly facile, marks the end of his long Obermann poem, but the sense of nature simply going on overrides it. Whatever man is doing, "Across the glimmering, / High in the Valais-depth," the sun rises.

The bright calm moon, ever the same and making little of life's fretful stir, confronts our restless pacings in "A Summer Night." Mycerinus, his term allotted, revels as death comes near, but "the murmur of the moving Nile" puts both events in perspective. *Sohrab and Rustum* merges its violence in the river's progress to the sea. At last we hear the "dash of waves," and the home of waters opens. Arnold, they said, had a passion for running water.

At the end of *Thyrsis,* he hears his dead friend's voice bid him "*Roam on! The light we sought is shining still.*" No proof backs this claim, and if the light shines, it leads nowhere. But without arguing, Arnold makes us feel that nature yields a "virtue," presented by loving reference to the physical world. His unemphatic voice, wistful, not pronouncing, inclines us to go with him when more assertive Romantic voices make us pause. "Under the flowery oleanders pale," Thyrsis sleeps in Florence, while nearer to home "The west unflushes, the high stars grow bright." This is consolation, not much but the best he can offer.

Nature's indifference doesn't move him to Tennysonian protest. To his sister he disparaged "the modern English habit (too much encouraged by Wordsworth) of using poetry as a channel for thinking aloud." Unwilling, perhaps unable, to wear his heart on his sleeve, he sought to be an impersonal maker. The time was against him, but even in his failures he set his chisel to a harder stone than others.

People who aspired to the life of the mind used to take his prose for their vade mecum, but it belongs in a class with Virginia Woolf's Professor Raleigh, well-bred, not otherwise distinguished. Clearing the decks for permanent Arnold, let me say what can be said for it, and move on. Audacious and catholic, Arnold didn't mind telling us what "the best that has been known and thought" was. His famous "touchstones," suggesting how the best might be recognized, put his widely traveled sensibility on the line. Not a relativist, he called some writers major, downgrading others. In today's climate of Reader Reception Theory, this makes him good for our health. Elaborating definitions was his habit, though not his talent, and he said great men were great only as they labored actively for the common good. His reading of conduct, obligating us to make reason and the will of God prevail, must appeal to the young who, if they promise anything, begin as Calvinistic and purposive.

But his precepts speak to the viscera, not to the mind, also argue a special cognizance of what goes on in God's mind. Dropping religion and culture into one bag, he gives a charter to literary professors. They justify literature, in particular poetry, because it makes us better men and women. Students in their carnal hearts know this isn't true, and the defense of poetry on moral grounds, breeding hypocrisy, has done a lot of damage.

Arnold, said Lionel Trilling, is "the father of criticism" in English, but Johnson is far more persuasive. Though no great critic goes wrong more often, he batters the house down, and his passion still dances above and under the lines. Arnold's obiter dicta aren't wrong exactly, only they don't latch the ear. *Bartlett's* reprints his definition of poetry: "nothing less than the most perfect speech of man," well said and needing to be said, but ask for particulars and you won't get them. Poems have to show "careful construction," be "excellent," "sound," or "true." Few comparativist critics have Arnold's credentials, but comparing French, German, and Italian poets with Wordsworth, he decides for Wordsworth because superior "in power, in interest."

His best-known phrase describes literature as "a criticism of life." So he isn't a sciolist, worth two cheers. But emphasizing literature's moral value runs him on another rock, relevance, his sine qua non. Ideas entoiled him, and he was able to say that "modern poetry can only subsist by its *contents*." Matters of style were beside the point, and if you paid them much heed, you were like the man who, "journeying home," finds a nice inn on the road and elects to stay there. "Home" is the ideational kernel.

In the poetry, however, the end of the journey is less important than the journey itself. Having faulted Tennyson for dawdling with the painted shell of the world, Arnold does something like this, and "dawdles," his word, is just right. I don't say he isn't serious, but that, paying close attention to the husk, he leaves the kernel to be what it is. Oddly, this creates a poetry of ends, not means.

Others in his time—Meredith, D. G. Rossetti—intending to be serious, come home as portentous, while genuine poetry like Emily Brontë's is damp with a woe she can't cope with. Though acquainted with woe, Arnold raises our spirits. In the best of his Marguerite poems ("Yes! in the sea of life enisled"), life is sad but details cross it "divinely": balms of spring, the nightingales' singing. Yes! a startling affirmative, says our sufferings declare us. Even in the depths, his voice lifts with bravura, "braving" the world. In "The Last Word," he looks at the wreck of his hopes:

> Charge once more, then, and be dumb!
> Let the victors, when they come,
> When the forts of folly fall,
> Find thy body by the wall!

Newman in his *Dream of Gerontius* has something of the intonation:

> When all was sin and shame,
> A second Adam to the fight
> And to the rescue came—

and you hear the pulsing beat, a touch mechanical, in Swinburne:

> In a coign of the cliff between lowland and highland,
> At the sea-down's edge between windward and lee . . .

One of Arnold's early poems got Swinburne's attention, perhaps because, Arnold said, it mirrored "that animation of movement and rhythm of which his own poems offer such splendid examples." But this is too polite, and Arnold isn't an imitator. In the kind of poetry that gets us off the mark, the poet of *Rugby Chapel* stands by himself.

Browning has a bigger voice, and it does more things than Arnold's. Leavening the couplet, i.e. raising it from flatness the way you leaven bread,

he harks back to Donne. But he looks forward too, and Pound isn't think-
able without him: "so smiled and talked his hour / Sylvester Blougram,
styled *in partibus* / *Episcopus, nec non.*" Girls come and go in his "Englishman
in Italy":

> With basket on shoulder,
> And eyes shut against the rain's driving;
>> Your girls that are older [and] . . .
> All the young ones . . . kneeling and filling
>> Their laps with the snails
> Tempted out by this first rainy weather.

Later they eat lasagna and purple eggplant, "that color of popes."
    Arnold, compared to this, seems a niggard of detail and too refined for
prose-in-poetry, Browning's special achievement. Nothing in him like
"The Bishop Orders His Tomb": "Nephews—sons mine . . . ah God, I
know not! Well." After the high Romantic thing, we want this judicious
lowering, but Arnold's knees aren't as supple as Browning's. Both go in for
exotic settings, risking costume drama. Browning's are Englished, though,
even his Spanish Cloister:

> 'St, there's vespers! *Plena gratia*
>> *Ave, Virgo!* Gr-r-r—you swine!

A belated Elizabethan, like Shakespeare of the "russet yeas and honest
kersey noes," he came in the tail of time but nicked the minute. Arnold
lacks this sense of an inevitable presence. But he isn't chummy or robus-
tious—Browning on a bad day—and invites you to a more intimate
communion.
    Rarely does his fluency approach Tennyson's, whose coin flashes out
"from many a golden phrase." The best of Tennyson is "here and there,"
though, his characterizing phrase in the long poem, "The Daisy," and the
parts are often more impressive than the whole. Mood painting, his
strength, implies a limitation. Poems like "Mariana," "The Kraken," "The
Eagle," prompt us to ask if there isn't more to be said. But he has done what
he wants to do, perhaps what he can. Like Arnold, only more devotedly, he
harps on a single string, and morning seldom wears to evening "but some
heart did break" (*In Memoriam*, VI). Maybe the gloom is too thick, its
instances felt as "topics," expedient for priming the emotional pump. The

famous songs from *The Princess,* "so sad, so fresh," make us feel that. Our greatest literary poet, partly meaning reminiscent, Tennyson thinks we

> Shall never more, at any future time,
> Delight our souls with talk of knightly deeds,
> Walking about the gardens and the halls
> Of Camelot, as in the days that were.

He said he could write blank verse in his sleep, and behind the stately iambs you hear the metronome.

But Tennyson's best is as good as anyone's, and judgment that discriminates is only his due. No blank verse in English more thrilling than his in "Ulysses":

> though
> We are not now that strength which in old days
> Moved earth and heaven, that which we are, we are.

But, like Mendelssohn's music, the great poem looks backward. Tennyson appeals to a taste that likes its poetry gorgeous, also pointed with big questions. Arnold, though he has his "Thus we see" side, is more prosaic and less intentional, making him easier to live with.

Like Andrew Marvell he is emotionally fastidious, not skimpy but reined in. The Marguerite poems describe him: "Thou hast been, shalt be, art alone." He doesn't offer reasons, and you can infer that this diminished condition is natural to him, perhaps on his reading to all. Once we were "parts of a single continent," or undivided like the sorb apple, no more. The bereaved man craved authority but had no system to support it, or what he had didn't always hang together. Some may like him better for this. His favorite sister, Jane, the Fausta of his poem "Resignation," oughtn't to hunt for a consistent meaning in his work, there being none "through my weakness." "My poems are fragments," he said. "I am fragments."

Suiting his modesty or chiming with his content, he is primarily a short-lines poet. He doesn't allow much discretion to content, and though he takes thought, doesn't chew things over. This aligns him with innovative poets like Dickinson and Hopkins, each of whom shares his antidiscursive bias. Dickinson, a provincial who got her prosody out of the hymnbook, seems antipodal to Arnold, but both mine riches in a little room. For her "common meter," she revises old narrative forms, or Protestant church music does this for her. The 14er is one, seven feet to the line, poulter's measure another, six feet alternating with seven. In earlier days, you gave just measure, an even dozen, or got hanged, and poulterers, playing it safe, gave one more. Dickinson, like Arnold, thinks more is less, and breaks down her models to units of three or four lines. Moments of *éclaircissement*, they lack breathing room, and are meant to.

Hopkins, much freer with words, doesn't ruminate either:

> Brute beauty and valor and act, oh, air, pride, plume, here
>   Buckle! and the fire that breaks from thee then, a billion
> Times told lovelier, more dangerous, O my chevalier!

Arnold, denied the chance to estimate Hopkins, might have objected that he has his cake and eats it. Behind his new poetry stands the ghost of iambic pentameter, and interjections, like "oh" in the first line, resembling Racine's all-purpose *hélas*, are there for the "meter's" sake, not for meaning. Much freed-up modern verse is like this, carrying with it the past it wants to be free of:

> I celebrate myself, and sing myself,
> And what I assume you shall assume.

Characteristically, modern poets break more sharply with the past, abandoning the formal structure you get from meter and rhyme in favor of rhythmic or syntactic recurrence, gerunds in sequence, alliteration, anaphora. All this, Whitman does elsewhere, but his loose and baggy reticule carries less goods than before. Arnold, paying his respects to "Mr. Walt Whitman's powers and originality," wants a tighter fit between form and content. Browning's Bishop says what he wants, content like the snake, form like the vigilant Archangel who stands above it, "calm just because he feels it writhe."

Arnold isn't an innovator in poetry, despite some freely cadenced poems that do without rhyme, and his chariness of the no-man's-land between liberty and license probably debars him from the first rank. But though his means are abstemious—he would say because they are—they bring him on extravagant ends. Sometimes his clipped tetrameters sound like a greater poet, Yeats or Jonson:

> They out-talked thee, hissed thee, tore thee?
> Better men fared thus before thee.

Anticipating much modern poetry, many of his lines appear to stand by themselves:

> on the French coast the light

> The autumn-evening. The field

> In the summer-morning, the road.

This last is a road "Of death," though we don't know that until we move on.

Often difficult, his syntax sponsors confusion, leaving different senses in possession of the field. In *Rugby Chapel,* "some of us strive / Not without action to die / Fruitless." If your habit is single-minded, you will likely revise to read: "Not to die without action and not to die fruitless," but this unpacks the reticule. Arnold's, packed with more goods than most, is best left to its ambiguous self.

Though shunning free verse, he mixes different line lengths in his narrow compass, made narrower by emphatically returning rhyme. In "The Buried Life":

> And then he thinks he knows
> The hills where his life rose,
> And the sea where it goes.

Form in "A Summer Night" intimates content, an inadequate way to put it, but these matters are difficult. Mimicking the violent to-and-fro of the sea, a five-line unit accommodates four different line lengths. But violence is realized only as restraint confronts it, and rhyme supplies the needed centripetal pull. In *Rugby Chapel,* however, Arnold's trimeters ring with such power that the poem doesn't need rhyme at all.

Most of him is "Quiet Work," the title of the poem that leads off his first volume. The Arnold country or Scholar-Gipsy country is like the poetry, not bristling with menace or the beauty that assaults you. Oxford lies in its northeast corner, and though Arnold makes obligatory noises about the heart-wearying town, he ranks it among his dear places. But his hold on the world of the senses is sure. He hears "the volleying rain," trails his fingers in the water "as the punt's rope chops round." *Thyrsis* raises the question: "Who, if not I," know the wood, the tree, the river's harvest? Even in *Empedocles,* where disquisition wearies, mossed roots, veins of turf, and dark shoots of ivy refresh us.

But Arnold, having our good at heart, is too much the teacher for his good. Sometimes he racks his poetry, or lays on conclusions like bills on a billboard. This isn't the same as finding things out, and perhaps the conclusions are false. Characters in *Empedocles* come down to the footlights and sing. Or rather they talk at us, a version of *Sprechstimme,* halfway between song and speaking. In "A Summer Night," the scenery sets him thinking and "the calm moonlight seems to say," etc.

Worrying the facts until they say what he wants them to, he violates his best-known poem, "Dover Beach." Plenitude breathes in its opening lines, as perfect as Yeats's in "The Wild Swans at Coole," and the return to metaphor at the end, a darkling plain swept with struggle and flight, is very taking. For the purposes of rhyme, "fight" might do as well but isn't what the metaphor argues. Meanwhile, however, saying gains on showing. The waves bring in "the eternal note of sadness," more than we need or the poet ought to give us, after their "tremulous cadence slow." Detecting a "thought" in the sound of waters, he says what this is. Perhaps his sound is enough for sense—

Begin, and cease, and then again begin

or

Only from the long line of spray—

metrically, the poem's most irregular line and a sufficient index of meaning.

Arnold's material, all half-extinguished gleams, is hard to handle artistically. It resists closure, and the shape under the artist's hand is amorphous. Coming to the point is tricky, perhaps a contradiction in terms. *Empedocles* doesn't end inevitably but stops. Willing an end to all the talk, Arnold pitches his hero into the crater. This violent gesture gets nothing done except by fiat, but is the only conclusion possible for his irresolute temper. At his wits' end, like Conrad in *Victory* or James in *The Spoils of Poynton,* he lights a fire, begging all questions.

The critic in him objected, and in his Preface of 1853 said you couldn't enjoy a poem "in which the suffering finds no vent in action." But all his best is "Empedoclean," that is, like the play before the last curtain. Some of the poems don't narrow to a conclusion but end with him knuckling his forehead. On the rim of the volcano is where he takes his stand. For the man, the torment must have been grievous. Aesthetically, though, agonizing becomes a poet who hovers but doesn't touch down.

In *Empedocles on Etna,* Arnold appeals from the present to the past when "we had not lost our balance." But he isn't a spokesman for the good old days, tiresome people are that, and his affiliation to the past is pretty much faute de mieux. "Now" is the iron age, a wintry clime of doubts and fears, Europe's dying hour ("Memorial Verses"). He himself, like Empedocles, last of the Greek religious philosophers, has lived on into "a time when the habits of Greek thought and feeling had begun fast to change, character to dwindle, the influence of the Sophists to prevail." According to the poem, things get worse each day "in Sicily."

"When we were young," says his lookalike, every natural joy gave pleasure. This included for Empedocles "the village-girl at her wheel." Where is she now? Arnold asks in *Thyrsis,* partly a threnody for his lost youth. But the Eden behind him, when we were like lambs and all was permitted, is a garden of sexual love. Reticent like his century, he never said so, perhaps not to himself. His view of sex is frosty, shading to embarrassed. He admired the French but regretted their enthusiasms, especially erotic. Keats's vehement sexuality made him cringe.

But the poetry and random jottings in his notebooks tell a different story. Wary of his body and fending it off, he is struck by a line from *Coriolanus:*

> your affections are
> A sick man's appetite, who desires most that
> Which would increase his evil.

Or St. Matthew's Gospel caught his eye: "The things from within, out of a man's heart, *they* defile him!" He kept the heart under lock and key, but sometimes in crowded streets a bolt shot back. Then "a lost pulse of feeling stirs," he said, releasing "unspeakable desire" ("The Buried Life"). Torment without a name, it hurt him into poetry.

He preferred the past for his stories and settings, but wasn't an escapist, and looking in a distant mirror, looked at himself. "And is she happy?" he asks in *Tristram and Iseult,* where the hero dies and the wife lives on. But the question is rhetorical, also personal to him. Quoting, I switch his pronouns, substituting a man for the woman:

> Does he see unmoved
> The days in which he might have lived and loved
> Slip without bringing bliss slowly away,
> One after one, to-morrow like to-day?
> Joy has not found him yet, nor ever will.

The Marguerite poems, seven titled "Switzerland" plus others cut from the same cloth, perhaps twenty all told, remember love won, then lost. Arnold's heroine doesn't stand on a pedestal—men before him have pressed her lips—and she isn't sugar and spice but has a figure worth noticing, blue eyes, pale skin, and "soft, ash-color'd hair." On the stairs or by the half-opened door, he hears her voice, and once, when out boating, sees her looking down at him, strawhatted, flowers in her breast, blue ribbons dancing on her shoulders. For a moment his boat hangs poised, then the darting river, or river of Life, bears him on. The when . . . then sequence is close to his bone. "When the moon their hollows lights," sexual longing sweeps the lovers, but then they know their bounds, and poem and life are over.

Reaching out to embrace her, he hears himself say: " 'Tis in vain." Sad, she must have thought him, perhaps an innocent. She was French. Arnold's family, denying her existence, destroyed the letters that might have confirmed it. But two letters to Clough survive, telling of a blue-eyed woman, possibly from Paris, and staying at the hotel in Thun. Evidently smitten, Arnold is "apt to hoist up the mainsail to the wind and let her drive." More exactly, he is "too apt," and lets the opportunity pass. Trilling says they read Foscolo, that unhappy Italian poet, together.

He judged himself, as he watched the parade go by, a man never quite possessed by passion or benumbed by the world's sway. Others went with the drifters, "men of the crowd," or the doers, "souls temper'd with fire." *Rugby Chapel* lays out these alternatives. Moving uneasily between his two worlds, Arnold followed neither. The poetry, where stasis governs, put him at ease, though. "Weary of myself, and sick of asking / What I am, and what I ought to be" ("Self-Dependence"), he faced a problem, at the very least artistic. Addressing it, he didn't furnish answers but dramatized his native frailty. Paradoxically, his poems take strength from this, their power like an old Elizabethan's, Fulke Greville's, divided by reason and passion.

His unwillingness to choose doesn't lower his credit but separates him from the many who want to know what the problem is. In his *Stanzas from the Grande Chartreuse,* we climb with him to a high place where he glimpses, through the scud of cloud, "something" shining. This is the lure of faith. Unlike his godfather Keble, yearning after a "dead time's exploded dream," he saw through it. But he didn't scoff like Huxley or revel like his Mycerinus, and recognizing a will-o'-the-wisp, regretted that it wasn't substantial. This impersonal regret makes him the time's exemplary poet.

So far, my praise is muted, and Arnold, though he bears it out, is more

than a judicious man who didn't or wouldn't. At his best, he joins like to
unlike:

> The day in his hotness,
> The strife with the palm;
> The night in his silence,
> The stars in their calm.
>
> > (*Empedocles on Etna*)

Fleeing "the infection of our mental strife," he heads for the sidelines, but
wants to live before he dies, so throws himself into the fray. More intelli-
gent than some whose talent was greater, he orchestrated the back-and-
forth, his poetry's distinctive condition.

In the great poems, he worked out a concordat between pro and anti-.
But though sharing the same reticule, they pull in opposite directions, cre-
ating a tougher compound than you get in poems where the parts are the
same. "Averse" like Dido to the blandishments of the new age, he breaks
with the old, like Aeneas. Or he accepts what he rejects and the other way
round, "the line of festal light in Christ-Church hall" from which his
Scholar-Gipsy turns, the merry Greeks in the poem's last two stanzas. Laden
with wine and "green, bursting figs," they gladden the heart but usher in an
evacuated future. In the courts of the Grande Chartreuse stone basins take
the icy water, white-cowled forms summon to death in life. But troops of
soldiers, going forth to the world, make the blood dance, and from far away
he hears the laughter of women.

Chapter 16

How Yeats Came into His Strength

"We were the last Romantics," said Yeats, and the poetry, vivid with felt experience, largely his own, approves him. No major poet speaks more often of himself, a matter of temperament, subsequently of style. The imperious or poignant voice, raised for the first time in epigrams and never mistaken, is recognizably his in "The Wild Swans at Coole," his volume of 1919. Though it begins with ego, art is uppermost in the Yeatsian style, as Ben Jonson said it must be: striking a second heat on the Muses' anvil. Intellect seals it, but not a philosopher's, a poet's. By the distinction I mean that his attention goes less to ideas than to form. The Ireland most know takes shape from him, more than it shaped him.

His career is flecked with impurities, some facile poems and too many abstruse ones. When he is abstruse, he is merely personal. He had a long career, beginning in the Victorian Age, ending on the outbreak of the Second World War, and toward the end his power flagged. But his recovery in the "Last Poems" (1939) is immense. He said he wanted "to make a last song, sweet & exultant," and did this.

At first the world he manipulated in art pressed him hard, a solitary boyhood, no good at games or his studies. Intended by his father for Trinity College, Dublin, he chose instead the self-instructed life. No doubt the powerful temperament will take off on its own, but better if it takes off from something substantial. Yeats's choice helped create the autodidact, too respectful of the formal learning he never acquired, and not always able to separate its wheat from chaff.

At fifteen, sex came on him "like the bursting of a shell." Horrible and splendid, words he used in "The Tower," it enthralled him for the rest of his life. In his last years he wrote to Olivia Shakespear, once his mistress: "I shall be a sinful man to the end, and think upon my deathbed of all the nights I wasted in my youth." Waste meant unconsummated love, but he made a good thing out of sexual frustration. Maud Gonne, the unrequited love of his

life, animated his old man's reveries, stunningly to our profit. Summoning
friends in the poem of that title, he remembered "what she had,"

> While up from my heart's root
> So great a sweetness flows
> I shake from head to foot.

In the 1880s, when he first met her, he became a devotee of the occult,
and like Blake forged his own worldview. Any handle on things is better
than none, and readers will want to look beyond its craziness. He said it fur-
nished him an "orderly background to work upon," absent in his youthful
unlocated verse. Not that he doesn't specify locations, but they are like the
painted cloth at the back of the stage.

Had he left nothing more than the first *Collected Poems* (1895), he
wouldn't rank higher than his friends of the Rhymers' Club, Ernest Dow-
son and Lionel Johnson. Christina Rossetti, who overlapped him, is a bet-
ter poet than early Yeats. She has edges, an individual voice, and her pas-
sion, not confected, forces its way to the surface. "High and airy," his own
self-mocking phrase, he is all surface. A decadent, he went heavy on hair,
"Passion-dimmed eyes and long heavy hair." "With a rhythm that still
echoed Morris," he prayed to the Red Rose and Shelley's Intellectual
Beauty.

But he remade himself, and outliving his palely loitering youth, created
the most impressive body of poetry in English since the seventeenth cen-
tury. The man who stands up and says it takes first place among theatrical
poets, and if sometimes you smile when smiling isn't asked for, that doesn't
diminish but endears him:

> We the great gazebo built,
> They convicted us of guilt;
> Bid me strike a match and blow.

"Superbia" is what he had, like the Rhymers, especially Dowson of the
Cynara poem, but raised to the ultimate power:

> John Synge, I and Augusta Gregory . . .
> We three alone in modern times.

His pride goes before a fall, not a moral sequence but signaling inclusiveness.
The Capitol with him is built over against the Tarpeian Rock. Like most

we call great, he is a poet of antinomies, holding both in suspension and honoring both, "the horn's sweet note and the tooth of the hound."

Despite a mind abuzz with esoteric learning, he lived in the mainstream. His sensibility, doing little with the Logos, vindicated the Word Made Flesh. In "A Prayer for My Son," he addressed the Creator, fashioned like himself from the dust of the earth:

> You have lacked articulate speech
> To tell your simplest want, and known,
> Wailing upon a woman's knee,
> All of that worst ignominy
> Of flesh and bone.

The Theosophist in him craved real apparitions, a contradiction in terms, and after a while his fellow communicants expelled him. Even in those early days, he walked in fear of "the dragon of the abstract."

His poems are an opportunist's, "like a child playing with bricks in the corner." Never mind his argument: it is his meter that persuades us, and when he falters, as in a trivial poem like "Politics," the meter, too easy, lets you know it. He doesn't intellectualize, and tackling important questions, has more wit than to answer them. "O when may it suffice?" is the question he raises in his great poem for the Easter Rebellion. The referent is mysterious, "it" standing for Ireland's struggle, also the evil that besets us but whose cause we can't know. Answering the question is Heaven's part, "our part"

> To murmur name upon name,
> As a mother names her child.

This activity, ceremonious like incantations, comprehends essential Yeats. Though he draws to conclusions, memorably in "Lapis Lazuli," "A Prayer for My Daughter," "A Dialogue of Self and Soul," they aren't argued but declared. E.g. in his "Dialogue": "I am content to follow to its source / Every event in action and in thought." It is the acceptiveness that marks him. Under the self-dramatizing, the poet he most resembles is Shakespeare, whose deepest wisdom is proverbial. "The readiness is all," Hamlet tells us. Here are some sententious lines of Yeats's:

> All things fall and are built again,
> And those that build them again are gay.

> My medieval knees lack health until they bend.

> Man is in love and loves what vanishes,
> What more is there to say?

Yeats is also the public man, a senator of the Irish Free State who held "views" like the rest of us. In old age he flirted with General O'Duffy's Blue Shirts, hoping to write songs for the "marching men" of Ireland. But his songs, though they storm heaven, are the reverse of kinetic. In his two-in-one nature he resembles many poets, Marvell the MP, Whitman the political journalist, Arnold the schools' inspector. Yeats wore this hat too. Herbert, a type of the man who lives for others, has the same comprehensiveness, and let us add Hopkins and Father Robert Southwell. Jesuit and martyr, he wrote a famous poem Jonson had the wit to envy. The mingling in one person of the active man and the contemplative who gets nothing done is a mystery. I think it means, at least for my exemplary cases, that laboring for the common good is noble work, but seeing into the life of things, work for a poet, transcends it.

Yeats saw farther than anyone else in his time. In the end, this serious man came to nonsense, as possibly all do who answer to the name. "Fol de rol de rolly O." Some of his last poems, like "John Kinsella's Lament," yield nothing to intellectual poking and prying. Commentators, worrying his balladlike "Three Bushes," have it instructing us that "Body and Soul are one," but the poem itself, all integument, not the same as superficial, shrugs this off. Sometimes all you get is a tissue of gratuities, and as near perfect as our century can offer. I quote only the ending of "Beautiful Lofty Things":

> Maud Gonne at Howth station waiting a train,
> Pallas Athene in that straight back and arrogant head:
> All the Olympians; a thing never known again.

The celebrant of "blind, stupefied hearts" is at the same time one of poetry's scholars, and shows you how "a good poet's made as well as born." Going to school to the past, he salutes his genuine peers, changed to his collaborators. He stands on the shoulders of poets before him, acquiring a larger and humbler perspective than you get from looking into your heart. "Speak to me of originality, and I will turn on you in rage," he said. Though Gaelic was his national language, he owed his soul to English poets, Shakespeare, Spenser, and Blake, perhaps William Morris. A patriot, he deplored this debt. But the grass must keep the form where the mountain hare has lain, and it gave his poetry its bent, straight and crooked.

Morris stands for the "swishiness and slushiness of the post-Swinburnian line," the matrix he had to get free of. "I am he," said this attractive man, more attractive as a man than a poet, "Who strive to build a shadowy isle of bliss," the Earthly Paradise. Blake speaks to the hermetic impulse in Yeats and his fascination with polar opposites like Self and Anti-Self, "Hic and Willie." In *The Rose*, his second volume, he tried to reconcile Peace and Battle, Heaven and Hell, but so far his words weren't up to the job. Thirty-five years later he wrote "Among School Children," where the chestnut tree flowers as the sum of its parts. Much of Yeats's psychic maundering is justified in this image, neither bole nor blossom—or Sad and Happy Shepherd, Soul and Body, Innocence and Experience—but an integer that most of us halve.

He took Spenser for his model (along with Shelley) in juvenile poems and labored imitations like "Shepherd and Goatherd." Spenser, restricted by temperament, "delighted in sensuous beauty alone." It offered too little, and he flew on the nets of allegory. In his partly failed poetry, said his former disciple, "the gyre ebbs out in order and reason." But Yeats's version of the good naif who took a wrong turn is made in his own early image and likeness, not auspicious for major poetry. Spenser doesn't suffer from an overplus of reason, and Yeats in the Nineties wouldn't be worse for a pinch of the same. Primarily pictorial, he worked from inferior copies, "Burne-Jones cartoons," Pound called them. Art bade him "touch and taste and hear and see," but he didn't honor the injunction when the Platonizing fit was on him. Platonizing means for him an abstract diagram—Swedenborg and Boehme, "my initiation into the 'Hermetic Students,'" cabalistic imagery—hung before the visible world.

At forty, he had lived too long in "a country of shadows and hollow images," so sailed for another country, England in the time of Shakespeare. Downplaying self-knowledge—Yeats's way of putting it but we might revise and say, not absorbed in the self—Shakespeare's English cultivated knowledge of some other, Hamlet or Lear. Know thyself is the precept most of us put first, and this doesn't sound hopeful, but wait. Shakespeare is the master of the impersonal voice, and Yeats came into his own as he learned it. In "Ego Dominus Tuus," a great poem marred by the hermetic student he never quite got rid of, he says he wants to find himself, not an image. But a shrewder self or Anti-Self reproves the callow poet:

> That is our modern hope, and by its light,
> We have lit upon the gentle, sensitive mind
> And lost the old nonchalance of the hand.

To recapture what was lost, he put on a mask, picked from the wardrobe and more compelling than the face he was born with. Elsewhere he wrote: mask is "the image of what we wish to become," and you can say he lived the role he played so well that it became him. This is the reason for role-playing, more fruitful than preachments that bid us be true to ourselves.

The drama in Shakespeare's age, objective work, converted the soul from a mirror to a brazier, burning off all that was only personal, hence of little account. Shakespeare's actual personality seems faint, or neutral like litmus paper. Through mask and image, however, "he created the most passionate art that exists." He had his neurasthenic side, a biographer's business, but feeling his way into Hamlet and Lear looked with "tragic joy" on the nightmare of history. Tragic joy isn't heartless but how you feel in the last exigent, or rather how they do, not breaking up their lines to weep.

Readers who don't love Yeats, warts and all, will likely jib at the talk of masks, anti-self, and the rest of it. Probably he talked too much about his ideas, using a made-up idiom that bristles with big words. "I must leave my myths and symbols to explain themselves," he said, but didn't always do that or couldn't. In well-known poems like "Byzantium," "The Second Coming," and "The Phases of the Moon," the intellectual freight, an unleavened lump, drags the poem earthwards. Perhaps there wasn't any help, Yeats's purity needing its dross.

A comprehensive worldview buoyed up his heroes Dante and Shakespeare, telling them what they ought to believe. Whether they believed or not mattered less than the availability of this frame of reference, and quarreling with it they pushed against a tangible thing that pushed back. Both depart from a norm and it gives their departures meaning. Yeats, like his Spenser, came on the scene when old certainties were crumbling. Denied a framework, he invented his own, and sometimes it leaves the rest of us on the outside looking in. Yeats isn't perfect and a just estimate will notice the warts.

But as his "system broadens out, it merges with the traditional insights of our culture, it tends to disappear into its specific aspects." This discrimination—Allen Tate's—is a good point of access to Yeats's philosophic work, scaffolding he should have kicked away and didn't. But it helped an anxious poet "hold in a single thought" the vexed matter of history. He marked off the past in "phases" of his own devising, and wouldn't be drawn if you asked him did they really exist. "Stylistic arrangements of experience," he called them, "comparable to the cubes in the drawing of Wyndham Lewis or to the ovoids in the sculpture of Brancusi." Much of *A Vision* works out to first-rate criticism, though written in tongues, and much, if you come to the kernel, demands assent. E.g. clapping on the mask, you find yourself as you go out of yourself. Actors and credentialed poets understand this, and Yeats as he prospered stood behind a screen, better than speaking directly "as to someone at the breakfast table."

The poet who expressed personal love or sorrow risked the twin rocks of egotism and "indiscretion" (not telling too much but telling it loosely). Keeping clear of the rocks required the constraints of traditional form. Our preeminent modern poet, Yeats shied from free verse, the particular idiom of the modern age. Ancient salt was best packing, and he stowed his decaying body in an old tun or fitted his neck to the yoke of old stanzas.

Ottava rima was one, annotated by Tudor poets, later by Byron. In a trio of great poems, "Sailing to Byzantium," "Among School Children," and "The Municipal Gallery Revisited," he made this stanza peculiar to himself, another way of saying how it becomes public property. He did the same in sonnets, though stamped with Shakespeare's *noli me tangere*. Experimenting, he wrote the Surreyan kind, couplets in series, or he imitated Shakespeare's kind but quit after twelve lines, leaving out the "Thus we see" part. He wasn't a modern for nothing. More than once, however, he dared break a lance with Shakespeare, and didn't come off second best. "Leda and the Swan," though close to Shakespeare's rhyme scheme, doesn't suggest him, doing something new with the form.

Under his hand, rime royal isn't reminiscent but alive with "images that waken in the blood," all telling of an old man's frenzy. You can call this man Yeats if you want to, half the truth, no more. It pleased him to say that he spoke his poems "through the mouth of some wandering peasant poet," but that was malarkey, and the voice you hear comes from Chaucer and Shakespeare. Resuming terza rima in the "Last Poems" he went back to Dante, at closer hand to Shelley. His work is of a piece, and for the first poem in his first volume, a half-century earlier, he chose the same form. With practice, it became second nature. No one practiced harder, and his study transformed him, like those shrouds in a late poem whose throats are changed to a bird's.

Heartfelt emotion takes all his heart for speech in the elegy for Major Robert Gregory, but his emotion, though real, is also managed. Some rhymes are faintly dissonant, marking distress, and an agitated poet—never more collected than when shaken by feeling—mixes different line lengths. Researching a pattern, he found his in Abraham Cowley, a late Metaphysical. Yeats's poem seems remote from painstaking, however, and says how true ease is art's offspring, those moving easiest "who have learned to dance."

Easy dactyls and anapests, every tyro's idea of poetry, make facile rhythms in poems of his first books. His pause for breath (caesura) doesn't dance much, and rhymes come trippingly, fortified by "running on the letter." Old rhetoricians, who knew a vice when they saw one, used this phrase for the alliterative mode. Yeats works it to a fare-thee-well, and many a creek gave the creel in his cart. "Unreality and cold rhetoric," words for the Miltonic style, enfeeble his early poems, and he only became his own man when (as he wrote Lady Gregory) he got Milton "off my back." You see this happen in his "News for the Delphic Oracle," modeled on Milton's hymn "On the Morning of Christ's Nativity." Cleaned-up shepherds in the hymn chat on the "lawn" outside "the courtly stable," and Pan, a type of the Good Shepherd, is piped on by "divinely warbled" music. Yeats's music is "intolerable," his Pan a foul goat head, and "belly, shoulder, bum" announce him. Milton doesn't write like that, preferring the high place convention decrees for poetry. As Yeats learned to climb down, his content grew more substantial, "solider" Aristotle besting Plato's ghostly paradigm. But the decisive change is linguistic. Yeats's philosopher plays "the taws upon the bottom" of a king, and genuine poetry waits on some such idiom as this.

Donne gave him a great shove in its direction. Few since Pope's time paid much heed to his mix of august and homely, and Pope only to correct it. Coleridge has a splendid epigram—his Donne wreathes "iron pokers into truelove knots"—and you meet Donne's craggy likeness in Browning. But restoring a great poet to his kingdom needed Sir Herbert Grierson's edition of the poems (1912), archaeology and much more. Yeats, immersed in this book, fished for pike, he said, planning out poems of his own.

He landed an important catch, diction, rammed with everyday life. Against convention, which likes its poetry high-toned, Donne favors the vulgate:

> were we not weaned till then?
> But sucked on country pleasures, childishly?
> Or snorted we in the Seven Sleepers' den?

Up the road are Yeats's "seven Ephesian topers," fabulous men but he brings them down to earth. Linguistic parallels don't tell the whole story, though, and the correspondence between Yeats and Donne, more than superficial, "the foolish hanging of a nether lip," involves new ways of seeing and presenting. Partly the new ways are technical. Form and content oppose each other when Donne's mistress imagines her lover "Assailed, fight, taken, stabbed, bleed, fall, and die" (Elegy XVI). Calm defines storm in his faultless iambics, and the same relation governs for Yeats. Many think this gets it backwards. They take Hamlet literally when he proposes that art hold the mirror up to nature. I.e. art, not giving life shape, mirrors it exactly, a one-to-one correspondence. Perhaps a chaotic utterance ought to represent chaos?

Yeats canvasses the problem in the light of his study, and his later poetry is more lifelike, but not because he has sacrificed form. "The discord had its value from the tune," he said, and the iambic pattern, broken, then resumed, makes his variations more telling. In "The Wild Swans at Coole":

> The woodland paths are dry,
> Under the October twilight the water—

and in "Among School Children":

> What youthful mother, a shape upon her lap
> Honey of generation had betrayed,
> And that must sleep, shriek, struggle to escape.

Running out the tether, he feels its tug, a salutary pressure, seeing how form, the warder of violence, controls but enables it too.

Beginning with his fourth book, *In the Seven Woods* (1904), he has got Donne's trick of speech. "The noisy set / Of bankers, schoolmasters, and clergymen" (like "school boys and sour prentices . . . country ants" in "The Sun Rising") call poetry effete, but he can tell you how articulating sweet sounds cracks the sinews.

> Better go down upon your marrow-bones
> And scrub a kitchen pavement, or break stones
> Like an old pauper.
>
>   ("Adam's Curse")

Yeats the anti-poet, less inclined to poetry than truth, begins with the opening stanzas of this poem, where "maybe" and "poetry" make a rhyme.

But he didn't renew himself all at once, and the Pre-Raphaelite poet keeps putting out new plumage—in "Adam's Curse" when the moon, "worn as if it had been a shell," is washed by time's waters. What went on in the kitchen didn't always detain him, or perhaps wasn't visibly there. In a poem from his first book, "peahens dance on a smooth lawn" and he moors his lonely ship in this landscape, like nothing in nature. He liked the peahens. "As to the poultry yards, with them," he said, "I have no concern." Giving his beloved "Certain Rhymes," he got their gist from "some old Gaelic legend. A certain man swears to sing the praise of a certain woman, his head is cut off, and the head sings." This song is disembodied.

Time passed, and in the person of Cosimo he imagined a library whence Italy—or turbulent Ireland—might draw delight in art, logic, and natural law. How should it do that but "by sucking at the dugs of Greece"? Yeats's line—it burns a hole in the early pastel pieces—doesn't imitate Donne but plunders by right of conquest. Donne's metaphysics, often pedantic, plus the obscenity, are naturalized in the rock and loam of Yeats's Eden. The man and woman who live there make a subtle knot of body and spirit. "Interinanimated" is Donne's word for what they make, meaning in this case of Yeats that you must feel your thought and experience your feeling as thinking. The language he wanted for his poetry ("a speech so natural and dramatic that the hearer would feel the presence of man thinking and feeling") is realized when thought rushes out to the edges of flesh. You hear it in the Robert Gregory elegy, celebrating a hero whose "mind and hand were one," or in that all-together poet who "thinks" in a marrow-bone. No good thinking your thought, as cogent as may be, unless the body's lineaments "even from the foot-sole think it too."

Deep in Ben Jonson by 1906, he came face to face with our greatest self-made poet. In poems of *The Green Helmet* (1910), the true dividing line between Yeats late and early, Jonson turns up everywhere, a bricklayer's prentice who wore his mask, as we might say his "persona," until he made it fit. The first and last poems in Yeats's volume are literary, but otherwise all are inflected with "the day's common speech." The phrase is his, but his poems, though written in the vernacular, set it ablaze. Flagrantly personal, remembering Maud Gonne, "what thing her body was," they get beyond themselves. Yeats's subject turns into "A Woman Homer Sung." He himself, who used to be a dandified provincial, is the singer.

The epigrammatic mode, terse, in the manner of Ben's *Epigrams,* distinguishes this poetry that withers into truth. In the titles Yeats does something different; he exfoliates. He is setting up an anti-model, the old loquacious poet. But he contradicts himself or does different things at once, and his long-winded titles illustrate and honor poetry's proper role. On this side, admonishing a poet "Who Would Have Me Praise Certain Bad Poets, Imitators of His and Mine," he is Petronius or Jonson:

> You say, as I have often given tongue
> In praise of what another's said or sung,
> 'Twere politic to do the like by these;
> But was there ever dog that praised his fleas?

On another side and all of a sudden, he is a modernist in poetry. He wants to be "colder and dumber and deafer than a fish." His tetrameter lines, truncated and pulsating, "Jonsonian," are riddled with light, though.

> Ah, that Time could touch a form
> That could show what Homer's age
> Bred to be a hero's wage.

Say these verses over and you endorse their sense, not won by intellect but the overflow of spontaneous (seeming) emotion. The emotion, apparently upended from the horn of plenty, is channeled through a narrow bore. Some call the last line sexist, true except for the neologism, but not adequate for the man it describes.

Jonson is chiefly an emotional poet, histrionic, romantic, and this is the temperament Yeats warmed to. Rhetorical questions, pointing his lines, give the effect of mind working. He got this strategy from Jonson, who raised questions to beg them, and their overlay keeps the poems from flying apart. (Exceptions prove the rule, like "Leda and the Swan.") Both Yeats and Jonson are great "ipse dixit" poets and depend less on cogitation than asserting, "thus he said." You need a personality, different from temperament, to beat down opposition, and Yeats, who didn't have one, made sure he found one. (It didn't lie in his way exactly.) Critics who rage at him, arguing from reason, founder in his shouldering sea.

Putting on the new man meant first of all an access of craft. Jonson's rhyming couplets suggested a form, but Yeats's rhymes, though often clamant, are often willfully slanted, or run-on lines efface them. Spondees, or what looks like them, intermit the tick-tock, appearing to break his iambic pentameter. "Our colt"—i.e. Pegasus, more "language such as men do use"—must

> Shiver under the lash, strain, sweat and jolt
> As though it dragged road-metal.

Sometimes the refrain makes too much music, Pre-Raphaelitish, so he takes it out when the ear expects its recurrence. He wants his poem to look accidental. As he gets on, his balladlike repetitions, not simply adhesive, work incrementally, and complicating meaning, assert it. What should he do for pretty girls, now his old bawd is dead?

The royal persona is Jonson's great gift to Yeats, and signals the transition from private rhymester to the world's acknowledged legislator, everybody's business.

> Tonight, grave sir, both my poor house, and I
> Do equally desire your company;
> Not that we think us worthy such a guest—

but Jonson's pronoun and the magisterial voice deny this. His Penshurst, where for a long time "gentler spirits have sucked innocence," recomposes itself in Yeats's "Prayer for My Daughter." "All's accustomed, ceremonious" in the house he wants her to dwell in, but the coveted thing has to be earned.

A great pretender, aristocratic Yeats, known slightingly as "Willie" to skeptical Maud Gonne, came down hard on "knave" and "dolt," preferring "Distinguished Persons." He looks wryly at himself, though, and the self-consciousness saves him. But Jonson is the master in this aggrandizing-concessive style. Riffraff are out there, affronting his person, and he smites them. None can stand comparison with high-and-mighty Ben, "All that I am in arts, all that I know." Then, disarming protest, he punctures the balloon: "How nothing's that?" Friends are wise as they don't answer him, a national treasure and the cross they have to bear. Yeats at Galway Races is like this, his own hero and best auditor. "Sing on," he says, rehearsing Jonson's "Ode to Himself" ("sing high and aloof"), never minding clerk and merchant. The contempt cuts two ways, though. Introducing the "Wild Swans at Coole" volume, he likens himself to "a post the passing dogs defile."

In this volume's great poem, his elegy for Robert Gregory—our century's greatest poem, said Allen Tate in an aside—he gathers from Jonson how death has meaning only as it bereaves a poet. Egotism bears no part in this. Poets are priests "and say such truths," on Jonson's word in his Cary-Morison ode. His dead friend lives on in Ben "who sung this of him, ere he went / Himself to rest," and Yeats's close companions, though breathless, survive "in my thoughts," worth recording. The voice that speaks these thoughts, dignified but prosaic, judgmental but rarely captious, invokes natural truth, less consoling but more persuasive than the consolations of philosophy. Mostly spare and Anglo-Saxon, it allows for big words, always the exception, and this gives them their force. An arbiter's voice that brooks no disagreement, it seems passed back and forth between two absolute makers, echoing each other across a great gap in time. Jonson's tells of "early men"

> Who, ere the first down bloomèd on the chin,
> Had sowed these fruits, and got the harvest in.

Yeats is more ample, running the gamut from youth to age, but the yield for both is incandescence:

> Some burn damp faggots, others may consume
> The entire combustible world in one small room
> As though dried straw, and if we turn about
> The bare chimney is gone black out
> Because the work had finished in that flare.

Severe on his first fruits, almost all of them "a flight into faery land from the real world," Yeats said that nothing he did in his early time had merit. He hoped to find merit and when still in his twenties looked forward to writing poetry of insight and knowledge. Critics often suggest that insight flooded in as he switched allegiance from "India" and "Arcady," venues of his first book, to "mad Ireland." That seems a half-truth, meaning that it has its scruple of truth.

Arguing for poetry, he put it on a par with science, demanding "the same right of exploration of all that passes before the mind's eye, and merely because it passes." He was echoing Pater, the famous passage in *The Renaissance:* "Art comes to you proposing frankly to give nothing but the highest quality to your moments as they pass, and simply for those moments' sake." Much quality (if you can render it) in "that color upon cheek or hair." But "A mound of refuse or the sweepings of a street" have their interest, and I think for Yeats in his majority we want to adjust the role content plays, tipping the scales in favor of form. He went through different incarnations but stayed faithful to the Nineties, and at the end the cask still smells of the wine that steeped it first.

"Circus animals," including peahens, are grist for poetry's mill, and nothing in itself is right about Gaelic legends, even up-to-date ones. "We protest against the right of patriots to perpetrate bad verses," said Yeats's mentor, O'Leary, who knew how many sins go under cover of content.

Nothing wrong with "faery" land, not ipso facto. In Shakespeare's, elves are drawn to scale, hiding in the cups of acorns, and a snake's cast-off skin makes a "weed" or garment "wide enough to wrap a fairy in." This is a real world, but doesn't exist except as the poet creates it. Taking it for granted in his early poems, Yeats wants more art and less matter.

Titles of his narrative and dramatic work, beginning with "The Wanderings of Oisin" (1889), say that he is Irish, but only by intention. In the *Crossways* volume (1889), he points to "Sleuth Wood," a real place near Sligo, but this rocky headland might be anywhere or nowhere. "Irish folk song," say the commentators, footnoting his famous song, "Down by the Salley Gardens." I think we say "Housman," though, Yeats's mirror reflecting a mirror. Housman's near-perfect poems are too well-known to quote, but their just claim on us carries a reservation with it, and in none does the poet break new ground. The same is true of Yeats's first anthology pieces.

All that strikes the eye and ear in the poems of his age is there from the start, at least paraphrasably: the pairing of opposites, the Beautiful Woman, his contempt for huckster's loins, an autodidact's philosophy, the histrionic defiance (spitting into the face of Time). Already in poems of *The Rose* he means to "Sing of old Eire and the ancient ways." Later he said that "from the moment I began 'The Wanderings of Oisin' . . . my subject matter became Irish." Let us agree, but what follows? Having sat through a reading of Yeats's nonstop romance, Morris said enthusiastically, "You write my kind of poetry!" Promoters of content as the key to a great poet's metamorphosis will want to reflect on this praise.

Yeats on his change and where it comes from isn't helpful. He said poets in the 1930s, "new poets," were "like goldsmiths working with glass screwed into one eye." This seems a good prescription for poetry, written with eyes close to the page. But getting up on his soapbox—like late Wallace Stevens, another mandarin grown uneasy—he calls for Robert Bly poets, masculine men who "stride ahead of the crowd . . . looking to right and left." It comes near vulgarity, out in the open when Yeats specifies the hoped-for yield of his rough-and-ready poetics: "vast sentiments, generalizations." Margaret Fuller, from the same bad nineteenth-century mold, is sure "a great work of art demands a great thought." This sentiment also has its scruple of truth, and Yeats says what that is in his "Meditations in Time of Civil War":

> only an aching heart
> Conceives a changeless work of art.

But you needed "waking wits," in Sato's house or Yeats's, to make the conception real.

In another vein, he said a writer "bred to the tact of words can take what theme he pleases." He had to honor one commitment, though, and Yeats made it absolute. This was to style, "the only thing that is immortal in literature." These are fighting words today, ratified, however, by poets who worship language, Auden's phrase in his poem for Yeats. Some ideas shake the world but that is only as the orchestration makes them quick. The "ethical interest," or theme, could "escape no attentive reader" of Shakespeare's, said Pater, assessing the plays (in *Appreciations,* 1889). But artistic law demanded "the predominance of form everywhere over the mere matter or subject." This truth, from the ancestral homeland of the New Criticism, is the principal gain of Yeats's long journey. Brooding on form, not a carapace but words in their suggestive quality and the way they reticulate, he said that "the wild-winged and unbroken colt"—Pegasus, recycled from Jonson's "Fit against Rime"—had to drag a cart of stones, onerous work but it disciplined this steed of the Muses.

As he gave himself to the work, he learned how to draw from "the melancholy submissive dreaming soul" all that opposed it, savage indignation, "cold Clare rock and Galway rock and thorn," "porter-drinkers' randy laughter." This study, transforming him, forged a hero's intransigent soul, pitched "into the frog-spawn of a blind man's ditch" and willing to accept what it found there. The dreaming soul is Synge's in his nonage, but "peeping and botanizing" this friend discovered work for his hand. In the famous story, laying his ear to "that hole in the ceiling," he heard the peasants below-stairs canvassing "themes." More critically, though, he registered idioms, and though his great play is more than their sum, it wouldn't be thinkable without them.

Starting out as a poet, Yeats manipulated "quantities," said his father John Butler Yeats, doing this to suit an adolescent's taste. He liked declaiming and indulging it begot his "bad metres." (He always liked declaiming, but later the oracular voice sounds as from a cave in Delphi). Like technical skill, "the secret of sincerity" revealed itself, however, not as you spoke heart's truth but as you racked your brain. Maybe skill and sincerity are one and the same, though the million won't ever believe it. "Do you prefer to be sincere?" the hero asks the lady in one of Wilde's comedies. "Yes," she tells him, "but it is so difficult a pose to keep up."

Hardy is sincere, his subject often Yeats's, how Time, "to make me grieve," partly steals the heart, letting part of it abide. But Yeats with his swagger, put on for the occasion, cuts deeper: "What shall I do with this absurdity— / O heart, O troubled heart?" That his poems of baffled love still reverberate a century later is less a function of truth telling than craft. Hardy tells the truth; Yeats, a performer, has the crowd on his side. "Malachi Stilt-Jack am I."

In none of what he does do the seams show. Though a line may take us hours,

> Yet if it does not seem a moment's thought,
> Our stitching and unstitching has been naught.

Sprezzatura, meaning "no sweat," is a word for his pose when it becomes habitual. Plucking the word from Castiglione's *Courtier,* this son of Oscar wore it in the world's eye. Not all that wicked, whatever he let on, he wasn't good beyond the ordinary either. It seems on one side he was daft. Padriac Colum, back in Ireland after many years' absence, tells of running into him on Dublin's O'Connell Street. "Willie!" he cried. "I hear a voice from over the sea," said Yeats, looking through this old friend, and passed on.

But he had a singular passion and it sets him apart from the poets he knew in his youth, "companions of the Cheshire Cheese." This was art, not a one-night stand as for most who aspire, and his enduring attachment puts his more glamorous attachment for the woman loved and lost in the shade. (For certain, she knew this.) Wooing art all his life, he revised endlessly, meditating new strategies, or call them fresh overtures that might get the business done. At last art gave itself to him. "I have come into my strength," he wrote in triumph, "And words obey my call."

In his fifties, looking back at "The Lake Isle of Innisfree," everybody's favorite poem, he told of loosening its rhythm to escape from rhetoric, that cold rhetoric out of Milton's Pandora's Box. "Use nothing but the common syntax," no inversions, no "pavements grey." Then, upping the ante, he saw that the "powerful and passionate syntax" he wanted meant more than the clarity that comes with everyday speech. At its highest pitch, it meant yoking things together in combinations no one had thought of. This defines the oxymoron, a contradictory-seeming figure, at first exotic, subsequently once-and-for-all.

But let me illustrate from one of Yeats's perfect poems. Death, sleep, and drinking, the three terms his cards deal him in "A Deep-Sworn Vow," have something in common, as for Shakespeare in Macbeth. As Yeats's poem unfolds, the order his terms take ought to decrease in magnitude, first death, the ultimate, last of all drinking. Common logic suggests that comparison must dwarf it. But "syntax," composing itself beneath the surface, belies this. Making a new order, it says how the last shall be first.

> Others because you did not keep
> That deep-sworn vow have been friends of mine;
> Yet always when I look death in the face,
> When I clamber to the heights of sleep,
> Or when I grow excited with wine,
> Suddenly I meet your face.

Near the end of his life, Yeats thought back to Spenser and his allegorical wrestling match in *The Faerie Queene*. Old Antaeus is almost bested in this contest, but touches earth, so comes into his strength. Surely it was like that for a poet and his friends?

>   all that we said or sang
> Must come from contact with the soil, from that
> Contact everything Antaeus-like grew strong.

This truth needs restating, though. The right emblem for Yeats is less Antaeus than Vulcan, the bandy-legged artificer who hammered out his art on the anvil.

Index